CULTURAL TREASURES

First published in Australia in 2007 by
New Holland Publishers (Australia) Pty Ltd
Sydney • Auckland • London • Cape Town

1/66 Gibbes Street Chatswood NSW 2067 Australia
218 Lake Road Northcote Auckland New Zealand
86 Edgware Road London W2 2EA United Kingdom
80 McKenzie Street Cape Town 8001 South Africa

Bradley, Pamela.
        Cultural treasures of the ancient world.

        Bibliography.
        Includes index.
        ISBN 9781741104950.

        1. Antiquities. 2. Civilization, Ancient. 3. Cultural
        property. I. Title.

        930

Publisher: Martin Ford
Project Editor: Lliane Clarke
Editor: Geraldine Coren
Designer: Simon Rattray
Cover Design: Hayley Norman
Production Manager: Linda Bottari
Printer: Everbest Printing Co (Ltd) China

10 9 8 7 6 5 4 3 2 1

CULTURAL TREASURES
OF THE ANCIENT WORLD

PAMELA BRADLEY

NEW
HOLLAND

CONTENTS

PART V

1st Millennium CE: A cultural turning point, synthesis and synergism   248

INTRODUCTION

Cultural treasures provide a record of our human condition on both a spiritual and human plane. To decipher this record is to know our past. And, so ourselves. To preserve it is to pass that knowledge on to future generations. —Miguel Angel Corzo, Director of the Getty Conservation Institute

What is an 'ancient treasure'?

The term 'ancient' is defined with different parameters in different cultural and geographical areas. In Europe, the ancient world is seen as that period of time before the fall of the Western Roman Empire around 476 CE (Common Era), while in parts of Africa, the Near East and Southern Asia, 'ancient' is pre-Islamic and varies from place to place. In China, 'ancient' refers to the time before the Song Dynasty of the tenth century CE, and in South and Central America it means pre-Columbian.

'Treasure' is an evocative word, conjuring up images of gold, silver or precious gems. Its legal definition in certain parts of the world is quite narrow, but to archaeologists and historians, all finds can be considered 'treasures'. Some of the criteria used to define a treasure in this publication are rarity, workmanship, the technological skill involved in its production, and significance within the society from which it originated. Also, its value as a source of information on an ancient culture has been taken into consideration. 'It is the stories which these treasures can tell us about our past that really matters' (Richard Hobbs, *Treasure: Finding our Past*, 2003).

As the pool of ancient treasures is immense, the choice of time frame and artefacts for this book is purely arbitrary. Most tend to come from a high point, or defining moment in a particular culture. For example, the first entry deals with the painted and sculpted treasures of a mysterious

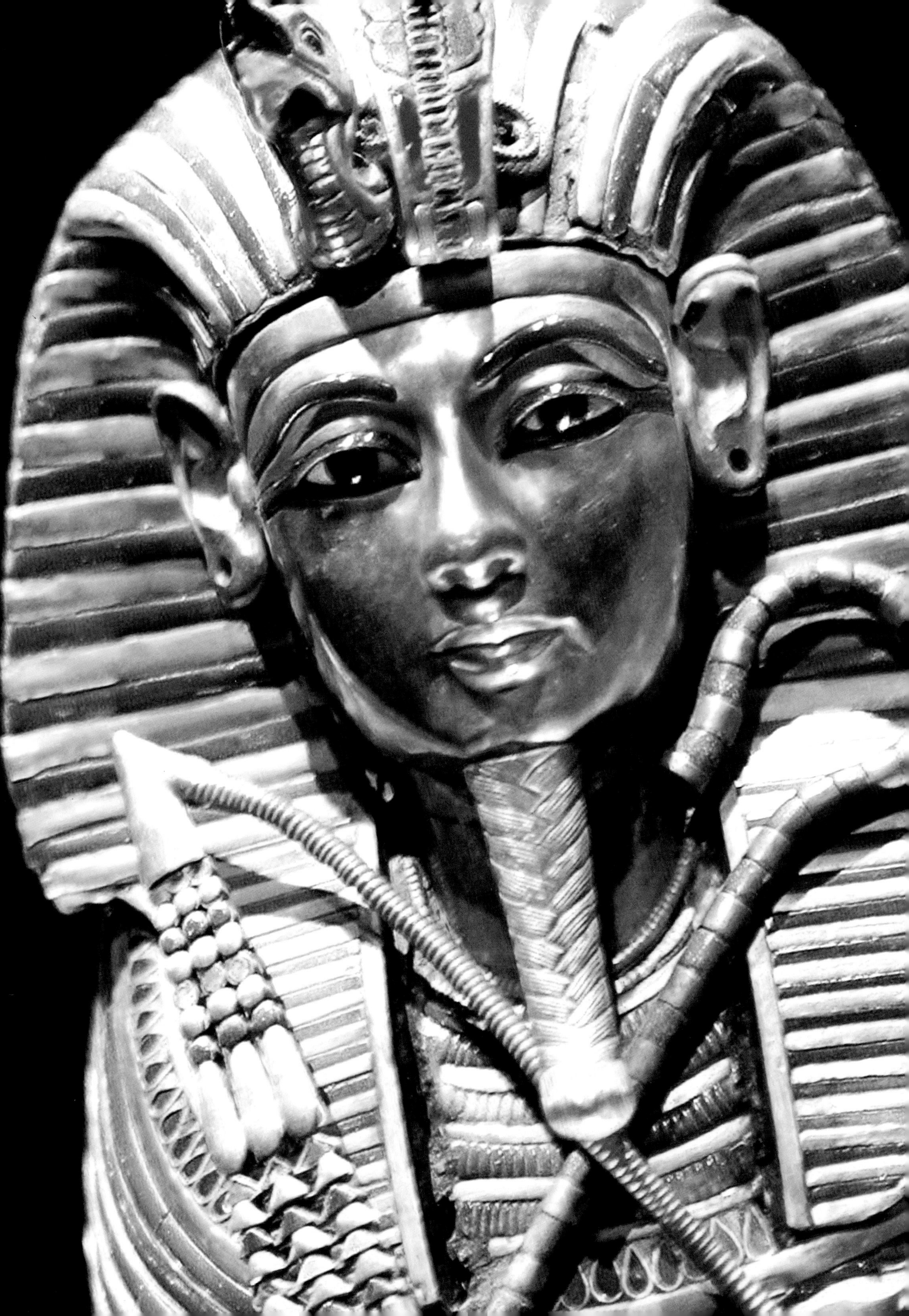

culture 'on the verge of civilisation'—Catal Huyuk in ancient Anatolia (Turkey)—while the final entry describes the treasures that provide a window into Mayan society of Central America just before its demise. This covers roughly a period from ca. 7000 BCE (Before the Common Era) to the end of the first millennium CE which provided a convenient cut-off point. The text is loosely arranged in chronological order rather than following a thematic approach, although in ancient times there is often no precise date that can be attached to an object.

Wherever possible, there has been an attempt to include artefacts made from a variety of materials: gold, silver, bronze, stone (basalt, granite, marble), semiprecious stones (jade, lapis lazuli, turquoise, carnelian, amethyst), pottery, terracotta, timber and textiles. However, objects made from wood, leather and textiles often do not survive the ravages of time and the elements.

Also, the 'treasures' have been selected from ancient urban communities with a social and technological level above that of hunters and gatherers. Unfortunately, this precludes outstanding Palaeolithic 'treasures' such as the European cave paintings of Chauvet, Lascaux and Altamira, and the enigmatic rock art of the Australian Aborigines and other groups on all continents. Not included in this book are the large-scale structural 'treasures' on the World Heritage List, such as Stonehenge; the Pyramids and Sphinx; Sumerian ziggurats; the Great Wall of China; Egyptian, Greek, Roman, Hindu and Buddhist temples; the ceremonial centres of pre-Columbian Central and South America, and the spectacular town and city sites such as Pompeii and Machu Pichu. However, some of the artefacts selected were, or still are, an integral part of larger structures in situ.

There tends to be a disproportionate number of surviving treasures associated with the spiritual/sacred life and burial practices of the upper echelons of ancient societies, although many of these do throw light on the everyday lives of ordinary citizens.

Most of the treasures presented here are housed in the world's greatest museums. A few are already familiar, such as the treasures of Tutankhamun, but many may not be so well-known to the general reader. Unfortunately, the provenance of some of these is unknown due to the practices of looting and smuggling over the centuries, which means that their cultural context can only be a matter of conjecture. Early treasure hunters, and even respectable archaeologists with or without permission, in the past removed many items of great value from their country of origin. Today some governments are actively seeking their return and the question of cultural 'ownership' is an ongoing debate.

ANCIENT CULTURE	TIMELINE OF					
	7000 BCE	6000 BCE	5000 BCE	4000 BCE	3000 BCE	2500 BCE
ANATOLIAN (Turkey)	Images of Catal Huyuk					Treasures from Troy
CHINESE		The Liangzhu Jades				
MESOPOTAMIAN				The Warka Vase	The Death Pits of Ur	
EGYPTIAN				The Narmer Palette Hard Stone Vases	Royal Statuary Private Statuary Furniture of Hetepheres Cedar Boat of King Khufu Old Kingdom Tomb Paintings	
AEGEAN/MYCENAEAN					Marble Sculptures from the Cyclades Islands	
INDUS VALLEY/ GANDHARAN/DECCAN					Miniature Animal Seals from Indus Valley	
BRONZE AGE BRITAIN						
MESOAMERICAN						
GREEK						
SCYTHIAN						
CELTIC						
PERUVIAN						
MACEDONIAN						
PERSIAN						
HELLENISTIC						
NOK/NIGERIAN						
VIETNAMESE						
ROMAN/BYZANTINE						

| 2000 BCE | 1500 BCE | 1000 BCE | 500 BCE | BCE CE | 500 CE | 1000 CE |

Oracle Bones and Ritual Bronzes

Ceremonial Bronze Bells

Buddhist Art of Dunhuang

Terracotta Army

Jade Burial Suits

Tang Pottery

The Nimrud Treasure

Meketre's Wooden Models

Portraits of an Egyptian Family

The Faiyum Mummy Portraits

Middle Kingdom Royal Jewellery

Treasures of Tutankhamun

Paintings in the Tomb of Nefetari

Minoan Treasures from Knossos

Murals of Akrotiri

The Mask of Agamemnon

Greco-Indian of Gandhara

The Caves of Ajanta

Hindu Treasures of the Deccan

British Gold

Ritual Art of the Olmecs

Mayan Murals and Figurines

Greek Vase Painting

The Parthenon Frieze

Greek Bronzes

Ancient Aphrodites

Scythian Gold and Nomadic Textiles

Celtic Metalwork

Paracan Textiles

Moche Gold and Ceramics

Treasures from Tombs of Derveni and Vergina

The Oxus Treasure

The Alexander Mosaic

Paintings from the Villa of the Mysteries

Pompeian Silverware

Monumental Sculpture

Nok Terracottas

Dong Son Drums

Coinage of First Caesars

Roman Silver

Roman Cameo Glass

Ravenna Mosaics

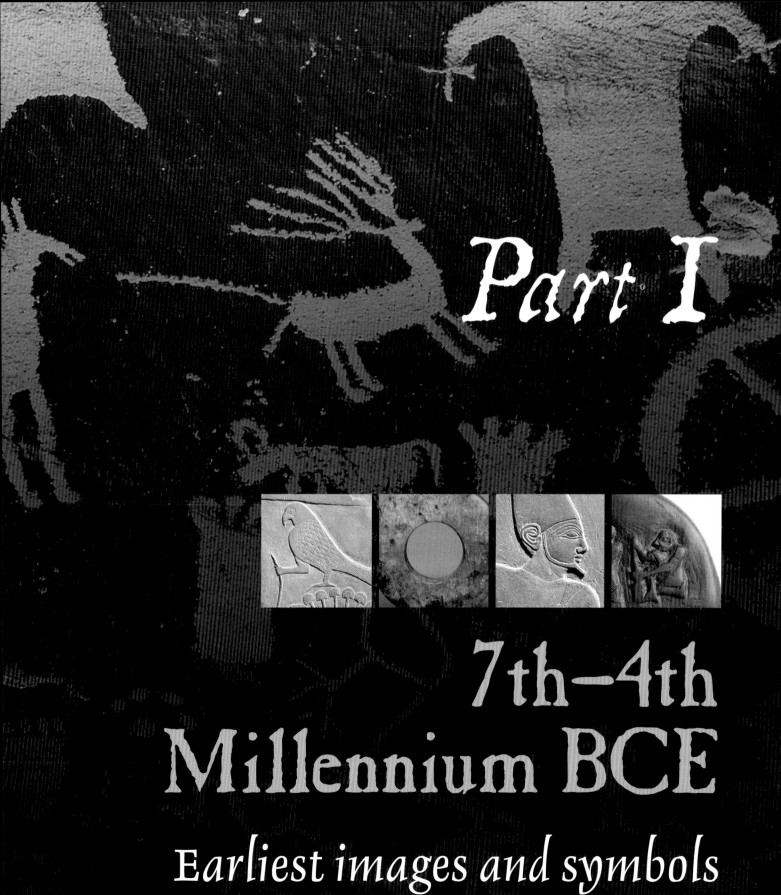

Part I

7th–4th Millennium BCE

Earliest images and symbols

A MYSTERIOUS SYMBOLIC WORLD

Painted and sculptured images from Catal Huyuk

Catal Huyuk is undoubtedly a site of deep mysteries. The high level of preservation appears to take one closer to a very distant and different world. And yet the strangeness of it all is confronting and distancing. It intrigues and baffles us.

—Ian Hodder, *The Leopard's Tale: Revealing the Mysteries of Catalhöyük*

Between 1961–1965, a community on the verge of civilisation was unearthed at the site of Catal Huyuk in central Turkey (Anatolia). What James Mellaart, the British archaeologist, discovered when he dug into a mound dominating the fertile Konya Valley staggered the academic world: a primary source of western civilisation 3000 years older than the earliest Sumerian cities of Mesopotamia.

Catal Huyuk, which was occupied between ca. 7400–6000 BCE, revealed the origins of settled farming life and the rise of the first towns, as well as an amazing concentration of art that pointed to a mysterious symbolic world.

Catal Huyuk's ritual artwork took the form of dozens of unique sculptures and wall paintings, the first ever on plaster, as well as an abundance of corpulent female figures carved and moulded

ABOVE: A leopard sculpture.

predominantly from clay and blue and brown limestone. Mellaart described Catal Huyuk as 'a supernova among the rather dim galaxy of contemporary peasant cultures' (*Catal Huyuk: The Temple City of Prehistoric Anatolia*, William Carl Eichman).

Under the 21-metre mound, he excavated hundreds of mud-brick buildings and courtyards crammed together in a honeycomb-like maze with no paths or streets between; some house walls were mere centimetres apart. Entry to, and exit from, these dwellings was through openings in the roofs, via exterior and interior ladders. Each house comprised a main room divided into functional areas by plastered and painted platforms of different heights, as well as small side rooms for storage and food preparation. The population buried their dead beneath the high, white plastered platforms in the northern and central part of the main room away from the ovens. The bodies were arranged in a flexed position; a few, possibly those with some special social significance, had their heads cut off after the initial burial and these heads were circulated for some time before a final reburial.

Although most buildings appear to have been domestic dwellings, some, larger than the rest, contained more female figurines, paintings and reliefs. Mellaart labelled these as 'shrines'. However, the present project team (*Catal Huyuk Research Project* led by Ian Hodder) believes they are all houses 'with varying degrees of symbolic and ritual elaboration . . . in the house, symbolic and practical aspects of daily life are thoroughly integrate' (*The Leopard's Tale*).

The inhabitants of the town, who may have numbered between 3000–8000, engaged in agriculture, herded sheep and goats, hunted cattle, horses and deer, and wove textiles. A vital part of their economy appears to have been based on obsidian (fine, black volcanic glass) which came from the vicinity of a twin-coned, active volcano known as Hasan Dag, 170 kilometres away.

Even though the people had domesticated animals, their art focused on wild species (solitary hunters like the leopard, the massive and terrifying scythe-horned auroch bull, and scavenging vultures), and the dangerous parts of wild animals such as horns, mandibles, teeth, antlers and tusks. There seems to be some link in their art between violence, initiation and death which the archaeologist Mortimer Wheeler in a foreword to Mellaart's book said 'represents an outstanding accomplishment in the upward grade of social development' (*Catal Huyuk: A Neolithic Town in Anatolia*).

The walls of Catal Huyuk houses were not always covered in paintings. Sometimes earlier ones were plastered over and the walls remained blank; maybe they were painted only at times of important events in the house such as births, initiations and deaths. Some of the most stunning wall paintings that have survived depict scenes of hunting or baiting a giant bull, another of hunting the red deer and one showing a vulture with human legs and outstretched wings hovering over a headless body. Another unique painting dated to ca. 6200 seems to represent a landscape featuring a stylised portrayal of the town itself with its terraced houses, behind which is an erupting volcano, clearly the twin-peaked Hasan Dag.

The sacred leopard

Judging by the percentage of representations of leopards in paintings (65 per cent) and reliefs (35 per cent), it appears that it was a 'sacred' animal. People depicted in the paintings wear leopard skins or garments, and leopards in pairs are moulded into the walls. Their spots were periodically repainted. Also, they are often found associated with 'goddess' figures. One unique figurine, found in a grain bin, depicts a woman sitting on a throne, her hands resting on the heads of two leopards. Leopard-like spots were a common motif, even painted onto an image of the volcano.

However, unlike with wild cattle and vultures, the bones, skulls and teeth of leopards were never part of the house installations fixed to the wall by pegs or attached to pillars and plastered over. There appears to have been a taboo on bringing leopard bones into the settlement. Ian Hodder, in his recent work, *The Leopard's Tale*, suggests that the qualities of a leopard—its individual markings and strong and enduring maternal bonding—may provide some clue to its symbolism.

The art of Catal Huyuk appears to be a survival of the Palaeolithic shamanistic cave art found in France and Spain. Perhaps some of the inhabitants believed they could acquire the powers of the wild animals they depicted in their art, and in an altered state of consciousness, could enter the spiritual realms to 'intervene in the world, to understand how it works, to change it' (*The Leopard's Tale*). Like Palaeolithic, and some modern-day hunting and gathering shamanistic practices, the artists of Catal Huyuk may have utilised psychoactive drugs.

The geometric designs in their paintings (spots,

circles, spirals, linear networks, horizontal grids and handprints) are typical of the reported first stage of a shamanistic hallucination. During the next phases of the experience, the visionary often reports seeing felines. Such speculation about the use of psychedelic drugs at Catal Huyuk is supported by the fact that a shrub called Syrian Rue grew in the vicinity of the settlement. Its seeds contained the psychedelic compounds of harmine and harmaline; harmine is supposed to cause visions of big cats. The spotted sacred mushroom known as *Amarita muscaria* was also found in Anatolia. Its psychedelic effects and its spots connect it with leopard imagery, (see John Allegro in *The Sacred Mushroom and the Cross*, and R. Gordon Wasson in *Soma: Divine Mushroom of Immortality*).

> The ritual artwork of Catal Huyuk took the form of dozens of unique sculptures and wall paintings, the first ever on plaster, as well as an abundance of corpulent female figures carved and moulded predominantly from clay and blue and brown limestone.

Without knowing what the inhabitants of Catal Huyuk intended in their rituals and art, all the experts can do is speculate. During his four seasons of excavation from 1961–5, James Mellaart found an abundance of what he described as 'goddess' figures, many with their heads removed. The most impressive is the one previously described of a woman sitting on a 'throne' resting her hands on two feline heads and with what appears to be either a baby or a skull between her legs. Whether this pointed to a Mother Goddess cult as suggested by Mellaart, the powerful image of the woman on her feline throne certainly points to the importance of women in the symbolism of Catal Huyuk. This was further reinforced when two important discoveries were made in 2004.

The first was a unique clay figurine of a female. On one side it had full breasts and extended stomach, on the back the figure appears skeletal with its scapulae, ribs, vertebrae and pelvic bones clearly visible. It has been suggested that it could be a depiction of a woman becoming an ancestor, or associated with life and death. 'Whatever the specific interpretations, this is a unique piece that extends our knowledge about the associations of female imagery' (*The Leopard's Tale*). The second find was the skeleton of an adult female, holding a red plastered skull to her chest and face, with a leopard-claw pendant below her body. This was the only bone of a leopard ever found in the settlement.

The unique ritual art of Catal Huyuk provides an ongoing and 'unprecedented opportunity to get into the minds of Neolithic settlers' (Michael Balter, *The Goddess and the Bull*).

THE ESSENCE OF HEAVEN AND EARTH

Jade artefacts from the Liangzhu culture

Jade is woven into the very fabric of the Chinese ethos and it has been from the earliest Neolithic cultures that thrived in what became known as China.

—Gary N. Davis, *About Chinese Jade*

There is an old Chinese saying that 'gold is valuable, but jade is invaluable'. Regarded as having spiritual or mystical properties, it has been worked creatively for more than 6000 years. The exquisite jade ornaments, ceremonial tools and ritual objects found in the burials of Chinese Neolithic cultures are believed to have influenced the craftsmen of the later dynasties.

The earliest jades from ca. 6000–5000 BCE were simple items, but between 4000–2000 BCE, the coastal cultures of Hongshan, Longshan, Dawenkou and Liangzhu 'progressed to a true jade industry with specialised technology . . . and jade became a significant part of the socio-economic structure' (Paola Dematte, 'The Chinese Jade Age', *Journal of Social Archaeology*, Vol 6 (2) 2006). It is thought that perhaps the material was used by elite groups to achieve and maintain social control. This has led some scholars to suggest that this period before the Bronze Age in China could be referred to as the Jade Age.

OPPOSITE: A collection of neolithic jade *bi* discs and *cong* cylinders from the Liangzhu culture.

This beautiful stone, appreciated for its lustre and colour (ranging from milky white to dark green and almost black), was the favoured material for ceremonial and funerary objects during the Neolithic period, often comprising up to 90 per cent of all burial goods. Out of 128 artefacts excavated from a tomb at Sidun, 115 were jades. Exactly what spiritual, magical or healing qualities these ancient cultures attributed to it are not known, but throughout Chinese history, jade has been regarded as the 'essence of heaven and earth', the embodiment of a higher morality, and even immortality. The first Chinese dictionary (100 CE), describes five virtues embodied in jade: humanity, justice, wisdom, courage and honesty. Today, it is still regarded as a talisman of protection and good luck.

The dawn of Chinese civilisation

Of the late Neolithic cultures, it was the Liangzhu culture in the lower Yangzi River Valley of the south-east (ca. 3310–2250 BCE) that produced the most varied and sophisticated jades. Many jade experts consider that archaic jade work reached its high point with this culture. The eighteenth century emperor, Qianlong, who collected ancient jade treasures to decorate his palace, would have agreed with them; he prized above all others those from Liangzhu.

The Liangzhu culture developed on a peninsula formed by the lower Yangzi River near Hangzhou Bay in modern Zhejiang province. The hundred or so sites have been included on the World Heritage List. Archaeologist Shi Xigeng first discovered the site in 1936 and excavation continues to the present. The Liangzhu complex has revealed evidence of a society that grew keng rice, made black-based pottery, had a well developed social structure, an iconography of authority, and built high platform-shaped earth mounds, which appear to be combinations of altars and opulent burials. These were built around the 'Earth Pyramid of Mojiaoshan', a rectangular ritual terrace of 310 square metres.

The people of the Liangzhu culture buried their dead in tombs surrounded by fine jade objects and accompanied by sacrificial victims. The purpose of the human sacrifices may have been to please the gods; it was certainly a reflection of the political power of the Liangzhu elites.

While the jades from the Hongshan culture of north-east China are predominantly confined to ornaments—coiled pendants known as 'pig dragons' (a curved dragon-like body with a pig-like snout), body plaques and animal-faced combs, as well as figurines of birds, turtles and fish—those of Liangzhu include weapons, tools, jewellery, monster masks and the mysterious ceremonial objects called *bi* discs and *cong* cylinders. Angus Forsyth in *Jades from China* says 'There is a fearsome cold reality . . . about the high precision detail and volumetric organization of the two register congs which sets them apart from, and above all other Neolithic jades.'

According to later Bronze Age sources, the flat round *bi* discs and rectangular *cong* cylinders are believed to have represented heaven and earth respectively. Perhaps the idea of a round heaven and a rectangular earth may have first emerged during Neolithic times, and the presence of *bi* and *cong* within a Liangzhu tomb may have provided a symbolic link between the earthly and spiritual realms. In one tomb excavated at Sidun there were 25 jade *cong* and 33 jade *bi*. C. N. Yang, Nobel laureate in physics in 1957, suggested these jade objects could have been used by the ancient Chinese to observe the skies.

> The flat round *bi* discs and rectangular *cong* cylinders are believed to have represented heaven and earth respectively.

Thousands of years later both discs and cylinders were still in ritual use, and the enigmatic face-like mask designs with prominent eyes found on many Liangzhu *cong* appear to have been the forerunners of the later stylised *taotie* motif (dragon/animal/monster face) on Shang and Zhou bronzes.

What is amazing about the finely-worked Liangzhu jades is that nephrite (the only true jade used in China until the eighteenth century when jadeite was imported from Burma) is a very hard, compact stone, and these pieces were fashioned several thousand years before metal tools appeared in China. In fact, jade cannot be carved by

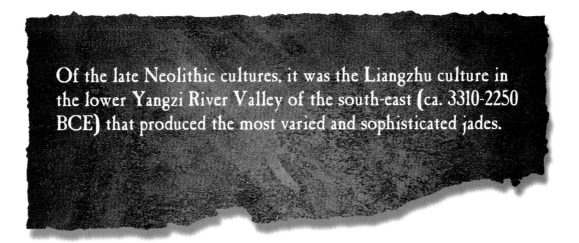

Of the late Neolithic cultures, it was the Liangzhu culture in the lower Yangzi River Valley of the south-east (ca. 3310-2250 BCE) that produced the most varied and sophisticated jades.

chiselling or chipping; it must be worn away by abrasion using hard quartzite sand, making it a slow and labour-intensive process. These Neolithic craftsmen used tubular bamboo drills, awls for piercing small holes on pendants, and sharp flint blades to produce the fine line decorations on *cong* tubes.

It appears that the specialised jade technology of Liangzhu grew out of a steady increase in demand for this 'finest of stones' judging by the number and quality of artefacts in the graves of the elite; over 1100 objects were excavated from a mere eleven graves at Fanshan. The need for mass production and the cost of obtaining the rare stone from the riverbeds of mountainous areas and transporting it required a high level of social organisation. Also, the link between cosmological knowledge and jade points to the direct involvement of an elite group in jade production.

According to the World Heritage website, 'The Liangzhu culture contains the essential elements for the formation of oriental ideology. It is so rare among the discovered prehistoric sites in China or within East Asia that it was considered the dawn of Chinese civilization and an important cultural heritage of mankind.'

A VISUAL NARRATIVE
The sacred Sumerian Warka Vase

Significant historical and cultural events, and even literary traditions, are often recorded visually in objects before they are written down in texts.

—Professor Irene Winter, Harvard University

The Sumerian Warka (Uruk) Vase is a cultural treasure of great significance. It was produced when writing first appeared in Mesopotamia, and has been described as the first narrative picture of its time. The magnificent carved alabaster libation vase, 105 centimetres high and 36 centimetres in diameter, is dated ca. 3100 BCE. It was excavated at Tell al-Warka, the ancient Sumerian city of Uruk (the biblical Erech), in modern Iraq in 1940 by a German archaeological team.

Ancient Uruk is believed to have been the world's first fully urbanised city-state. Between 3700–3000 BCE, it was the most powerful Sumerian city in southern Mesopotamia, the so-called cradle of civilisation and traditional site of the Garden of Eden. Its influence extended the length of the Tigris and Euphrates valley.

Today, all that is left is a dry, treeless mound in the southern desert of Iraq. At its height, Uruk had a population of 30,000–50,000 people and covered an area of approximately 486 hectares with a temple complex (the prototype of later ziggurats) and a city wall 10 kilometres in circumference. Thousands of clay tablets, marked with a pictographic script recording the produce of the surrounding farms, were found in its ruins. Other Sumerian city-states flourished

ABOVE: An inscribed dark schist artefact of the same period as the Warka Vase. The figures on this artefact resemble those on the vase. The archaic script is the earliest form of writing.

under their kings, and there was periodic conflict between them, possibly over trade and commerce. By the end of the third millennium, Uruk's political power in Sumer was usurped by the city-state of Ur.

The importance of the Warka Vase cannot be overstated. It is the largest known piece of art from the late fourth millennium BCE and the world's oldest carved stone ritual vessel. Its sculptured images depict the earliest example of a formalised religious worship. The vase was so precious that when it was damaged in antiquity, the ancients carefully repaired it with copper rivets. This libation vase records the economic foundation of Uruk and what appears to be a Spring Festival dedicated to the worship of Inanna, the fertility goddess. From a modern perspective its images are important because 'they help to see the beginning of the interaction of art and writing' (Professor Denise Schmandt-Bessert, *The Case of the Missing Vase*).

The relief decorations on the vase are arranged in a number of registers. The lower one features the life-giving waters of the rivers and a strip of fertile land with alternating depictions of grain and date palms. Above this tier is a procession of well-fattened ewes and rams in alternating pairs winding its way around the vase. The middle register depicts nude and shorn offering bearers, possibly priests, carrying bowls, baskets and jars of food and wine: first offerings of the fields to the goddess. On the top register is a dignitary, perhaps the king, whose long tasselled belt is held, like a train, by a servant in a short tunic. In front of him is a priest, in ritual nudity, offering the robed goddess Inanna, or her high priestess, a basket of produce.

It has been suggested that this scene symbolises the sacred marriage between the goddess and her consort and anticipates the consummation from which all life in the land will spring. The goddess wears a horned headdress, a sign of supreme deity. Beyond her, further into the temple precinct, are what appear as two minor deities standing on top of a ram, possibly an offering table, and piles of offerings in baskets, plus libation vases similar to the one on which the images are carved.

The way the sculptured procession winds its way around the Warka Vase is reminiscent of an actual procession winding its way up the ziggurat to the temple on top.

Stolen treasure

This unique vase was housed in the Iraqi National Museum until April 2003 when it was stolen along with thousands of other priceless national treasures in the tumultuous days following the overthrow of the Iraqi dictator Saddam Hussein, during the Second Gulf War. This was a cultural catastrophe for Iraq.

The vase had apparently been left on display because it was believed to be too fragile to move into the underground vaults in the weeks before the war, although the world's Mesopotamian scholars had predicted the sort of looting that occurred. 'Few will forget the images of Iraq's director of museums, head in hands, sitting among the ruins of what was once Baghdad's treasure trove. A mixture of opportunistic looting and very specific theft to order had robbed the nation of its most priceless works of art. The list is long, but at the top is the Warka Vase . . .' (Sarah Woodward, *Stealing History*).

> A mixture of opportunistic looting and very specific theft to order had robbed the nation of its most priceless works of art.

Three months later, after an amnesty was granted to anyone returning a stolen artefact, a car turned up outside the museum and the unidentified occupants took the fragmented remains of the vase (one large piece and six smaller ones) from the boot and handed them over to guards at the museum's gates. The optimistic Director General believed the vase could be repaired once again.

A 'FIRST TIME' EVENT
The Egyptian Narmer Palette

The historical events commemorated here ... render this palette
one of the most famous and important pieces in our collection.

— The official catalogue of the Egyptian Museum, Cairo

The commemorative Narmer Palette, 64 centimetres high and 42 centimetres wide, is dated ca. 3100–3000 BCE. Named for the king whose reign it depicts, it symbolically represents what the Egyptians regarded as a 'First Time' event in their history: the political union of the 'Two Lands of Upper and Lower Egypt'. It is also a pictorial record of early Egyptian kingship. The palette was discovered in 1894 by archaeologist J.E. Quibell and was part of a cache of predynastic objects found in a temple at Nekhen in southern Egypt. Today the palette is housed in the Egyptian Museum in Cairo.

At the end of the fourth millennium BCE, Nekhen, later named Hierakonpolis or 'city of the falcon' by the Greeks, was one of the earliest urban centres of predynastic Egypt. It was the 'capital' of southern Egypt (the Kingdom of Upper Egypt). There is evidence of fortifications, a temple precinct, specialised crafts, social distinctions, and trade beyond the area. The city's furnaces for firing pottery were skilfully designed, hard stone vessels were hollowed out and polished and there were kilns for drying and storing foodstuffs. It was the seat of a powerful

OPPOSITE: The reverse of the beautifully carved ceremonial object known as the Narmer Palette, which reveals the beginning of hieroglyphics and the royal motifs that lasted throughout Egyptian history.

chieftain or king associated with the falcon god, Horus, and it appears that all the basic concepts associated with Egyptian kingship originated in this area. Tradition points to another Kingdom of Lower Egypt centred on the Delta.

Votive offerings, in the form of mace-heads and cosmetic palettes with relief ornamentation of chieftains/kings as bulls or lions tearing at their enemies and attacking fortified towns, indicate that the late fourth millennium in Egypt was possibly a time of warfare and struggle. These ornamental ritual objects represented the earliest attempt by Egyptian artists 'to express themselves in large-scale compositions on a high aesthetic level' (R. Schulz and M. Seidel, *Egypt The World of the Pharaohs*).

The Narmer Palette survived in perfect condition. With its carefully incised details, this largest of the extant ornamental palettes is a masterpiece of craftsmanship. Believed to be the last of this genre, it is the most archetypal icon of kingship ever discovered in Egypt. It brings together all the elements associated with the power of the Egyptian king 'in a deliberately created art form' (Gay Robins, *The Art of Ancient Egypt*).

A defining moment in Egyptian history

The concept of the political union of the 'Two Lands of Upper and Lower Egypt', linked by one king, remained the ideal for three thousand years after this event and the symbolism was repeated ritually at every king's coronation and jubilee. Another motif on the palette, 'the King smiting his foes' (using his mace to smash the skulls of his enemies) was

endlessly reiterated in art until the end of pharaonic history in Roman times.

Horizontal lines divide each side of the palette into a number of pictorial registers, and the theme on both sides is of conquest. It combines both realistic and symbolic motifs with examples of a hieroglyphic script. The upper rims feature faces of Hathor, a sky goddess with cow's ears and horns. Between the faces is Narmer's Horus name (the earliest of the later five names of a pharaoh) written as a catfish and a chisel.

The use of scale on the palette designates importance; the king is shown larger than other figures. On one side, Narmer, wearing the conical White Crown of Upper Egypt and the archaic costume (bead apron and animal tail) of a primitive chieftain, is accompanied by his sandal bearer and foot washer. Even though a person of considerable rank, the bearer is shown as much smaller than the king. The king holds a mace, raised and ready to smash into the head of a kneeling enemy who he has grasped by the hair.

Although a hieroglyph identifies the name or territory of the prisoner, it cannot be read with accuracy. The motif above the prisoner, however, leaves little doubt that he comes from the north, possibly the Delta region, and is representative of the conquest of that area. A falcon holds a strip of land, with papyrus reeds, on a leash. Papyrus grew prolifically in the Delta and was the plant emblem of the Kingdom of Lower Egypt. The human head growing from the land probably represents the population of the north subjugated by the south, represented by Horus the falcon. In the lower register, below the king's feet, are two naked fallen enemies. This was another motif repeated in all periods of Egyptian history. The city from which they come is symbolised by the rectangular fortress.

On the other side of the palette, the king, wearing the Red Crown of Lower Egypt and accompanied once again by his sandal bearer, is preceded by a priest wearing an animal skin and four standard bearers.

There is a ship above two rows of bound bodies, their decapitated heads between their legs. In the centre register, the two intertwined snake-necked panthers, held by leashes, may have represented the union of the two lands. The emblematic figure of the bull in the lower register symbolises the king breaking through the fortifications of a town and trampling the enemy to death. The identification of the king with a bull was another constant theme during pharaonic times.

It is unlikely that this palette represents a single conquest, since the subjugation of the north and political unification probably occurred over a period of time, but it represents what the Egyptians came to regard as possibly the most defining event in their history.

> With its carefully incised details, this largest of the extant ornamental palettes is a masterpiece of craftsmanship. Believed to be the last of this genre, it is the most archetypal icon of kingship ever discovered in Egypt.

Part II

3rd Millennium BCE

Stunning achievements
in stone, timber and gold

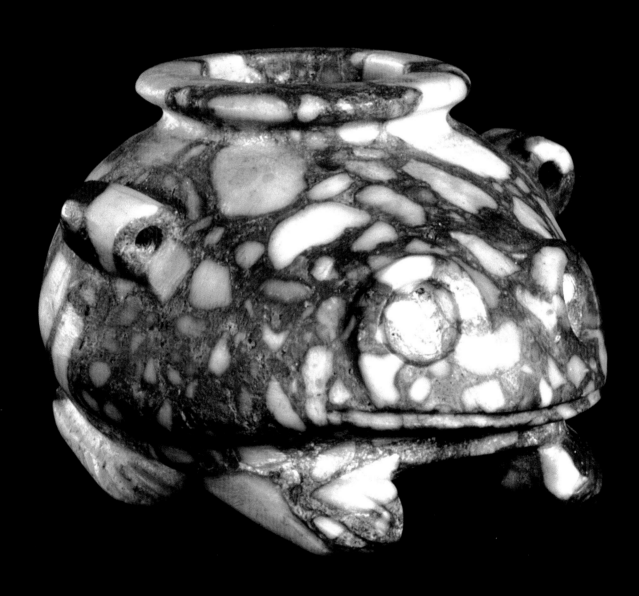

HARMONY IN FORM AND COLOUR

Hard stone vases of early dynastic Egypt

From the point of view of magnificence and skill in using hard and beautiful stones ... the Egyptians rose to their highest level in the late prehistoric and early dynastic times. — W. M. Flinders Petrie, *Diospolis Parva.*

The Egyptian genius for stone working can be seen particularly in the decorative vases, bowls and platters of the first–third dynasties (ca. 2920–2575 BCE). These beautiful artefacts, many made from coveted, multicoloured hard stones, were associated with beliefs about the afterlife and were intended to last for eternity.

Stone vessels formed the most valuable part of the funerary equipment of royalty and the upper class during the earliest dynasties. They were not only made to hold—and protect against deterioration—the costly divine provisions such as unguents, perfumes, oils, wine, and food for the afterlife, but were also of great value as ornamental and luxury items in themselves. Their value depended on the rarity of the material and the difficulty in working and transporting the stone. The production of these vessels was a royal monopoly and their existence in a private tomb was an indication of status.

OPPOSITE: An early dynastic Egyptian hard stone vase in the shape of a frog.

There were 200 found in the tomb of a second dynasty king (Kasekhemwy) at Abydos, and close on 40,000 of all shapes and styles, together weighing between 80–90 tonnes, in the subterranean galleries of the remarkable third dynasty Step Pyramid of King Djoser (ca. 2630–2611) at Saqqara. However, only a small number found under the Step Pyramid are datable to the reign of that Djoser; most belonged to his royal ancestors. The mystery is why Djoser appropriated the vessels of his predecessors for his own tomb rooms. Since most were not for food storage, there may have been a magical or symbolic reason behind their appropriation. Or perhaps Djoser did it out of piety, believing that his pyramid was inviolable.

Egypt was blessed with more stones of exceptional quality and variety than anywhere else in the ancient world, and its stone workers could identify the most appropriate sedimentary, igneous and metamorphic rock for particular projects. They understood the symbolism of stone, both in its form and colour. Some stones were associated with the sun, the heavens and the underworld, others with healing.

The ancient artisans knew what worked best for building, sculpting into statues of kings and gods, and crafting into amulets and beautiful vessels. The most common stones used for vases, bowls and plates were alabaster, travertine and limestone breccia, schist, basalt, diorite, porphyry, gneiss, quartz, serpentine, dolomite and granite. Semiprecious stones such as carnelian, amethyst and crystal were also used. Dr Patrick Hunt in *Egyptian Genius: Stone Working for Eternity* maintains that 'the ancient Egyptians were capable of working stone ranging from 1 to 9 on the ten-step, relativised Moh's scale of hardness'.

The work of these early craftsmen combined an aesthetic sensibility with experimentation. Other vessels have an almost modern simplicity to them.

Among the numerous stone vessels produced during the first and second dynasty and excavated from the royal cemeteries at Abydos and Saqqara, are a few of unsurpassed quality, revealing a flawless and harmonious combination of form and colour. Some imitated containers made from organic materials such as baskets, and

ABOVE LEFT: A carnelian and gold sealed jar. RIGHT: A dolomite and gold sealed jar. Both stone vessels were found in a second dynasty royal tomb at Abydos.

others reproduced the shapes of nature, at a time when architecture was also beginning to copy the features of timber, reeds and matting into stone. The work of these early craftsmen combined an aesthetic sensibility with experimentation. Other vessels have an almost modern simplicity to them. According to Francesco Raffaele in *Stone Vessels in Early Dynastic Egypt*, they reveal 'an awesome and skill-challenging' range of forms and materials'. Many of the hard stone vessels are of such precision that modern day artisans would find them difficult to replicate.

Sophisticated methods

The stunning examples of early dynastic hard stone vessels have raised questions about the tools used to execute such beauty and precision, just as questions have been asked about the technology used in the construction of the Pyramids and Old Kingdom sarcophagi. Despite the continued attempts by Egyptologists to insist that many of these early dynastic artefacts were produced solely with copper tools, examples of which are displayed in the Cairo Museum, modern technologists believe that while copper could be used for cutting and shaping limestone and alabaster, it is much too soft to cut and shape hard igneous stones.

The traditional view is that hard rock vessels were probably given their outer shape by pounding with diorite hammer stones and the interior bored with stone drill heads and quartzite sand as an abrasive. Modern stone experts, such as Dr Patrick Hunt, believe that the Egyptians used emery (corundum and magnetite), from the islands of the Aegean. Emery is harder than steel and any other stone except diamond.

Sir William Flinders Petrie, working at Giza during the late nineteenth and early twentieth centuries, found evidence of the use of bronze tubular drills, set with 'jewels' which would have been harder than the material of the work-piece itself. Marks were also found that suggested true lathe turning. He believed the Egyptians of that early period had lathes that would turn and polish hard stones like granite, diorite and basalt.'The lathe appears to have been as familiar an instrument in the fourth dynasty, as it is in modern workshops … However, no actual proofs of the tools employed, or the manner of using them, have been obtained …' (Sir William Flinders Petrie, *The Pyramids and Temples of Gizeh*). The skilled artisans who made these objects were in constant danger of stone splinters piercing their eyes, and their lungs filling with fine silica dust (silicosis) from polishing.

> Sir William Flinders Petrie believed the Egyptians of that early period had lathes that would turn and polish hard stones like granite, diorite and basalt.

There seems to have been a decline in both craftsmanship and number of vases produced by the time of the third dynasty, probably due to 'the increasing importance of other forms of *artistic* expression such as royal and private statuary' (Francesco Raffaele, *Stone Vessels in Early Dynastic Egypt*). Perhaps political and economic reasons played a part, such as the need to direct resources and manpower to pyramid building. Also, the need to store real food and wine in hundreds of stone vessels in tombs became redundant. The Egyptians came to believe that carved reliefs of food production on tomb walls could sustain the eternal existence of the tomb owner just as much as the real thing.

FIGURES OF GRACE AND SIMPLICITY
Marble sculptures from the Cycladic Islands

6

Transport yourself into the early childhood of nations, the first beautiful morning light of Europe, when all yet lay in fresh young radiance as of a great sunrise, and our Europe was first beginning to think, to be!

—Thomas Carlyle, *Heroes and Hero Worship*

Someone wandering the first floor of the Cycladic Museum in Athens could be forgiven for thinking they were in a modern sculpture gallery, or that they were looking at the sculpted heads and figures of one of the early twentieth century's greatest artists, Amedeo Modigliani. Instead, what are on display are 'human figures, elegantly carved with a breathtaking simplicity of line which constitute one of the glories of the prehistoric art of the world' (Colin Renfrew in the introduction to Christos Doumas *Cycladic Art, the N.P. Goulandris Collection*). The grace and simplicity of their style appeal to the modern eye despite the fact that they were carved in the third millennium BCE by artisans on a group of islands in the eastern Mediterranean.

For over a thousand years (ca. 3000–2000 BCE) this cluster of 30 or so rocky, barren islands, called the Kyklades from the Greek word *kyklos* meaning *a circle*, supported a flourishing culture quite distinctive from those around them. The populations of Naxos, Paros, Syros, Siphnos, Melos, Thera, Amorgos, Mykonos, Keos and others, who lived in well-fortified settlements, were engaged in fishing, shipbuilding, and the export of mineral resources such as copper, lead and emery.

The islands were favourably placed for trade, situated as they were between Crete, mainland Greece and the coast of Asia Minor. The people developed metallurgy and pottery and became accomplished sculptors. As most islands were rich in marble, particularly Paros and Naxos (famous for the quality of their stone in Classical times and still mined to this day), it was from this fine crystalline stone that the Cycladic artists carved their unique figures. The most stunning came from what is referred to as the Keros-Syros subculture ca. 2800–2300 BCE.

> The grace and simplicity of their style appeal to the modern eye despite the fact that they were carved in the third millennium BCE by artisans on a group of islands in the eastern Mediterranean.

The earliest abstract forms of the female figure with rounded lower torso, narrow waist, square shoulders, long neck and no head, are referred to as 'violin-shaped'. Later 'Cycladic idols' are termed 'folded arms' figurines. With their well-defined forms they reveal a considerable range of details which point to individual workshops and artists.

Celebration of the female form

Most of the figures are feminine, nude and with the arms folded over the abdomen; in some cases the belly is swollen as if indicating pregnancy. The breasts are shown as two slight protuberances and the pelvic area as an incised triangle. The slightly elongated almond-shaped, flat or oval heads, somewhat tilted back, are distinctive, with strikingly long noses as the dominant facial feature. Mouths and eyes may be absent, rendered in low relief, incised or painted. Some of these figures are large enough (150 centimetres) to be classified as statues.

Male figures are extremely rare in Cycladic art. Those that exist tend to be associated with specific roles, particularly as musicians. There are a number of exceptional examples of musicians playing the lyre, double flute and syrinx (a set of pan-pipes) in the Archaeological Museum of Athens and the Metropolitan Museum of Art in New York. A rare male figure in

OPPOSITE: A marble female figure of the 'folded arm' type found in the Cycladic Islands of the Aegean Sea.

ABOVE LEFT: The marble head and neck of a figurine. RIGHT: A pottery beak-spouted ewer.

the Cycladic Museum in Athens depicts a warrior/huntsman with a sword-belt in relief hanging from the right shoulder and an incised triangular dagger. Another masterpiece in the museum depicts a male sitting on a stool with extended arm holding a cup as if making a toast.

Some of the figures are mottled and encrusted with tan and ochre, while others have traces of colour on the face and upper arms. Scientific analysis has shown that some details were painted with mineral-based pigments such as cinnabar (red) and azurite (blue).

Although many of these figures were found in graves, not all graves contained them. Perhaps antiquities collectors plundered them over the centuries or perhaps they were not an essential part of the burial ritual. Many of the earlier discoverers did not document their finds so most have no archaeological context, and due to the lack of writing at the time, any discussion of their purpose and symbolism can only be based on conjecture.

The most popular view is that the female 'idols' represented a mother or fertility goddess. Another interpretation, based on the tilted nature of the heads and the slanting soles of the feet, suggests that they were ritual dancers in an ecstatic state performing to the music of lyres and flutes, while the males invoked various powers in song. Some scholars have suggested that the figures symbolised deities, revered ancestors, or acted as a substitute for human sacrifice. Still others think that they were believed to guide the souls of the dead on their journey into the afterlife or played some part in averting evil or bad luck. There is no evidence so far convincing enough to support any of these hypotheses.

Whether their purpose will ever be known, one thing is certain: in the harmony, balance and understatement of these treasures, the sculptors of the Cyclades in the third millennium BCE 'transcended the limitations of time and space to produce works which speak to us directly' (Colin Renfrew in Christos Doumas *Cycladic Art*).

RIGHT: A violin-shaped female figurine.

7

GIFTS TO THE GODS OF THE UNDERWORLD

Treasures from the royal death pits of Ur

I have found the greatest death pit of all yet discovered, containing women more magnificently attired, harps ornamented with beasts in gold and silver, and two statues of goats in gold and mosaic.

—Sir Leonard Woolley, telegram to the Director of the British Museum, December 22, 1928

43

3RD MILLENNIUM BCE3RD MILLENNIUM BCE

The exquisite Sumerian artefacts excavated from the royal tombs of Ur by Sir Leonard Woolley between 1926–1934, are amongst the greatest treasures from the ancient world. With their technical expertise in the processes of metallurgy, welding, filigree and enamelling, and their artistic skill in combining colours and materials such as gold, silver, lapis lazuli and mother-of-pearl, Sumerian craftsmen produced objects of stunning beauty and sophistication.

Such masterpieces include the jewellery of Queen Pu-abi, the bovine lyres and harps, a mysterious artefact referred to as the Standard of Ur, and ritual objects such as the enigmatic standing goats. Most of the treasures are dated ca. 2700–2600 BCE and are now housed in the British Museum, the University of Pennsylvania Museum and the National Museum of Iraq.

OPPOSITE: A he-goat hobbled to a golden tree, misnamed 'Ram in the Thicket', made from gold, silver, lapis lazuli, shell and red limestone and found in the 'royal cemetery' of Ur.

LEFT: Queen Puabi's jewellery.

The remains of the ancient city of Ur, which reached its height ca. 2750–2500 BCE, lie south of modern Baghdad, near the town of Nasiriyah. Before Woolley's discoveries, Ur was known primarily as the legendary birthplace of the biblical patriarch, Abraham, and for its great ziggurat, the three massive stepped platforms topped by a temple dedicated to the moon god Nanna.

It was while Woolley was digging trenches near the relatively well-preserved ziggurat that he saw evidence of ancient burials. Over a period of eight years he unearthed approximately 1850 burials, sixteen of which he designated as 'royal' because of the wealth they contained and the cylinder seals with inscriptions referring to royal titles.

The graves comprised a stone-built burial chamber with a domed or vaulted roof in a large pit with a sloping ramp leading from the surface. All of the burial chambers, except that of Queen Pu-abi, had been plundered. However, the adjacent pits contained magnificent artefacts as well as the remains of numerous males, females and animals. For this reason Woolley called them 'death pits'. The largest contained 73 attendants, 68 of them women. Beside many of the bodies Woolley found little containers of clay, stone or metal which probably contained a poisonous potion or drug, taken in a mass ritual suicide. It would have been necessary for someone to enter the pit later to kill the animals and arrange the bodies before the burial was sealed 'forever'.

A cuneiform text, *The Death of Gilgamesh*, mentions this bizarre practice. Gilgamesh was a legendary Sumerian ruler and according to the text his 'beloved wife and his beloved son, his favourite wife and junior wife', his singer, cup bearer, barber and palace attendants, lay 'down in their place with him as in the pure palace in Uruk'. Then Gilgamesh 'weighed out the meeting-gifts for Ereshkigal, weighed out the presents for Namtar ...' It appears that the Sumerians believed that kings would have palaces in the underworld and they needed their retinue to help them continue living as they had always done. The massive treasure buried with them was to offer as gifts to the gods of the underworld.

In the only intact tomb in the royal cemetery, Woolley found the remains of a woman about 152 centimetres tall, lying on her back on a bier, accompanied by three attendants. She was identified as Queen Pu-abi by a lapis lazuli cylinder seal written in cuneiform on her left shoulder and was judged to be around forty years of age. Her head was enveloped in three magnificent diadems—jewelled headbands—each smaller than the one below it and fastened to a wide band wound several times around her elaborate padded hairstyle (perhaps a wig).

The first diadem, which covered the forehead, was formed of lapis and carnelian beads supporting large interlocking pendant rings, while the second and third were made from realistically designed leaves in sheet gold supported by cylindrical lapis lazuli beads. Above the diadems were drooping gold flowers, decorated in blue and white, and on the back of her head she wore a gold comb decorated with golden flowers or rosettes with eight petals. A huge pair of golden, double-lunate earrings completed the adornment of the queen's head. She wore a necklace composed of three rows of semiprecious stones, while her upper body, from shoulders to stomach, was covered with a jewelled 'garment', perhaps a cape, of gold, silver, lapis lazuli, carnelian, agate and chalcedony beads. On a table nearby was another exquisite diadem.

Other magnificent treasures filled her tomb: a silver, lapis lazuli and shell head of a lion and a bull, which are remarkable examples of hollow-cast metal sculpture and which exhibit 'a masterful blend of naturalistic forms and abstract shapes' (Donald P. Hansen, *Treasures from the Royal Tombs of Ur*).

Precious offerings to the gods

The bovine lyre was the most common stringed intrument in the third millennium BCE. Some were small hand-held instruments while others had to be played while seated. Harps and lyres were referred to in Sumerian poetry as 'beloved' and 'holy'. Of the two harps and nine lyres discovered in the tombs, the most magnificent, largest and oldest was the 'Great Lyre' dated at ca. 2750 BCE.

The 'Great Lyre' was made of wood, but ornamented with a gold-sheathed bull's head with curly hair and a beard. The tips of the horns and forelock were fashioned out of lapis lazuli, and

The 'death pits' of Ur and their offerings have given us both a record of the fascinating, yet gloomy practice of ritual sacrifice as well as an abundance of beautifully made treasures.

the beard, also of lapis, was set in silver backing, while the eyes were of shell set in lapis. The front of the rectangular sound box featured a mosaic of mother-of-pearl plaques set in bitumen to highlight the ivory human, mythological and animal figures. Musical experts believe that the 'Great Lyre' would have produced a sound like a deep tone bass, perhaps as powerful as the bellowing of a bull.

The so-called Standard of Ur is the most informative object found in the royal cemetery. These side panels of what appears to have been a wooden box, possibly the sounding box of a lyre, feature mosaics of small, carved figures in shell, red limestone and lapis lazuli. They provide one of the earliest representations of the Sumerian army, and depict the roles of the king as warrior, protector, and mediator between men and gods, responsible for the fertility of the land.

Of all the objects recovered from the royal cemetery, the pair of statuettes each referred to as 'Ram Caught in a Thicket' are considered the most unusual. They were found in the largest death pit lying near to one another. Although recognising them as rearing goats hobbled to trees, Woolley rather fancifully misnamed them in reference to the biblical story of Abraham told in Genesis 22:13. One is in the Pittsburgh Collection, its counterpart is in the British Museum.

The goats, 42.5 centimetres high, with gold poles rising from their backs, stand on a base of shell, coloured stone and silver. The fleece of one goat is of carved shell and lapis lazuli; head and legs of gold foil; a silver stomach; ears of copper, and beard, horns and eyes of lapis. It has been suggested that these statuettes were associated with plant and animal fertility and that the goat was fertilising the tree, indicated by its symbolic eight-petalled flowers. A gold penis sheath and testicles were preserved on the British Museum statuette. Although their original function is unknown, Woolley believed they formed the supports of an offering table.

The 'death pits' of Ur and their offerings have given us both a record of the fascinating, yet gloomy practice of ritual sacrifice as well as an abundance of beautifully made treasures: 'Perhaps no excavation in the more than 150 years of archaeological work in Mesopotamia has excited as much public attention as Leonard Woolley's work at ancient Ur in the 1920s and early 1930s' (Richard L. Zettler, *Treasures from the Royal Tombs of Ur*).

GOD-KINGS OF GIZA

Royal statuary of Khufu, Khafre and Menkhaure

Any gods who shall cause this pyramid and this construction of the King to be good and sturdy, it is they who will be vital, it is they who will be respected, it is they who will be impressive, it is they who will control … it is they who will take possession of the crown. — Pyramid Texts, 1650

At Giza, on the outskirts of Cairo, stand the awe-inspiring trio of pyramids attributed to the god-kings of the fourth dynasty of Egyptian history: Khufu, Khafre and Menkhaure who ruled ca. 2551–2472 BCE. Herodotus, the Greek historian of the fifth century BCE, described The Great Pyramid, supposedly constructed for Khufu, as 'the largest monument of its kind ever constructed', and 'for workmanship, accuracy of planning and beauty of proportion, it remains the chief of the Seven Wonders of the World' (Herodotus, *The Histories*, Bk. 2).

It is particularly ironic, then, that the only portrait of Khufu is a priceless tiny ivory statuette, 7.5 centimetres in height and 2.5 centimetres in width, the smallest royal statue ever found. In complete contrast is the magnificent 168-centimetre seated statue of King Khafre (second Pyramid) carved from hard diorite, and the exquisitely modelled greywacke (a type of sandstone) triads featuring King Menkhaure (third pyramid) which reach 90 centimetres in height. All are housed in the Egyptian Museum in Cairo.

According to Herodotus, who supposedly heard it from Egyptian priests, Khufu (Cheops), 'brought the country all sorts of misery' (Bk.2, p.122). He closed the temples, forced his subjects to work as slaves on the construction of his pyramid, and sold his daughter into prostitution to help pay for it. Herodotus' sources believed that Khafre (Chephren) was 'equally oppressive', although the rule of Menkhaure (Mycerinus) was milder, as he reversed his predecessors' policies, 'reopened the temples and allowed his subjects, who had been brought into such abject slavery, to resume the practice of their religion and their normal work' (Bk.2, p.126).

Herodotus' views were based on his own standards and those of his age, 2000 years after Khufu's lifetime. It is unlikely that his informants of the fifth century BCE would have known a great deal about events so far in the past. The Greeks would have seen monuments as massive as the Great Pyramid, and that of Khafre, as evidence of *hubris* (excessive pride) on the part of the builder, and would have been unable to contemplate their construction by anything other than an army of slaves.

In fact it is now known that the vast numbers quoted by Herodotus (100,000) were not accurate and that it is possible that a force of 20,000–25,000 pyramid workers (not slaves) living in a 'settlement' close to the construction site, was all that was needed. However, it is quite possible that there was some truth in Herodotus' claim that Khufu and Khafre closed down temples, as there seems to have been religious changes occurring at the time, with a growing emphasis on the cult of the sun-god Re.

A 'dwelling place for the spirit': three regal figures

The rare and priceless ivory statuette of Khufu was not discovered at Giza, but at Abydos, an ancient cult centre in Middle Egypt. In 1903, the renowned British archaeologist, Sir Flinders Petrie, was digging in a temple at the site when one of his workmen came across a miniature headless statuette. Petrie realised the significance of the find when he deciphered the Horus name in the cartouche on the right side of the throne. It was the name of one of the greatest kings from antiquity: Khnum-Khuf (*the god Khnum is his protection*), or Khufu for short (called Cheops by the Greeks).

OPPOSITE: A seated diorite statue of the fourth dynasty Egyptian pharaoh Khafre, with the falcon god, Horus, perched on the back protecting the king.

Noting that the break across the neck of the statuette appeared fresh, Petrie believed that the head had been severed by one of his workman's picks. The story goes that he sent his men into a large town nearby with instructions to purchase all the sieves they could find, in order to meticulously sift the sand near where the body was found. It took three weeks to locate the head.

The diminutive statuette, carved with great attention to detail, appears realistic. It shows the king at an advanced age, seated on his throne, wearing the Red Crown of Lower Egypt, the short pleated kilt of royalty (*shendjyt*) and holding the ceremonial flail across his chest with his right hand. His facial features, with just the hint of a smile, if rather disdainful, suggest an iron-willed and uncompromising ruler of men. Rather than the oppressive tyrant suggested by Herodotus, the evidence suggests that Khufu 'was an able and energetic ruler during whose reign the land flourished and art reached perfection' (A. Fakhry, *The Pyramids*).

The remarkable seated statue of Khafre, made of extremely hard Nubian diorite, is the embodiment of the majesty and divinity of the god-kings of Egypt. This masterpiece was found, with the remains of seven other statues, in a large pit in Khafre's Valley Temple by Auguste Mariette in 1860. It was in a remarkable state of preservation, and the Egyptian Museum's catalogue describes it in the following way: 'The majesty of its pose, the perfection of its modelling and polish and the subtle symbolism of its component parts make it an ideal manifestation of Old Kingdom theocratic monarchy.' The statue is often called the 'Falcon Khafre', referring to the falcon god Horus perched on the back of the throne with its outstretched wings protecting the king who stares into the distance.

The statue reveals the iconic regalia of an Egyptian king: ceremonial false beard, the folded striped head cloth with pleated lappets (*nemes*), the royal cobra (*ureaus*) in raised relief, and the

LEFT: Ivory statuette of King Khufu.

short pleated *shendjyt* or kilt. There is a great deal of symbolism in this piece. Two lions, symbols of the sun and guardians of the throne, flank the king's legs while on each side of the throne is the motif of the union of the Two Lands (*sem-tawy*). This consists of the intertwined emblematic plants of Upper and Lower Egypt around the hieroglyph for 'union'. The falcon at the back is the symbol of Horus the sky god. Each king was regarded as the embodiment of Horus on earth and was given a Horus name, which was a statement of his god-like status.

It is believed that the statue once stood with twenty-two other life-sized statues of the king in his Valley Temple adjacent to the Sphinx. This temple, the gateway to Khufu's pyramid complex, is a masterful example of monumental architecture.

> The majesty of the seated Khafre's pose, the perfection of its modelling and polish and the subtle symbolism of its component parts make it an ideal manifestation of Old Kingdom theocratic monarchy.

Khafre's pyramid complex (Valley Temple, Causeway, Mortuary Temple, Subsidiary Pyramid, Pyramid and Temenos Wall) is the best preserved of all pyramid complexes, although his Pyramid is slightly smaller (in height) and less controversial that of his father, Khufu.

The beautifully carved and polished greywacke triad featuring King Menkhaure, wearing the White Crown of Upper Egypt, has survived in perfect condition. He stands between the goddess Hathor with her distinctive headdress of solar disc resting between two cow horns, and a female representation of one of the provinces (*nome*) of Egypt. The superbly rendered facial features, the delicately modelled torso of the king, and the artist's anatomical understanding of the female figure, make this another masterpiece of Old Kingdom art. This triad once stood in a chapel in the court of Menkhaure's Valley Temple.

Because the Egyptians celebrated the human form 'as an image of the spirit within', Egyptian craftsmen tried to create 'a fine dwelling place for the spirit, and an attractive focus for worship and offerings' (Zahi Hawass, *The Peak and Splendour of the Old Kingdom to the end of the Sixth Dynasty*). Unfortunately, during a time of economic and social collapse at the end of the Old Kingdom, there was a great deal of anger against the kings who had come before and many of these fourth dynasty sculptural masterpieces were smashed, making those remaining even more precious.

ALL THE KING'S MEN
Rare private statuary from fourth dynasty mastaba tombs

... the mason crawled into the narrow passage only to reappear several minutes later overcome with terror. Gabbling in fear he told Daninos (an Egyptologist) that there were two people staring at him from inside a hidden chamber. — Zawi Hawass, *Hidden Treasures of Ancient Egypt*.

The two pairs of eyes staring out of the dark at the terrified mason, described above, were made of opaque quartz and transparent rock crystal. They belonged to Prince Rahotep and his wife Nofret, whose life-sized double statue was secreted behind a limestone wall in a brick-built mastaba near the Pyramid of Meidum and discovered in 1871.

It is one of the earliest confident examples of private Egyptian statuary of illustrious members of the court who were involved in the construction of the pyramids. Two other treasures from the fourth dynasty are the impressive life-size seated statue of Hemiunu, 'architect' of the Great Pyramid, and the unique bust of Prince Ankh-haf.

It was the usual practice of nobles and dignitaries to build their mastaba tombs (an Arabic word meaning 'bench') close to the king to whom they were related or served. The Egyptians believed that the life force of the deceased (*ka*) could temporarily reside in a life-sized statue (*ka* statue) to

OPPOSITE: A perfectly preserved and coloured double statue of Prince Rahotep and Princess Nofret found in the Egyptian royal necropolis of Meidum.

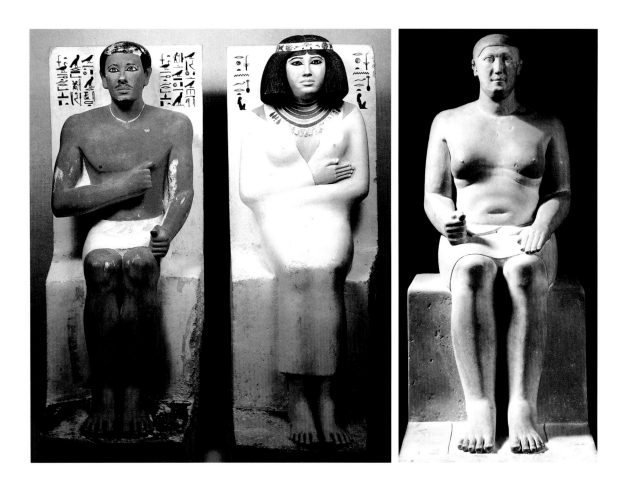

LEFT: Painted limestone statues of Rahotep and Nofret. RIGHT: Limestone statue of Hemiunu, believed to be the architect of the Great Pyramid.

accept offerings of food, drink and incense. However, possession of a *ka* statue, like the land for a tomb, was a privilege granted by the king in return for outstanding skill and achievement. For a time, during the reign of King Khufu, the *ka* statue was replaced with a slab stela (a pillar bearing an inscription) of the deceased sitting in front of a table of offerings, which explains the rarity of private statuary at this time.

The statues of Rahotep, Nofret and Hemiunu reveal the basic iconography of the human figure which changed little throughout Egyptian history. This strict canon, which included 'frontality', that is, the statue facing straight ahead, allowed the living person to interact directly with the deceased. Other elements of the sacred canon included a strict ratio between different parts of the body, and a standard pose for men and women, whether seated or standing. When standing, the woman has her two legs together, while the man has his left leg in front as if striding forward and he often holds a symbol of his rank in one hand. When seated, the feet are usually together and the left hand rests on the knee while the right hand is clenched. The skin of women was always painted a creamy yellow and the men a reddish brown.

Because sculpture had to follow sacred standards, most formal statues appeared to be of 'an unidentifiable age, neither young nor old, and show maturity as well as vitality. Their firm gazes are fixed straight ahead. Mood is neither happy nor sad' (Helmut Satzinger, 'Living Images the Private Statue', from *Egypt, the World of the Pharaohs*). However, during the fourth dynasty, dignitaries began to be fashioned more realistically, some portrayed as older and even corpulent, but in most cases reality was kept in check by the necessity of idealisation.

The marvellously preserved double-statue of Rahotep and Nofret is counted among the masterpieces of the Cairo Museum. It was in the northern mastaba field at Meidum, close to what is believed to have been the first pyramid of Sneferu, the founder the fourth dynasty.

Due to the location and size of Rahotep's palace-facade brick mastaba, as well as the titles painted on the statues, it is believed that he was either the brother of King Sneferu or his son. His titulary included: *Son of the King of his body; Great Priest of Heliopolis, General and Superintendent of Works and Expeditions.* Nofret, his wife, was referred to as *One known to the King,* indicating that she was part of the royal entourage. Rahotep must have died before Sneferu who built two more pyramids, including the first 'true' pyramid, at Dahshur where he was buried.

These painted limestone statues have a restrained naturalism, and clearly recognised identity. They were found virtually intact and retained their original vibrant colours. Their faces are skilfully crafted, revealing the solemn and dignified expression of personages of their rank. Their inlaid eyes heighten the life-like expression. Rahotep, shown in his prime with short hair and a fine moustache, wears a short white kilt and a heart-shaped amulet around his neck. Nofret has her eyes heavily made up and wears a shoulder-length wig. The artist has painted her real hair on her forehead. She wears a diadem (headband) of rosettes, a broad collar of concentric coloured beads and a cloak-like garment over a halter dress.

Loyal servants honoured in death

The monumental limestone statue of Hemiunu was discovered in the niche of his mastaba in the western cemetery at Giza not far from the Great Pyramid of Khufu in 1912. The statue has been described as revealing 'some of the ruthless exploration of form of which the geometrical perfection of the Pyramid is the architectural counterpart' (Cyril Aldred, 'The Rise of the God-Kings', from *The Dawn of Civilization*).

It is now displayed in the Roemer-Pelizaeus Museum in Hildersheim, Germany. At the time of its discovery, Dr Adolf Erman, a prominent German Egyptologist, claimed it to be the finest male statue that he knew of from Ancient Egypt, even though it was not found intact. Its head was lying nearby, its crystal and quartz eyes had been gouged out and it had only traces of the original paint left on the limestone.

Hemiunu was the grandson of Sneferu and the nephew of King Khufu who appointed him as his vizier (head of the civil administration and second only to the king) and *Master of all the King's Works*. He has been credited with being the 'architect/engineer' of the Great Pyramid. The statue is exceptional, because during Khufu's reign, life-sized statues were replaced with images of the deceased seated at a table of offerings. Skilfully sculpted heads—'reserve' heads—bearing the features of the deceased were placed at the bottom of their mastaba shafts. The quality of the statue of Hemiunu lies in its combination of realism and force. The mature corpulent image (double chin, sagging breasts and chest, heavy belly with a roll of fat, massive arms and legs) reveals the authority, privilege and prosperity of a member of the Old Kingdom elite who 'built' pyramids.

The portrait bust of Ankh-haf was found lying amongst the debris of his chapel in the eastern mastaba cemetery at Giza in 1925 and is now conserved in the Boston Museum of Fine Arts. He was obviously a royal prince as his mastaba was the largest single one in the field of royal burials (101 metres long, 52.5 metres wide and originally 10 metres high), and he bore the title *Eldest Son of the King's body*. He is believed to have been the brother and vizier of King Khafre, the builder of the second pyramid at Giza.

This extremely naturalistic and enigmatic bust is the finest portrait of the Egyptian Old Kingdom and one of the outstanding creations in all Egyptian art. It is almost possible to 'see' the personality of this mature dignitary with his 'intelligent gaze, ageing features, bags under the eyes and a receding hairline' (Andrey Bolshakov, *What Did the Bust of Ankh-haf Originally Look Like? Journal of the Boston Museum of Fine Arts*).

This unique portrait was never part of a statue, but was clearly made as a *ka* bust and may once have had arms in order to 'accept' food offerings. Ninety-four plaster models, including food, were found under the bust. It had been torn from its pedestal and its ears and nose were missing. Despite this mutilation, it is of great interest, as its creator (a master sculptor) employed a technical method unusual in Egyptian stone sculpture. He first covered the white limestone with a gypsum plaster of varying thickness to allow for more delicate modelling of the face, and then painted it. The statue of Hemiunu and the bust of Ankh-haf are two of five key items of Egyptian cultural heritage that Zahi Hawass, current secretary-general of the Egyptian Supreme Council of Antiquities, is lobbying to have returned to Egypt.

10

A ROYAL BOUDOIR

The furniture and possessions of Queen Hetepheres

Looking in from a small opening [we] had seen a beautiful alabaster sarcophagus with its lid in place. Partly on the sarcophagus and partly fallen behind it lay about twenty gold-cased poles and beams of a large canopy.

—George Reisner, Head of the Boston Museum of Arts Expedition, 1925

In 1925, a tomb found by accident within metres of the Great Pyramid revealed artefacts of inestimable value and significance: 'a private boudoir of a queen' (Mark Lehner, *The Complete Pyramids*). These finds were associated with Hetepheres, the most influential and powerful female of the Old Kingdom. Despite their simplicity and clarity of form, Hetepheres' elegant possessions are of the highest quality workmanship and comprise one of the most important finds of the Old Kingdom.

Queen Hetepheres was the daughter of a 'god' (Huni, last king of the third dynasty); wife of a 'god' (sister/queen of Sneferu, first king of the fourth dynasty); and mother of a 'god' (Khufu, second king of the fourth dynasty). Old Kingdom queens had a very high status and were regarded with great respect. During the fourth and fifth dynasties, they were buried in small replicas of their husband's pyramid tombs. Khufu supposedly built three small pyramids on the eastern side of the Great Pyramid for his queens and his mother. The northern one, which is no longer intact, is believed by some scholars to have been for Hetepheres.

ABOVE: The gilded wooden armchair of Queen Hetepheres which formed part of her funerary ensemble.

An Egyptian photographer, Mohammed Ibrahim, working for a team of American archaeologists near the causeway of the Great Pyramid of Khufu, was having difficulty getting his tripod to stand up straight because the ground was too hard and uneven. He moved it to another spot and one of the legs broke through the ground into a hole. On examination, it was found that the ground around the hole was covered with what appeared to be a plaster seal covering the entrance to a shaft.

The fact that the seal was not damaged in any way led to great excitement; it was possible that what lay beneath was untouched. The layer of plaster was removed, revealing twelve steps leading to a rubble-filled shaft. It took excavators thirteen days to clear the 27-metre-deep shaft, at the bottom of which they found a wall of limestone blocks. In his journal, George Reisner, the leader of the team, boasted that his discovery was '1500 years older than the royal tombs of the New Kingdom'. It should be noted that the Englishman, Howard Carter, had only three years previously found the intact tomb of Tutankhamun and was still astounding the world with its treasures. There was obviously some professional jealousy and one-upmanship involved.

When the first limestone block was removed, the excavators reflected sunlight into the burial chamber by means of mirrors. What they glimpsed was not just an alabaster sarcophagus, but according to George Reisner, 'several sheets of gold inlaid with faience' (fine glazed earthenware) and 'a confused mass of gold cased furniture.' It soon became obvious from the exquisite gold hieroglyphs on the remains of a sedan chair, that what they had stumbled upon was the burial of Queen Hetepheres, 'Mother of the King of Upper and Lower Egypt . . . one for whom everything she says is done, the god's bodily daughter, Hetepheres'.

It took two years to clear the tomb of the queen's funerary equipment which consisted of a wooden bed partially covered in gold, with a gold-panelled floorboard featuring a black and blue floral design; a canopy frame made of wood encased in gold, with its poles ending in lotus buds; a curtain box, and an alabaster headrest. There were two wooden armchairs encased in gold, and a magnificent sedan chair. Carrying chairs seem to have been the favoured mode of transport for the elite. The sedan chair featured an embossed gold pattern resembling woven matting, and panels of precious ebony wood from tropical Africa. Other items included a tube for holding walking sticks; eight alabaster vases filled with unguents and kohl; a gilded box containing 20 silver bracelets and anklets inlaid with lapis, carnelian and malachite in the shape of butterflies; gold razors and knives, as well as a gold manicure set.

Despite their simplicity and clarity of form, Hetepheres' elegant possessions are of the highest quality workmanship and comprise one of the most important finds of the Old Kingdom.

The furniture had to be reassembled, and was skilfully restored by Ahmed Youssef Moustafa where the original wood had not survived. Today it is displayed in the Cairo Museum, with reproductions in the Boston Museum of Fine Arts.

Missing body

Only after the queen's possessions were removed could the excavators turn their attention to her sarcophagus. Because the resinous remains of her internal organs were found in an alabaster canopic chest, Reisner was anxious to open the sarcophagus to reveal the royal mummy. According to Dows Dunham, chief team excavator, 'On March 3, 1927, a distinguished company [of eight people or so] assembled 100 feet underground . . . At a nod from Reisner, the jacks that had been placed for the purpose began to turn. Slowly a crack widened until we could see into the upper part of the box: nothing was visible' (Dows Dunham, *Recollections of an Egyptologist*). The team artist, Lindon Smith, continued, 'When it was sufficiently raised for me to peer inside, I saw to my dismay that the queen was not inside—the sarcophagus was empty. Reisner rose from the box and said, "Gentlemen, I regret Queen Hetepheres is not receiving." And added, "Mrs Reisner will serve refreshments at the camp."'

Although at first this appeared to be the oldest intact Egyptian royal burial ever found, upon closer examination the evidence pointed to a possible hurried reburial. There was no tomb superstructure, the shaft was left with rough walls; there were workmen's tools lying about; the burial chamber was left unfinished and holes in the walls appeared to have been plugged; pottery was smashed and linen lay disintegrated among the remains of boxes that once contained it. There were chips in the sarcophagus and the pieces of furniture had been jammed into the chamber. Also, Reisner noted that the contents of the chamber were in the reverse order usually found in tombs.

The manner of Hetepheres' burial has been the source of considerable scholarly controversy. Reisner suggested that Hetepheres was buried originally near her husband, Sneferu, at Dahshur. At some point, her tomb was plundered and her body stolen. According to this theory, in reporting the theft of valuables from the tomb, Khufu's officials did not inform the king of his mother's missing body and he arranged for a hurried reburial at Giza near his own burial place in an unmarked shaft for safety.

There are a number of objections to this theory suggested by Mark Lehner, an Egyptologist working on the Giza plateau for many years. He thinks that if robbers plundered her original tomb, they would have smashed the lid of the sarcophagus in their haste to steal what was on the body, as usually happened in tomb robberies. Also, why would robbers have left behind valuable portable items such as the 20 bracelets? He maintains there is no evidence of a burial at Dahshur, but even if there had been, Hetepheres would have been reburied there rather than at Giza. Lehner thinks it impossible that a shaft of 30 metres depth could have been built secretly at Giza. Finally, it is hard to believe that Khufu would have knowingly allowed his mother to have been buried with broken pottery and violated funerary equipment.

Lehner believes that Hetepheres died early in her son's reign and she was temporarily buried in the hastily made shaft while her pyramid was built. Her body was then removed to the burial chamber of the GI-a pyramid, one of the three smaller structures supposedly built for fourth dynasty queens, perhaps with a new set of funerary equipment. However, this does not explain why the canopic chest with its organs, needed by the deceased in the next life, would have been left behind in the shaft.

Zahi Hawass, head of the Egyptian Supreme Council of Antiquities, disagrees with both theories. He suggests that Hetepheres was originally buried in GI-a further suggesting that the bed canopy would have fitted exactly inside the pyramid's burial chamber. During a later period of upheaval, possibly at the end of the Old Kingdom during the First Intermediate Period, the burial was disturbed and her body stolen, the thieves looking for jewels. Afterwards, the priest associated with Khufu's cult moved the remains of the equipment into a shaft that already existed.

Another line of speculation is that Hetepheres was not the mother of Khufu and that her shoddily built tomb, without a notable superstructure, indicates dynastic conflicts over the succession. Whatever the case, Hetepheres' funerary items are unique examples of the Old Kingdom craftsmen's skill.

11

A JOURNEY TO THE NETHERWORLD
The cedar boat of King Khufu

*Be pure: occupy your seat in the barque of Re;... may you row over the
sky and ascend to the distant ones; row with the Imperishable Stars ...*

—*Pyramid Texts*, trans. A. J. Spencer, ***Death in Ancient Egypt***

In 1954, an Egyptian archaeologist, Kamal el-Mallakh, made a major find on the southern
side of the Great Pyramid: the funerary or solar barque, or boat, of King Khufu. Despite
being disassembled, it was in a remarkable state of preservation. Now reassembled and
restored, this full-sized 'papyriform' wooden boat, the only one in existence, is an impressive
expression of religion and the power of the king. Its discovery provided Egyptologists with insights
into the technology of ancient boat building, previously only gauged from the walls of tombs and
from miniature replicas of boats placed among funerary items. Khufu's boat is on display in its
own boat-shaped museum beside the Great Pyramid.

Due to the inhospitable desert and the lack of wheeled vehicles until ca.1600 BCE which
made overland journeys difficult, the Nile River was the country's main highway, linking the
scattered villages and towns along its 900-kilometre length. Travel up and down the river was

OPPOSITE: The reassembled full-sized papyriform wooden funerary/solar boat of King Khufu.

made easier by the prevailing wind which blew from north to south and the river current which ran from south to north. At any time on the river there could be papyrus or reed rafts and skiffs for fishing and fowling; wooden cargo boats laden with precious materials from the eastern deserts, Nubia and Aswan; boats with a deck cabin, a single sail and a large oar-shaped rudder used by officials carrying out their duties, and more substantial boats for trading beyond Egypt.

Even the sun god, Re, was believed to travel through eternity in his papyrus boat. In the *Pyramid Texts* (the oldest religious texts in the world), there are constant references to boats, boatmen and ferrymen and the king's journey to the afterlife where he joined the sun god, Re, sailing in his barque across the heavens. Linked to the barque of Re was another type of boat constructed from timber but in the form of a papyrus raft and associated with royalty. It was used for pleasure, on state occasions, and to transport a deceased king across the Nile to the *beautiful west* where his tomb was located.

Full-sized boats were buried adjacent to the tombs and pyramids of the earliest Egyptian kings. A 'fleet' of fourteen early dynastic wooden boats were found at Abydos, about 482 kilometres south of Giza. The timber hulls, sealed in brick boat-shaped casings and filled with mud bricks, are poorly preserved due to the actions of wood eating ants. In many cases all that was left of the hulls was frass, (ant excrement) that retained the shape of the original wood. The wooden planks that have survived do not appear to have been of cedar. These boats ranged in size from 19–27 metres in length with their prows towards the Nile. The planks were held together with woven ropes and the seams between the planks were filled with bundles of reeds to make the boat impermeable to water. These are considered to be the world's oldest planked boats. Although they predate the ones found at Giza by 300-440 years, Khufu's papyriform solar/ funerary boat is in a different class.

> Now reassembled and restored, this full-sized 'papyriform' wooden boat, the only one in existence, is an impressive expression of religion and the power of the king.

Associated with the Great Pyramid of Khufu at Giza are five boat pits which have been described as resembling 'a royal port authority or docking place on the journey from this world to the Netherworld' (Mark Lehner, *The Complete Pyramids*). Three of these, to the east of the pyramids, were boat-shaped, but were empty when discovered. It is not known whether they ever held actual boats or were just simulations.

In 1950, when an area on the southern side of the Great Pyramid was being cleared for a tourist road, Kamal el-Mallakh noticed a thin outline of mortar which delineated two long rectangular pits lying end to end. When he dug further down into one of the pits, he uncovered a

ABOVE: Hieroglyph for 'Son of Re', part of a pharaoh's titulary.

row of forty-one massive limestone slabs weighing between 17–20 tonnes each. Although Kamal el-Mallakh believed that the pits might contain Khufu's solar boats, it took until 1954 for the authorities to give him permission to excavate. He described how he scraped between two blocks in the easternmost pit, making first a chink, then a hole, continuing to cut until his hand eventually broke through into nothingness, then how an almost imperceptible smell crept into his nostrils. At first he thought it was incense, then he realised that it was cedar wood. With the use of a mirror reflecting a shaft of sunlight into the hole, he was able to see a large wooden oar. 'It is the boat, it is the boat!' he apparently shouted.

In the 32.5 metre-long pit, he found the dismantled boat of Khufu, carefully buried in 651 separate pieces, varying in size from ten centimetres to 23 metres, and arranged in thirteen layers. The ancient builders had even indicated on some pieces which parts of the boat they had come from. The almost perfectly preserved timbers were made of precious cedar imported from Lebanon, while the pegs and other small parts were made from native acacia and sycamore wood. The ancient boat builders did not use nails; there were holes in the timbers so that the boat could be 'stitched' together using ropes made of vegetable fibres. It is believed that when the wood was swollen by water the ropes would tighten and make the boat watertight.

For fourteen years, the expert conservationist, Hag Ahmed Yousef, made sure each piece of the boat was recorded, chemically treated to preserve it and then carefully put together like a jigsaw puzzle. The reassembled boat is 43.3 metres long and 5.9 metres wide, its prow sweeping upward with a papyrus end while the bow curves inward and is tipped with a magnificently carved papyrus blossom. It is a perfect papyriform boat with twelve oars averaging seven metres in length, one pair at the stern to act as a rudder. There is a panelled cabin nine metres long, with palm-form capitals with an open canopy supported by poles, and a smaller enclosure at the fore, probably for the captain. The boat is a very impressive piece of technology.

In 1987, the second rectangular boat pit was examined with a micro camera inserted through a hole, which confirmed that its contents were similar to the excavated pit. A decision was made to leave it untouched.

A symbolic or actual voyage?

As with many discoveries in Egypt, this boat has provided endless speculation and conjecture as to its purpose. Was this boat a symbolic part of the burial of Khufu, meant to carry the king's soul through the heavens with Re (a solar boat)? Or was it used during the funeral procession to transport the king's body across the river to its final resting place (a funerary boat)? If it was a funerary rather than a solar boat, had it been used during the king's lifetime or was it built specifically for the funeral?

Zahi Hawass believes it was a symbolic solar boat constructed close to where it was buried as there were shavings of cedar and acacia found nearby. Also, due to the complete absence of water marks and the lack of a mast, he maintains the boat had never been in the water. The *Pyramid Texts* do mention that the sun god used two boats: a day boat and a night boat. As the representative of the sun god on earth, it is possible that the king also needed two symbolic boats, but would they have needed a large deckhouse and a hut for the captain?

Other scholars, like Mark Lehner, believe that the two southern boats were not part of the symbolic layout of the whole Khufu complex, but were used for Khufu's funeral voyage to the pyramid. Lehner suggests that they formed part of 'a deliberate ritual disposal'. He bases this on the fact that the pits are rectangular, not boat-shaped, and their location would have placed them outside the sacred enclosure wall (*temenos*) of the pyramid. He also maintains that 'items connected with the royal funeral were considered in some sense to be highly charged. To neutralise them, they were dismantled and buried separately, close to, but outside the funerary complex' (*The Complete Pyramids*). On the other hand, it has been suggested that its oars were too heavy to be used for rowing.

Although the function of the boat, whether solar or funerary, continues to be debated, it does nothing to detract from the significance of this unique ancient artefact.

12

BIRDS AND BEASTS IN THE 'HOUSES OF THE DEAD'

Old Kingdom Egyptian masterpieces from the tombs of the nobles

Make good your dwelling in the graveyard,
Make worthy your station in the west
The House of Death is for life.

—From the tomb chapel of Prince Hardjedef

The incised and painted images in the tomb chapels and on the slab stelae of the nobles of the fourth and fifth dynasties (ca. 2575–2325 BCE) are remarkable for their quality, originality, attention to detail, and their excellent preservation after four-and-a-half millennia. They also provide a vibrant picture of the flora, fauna and life along the Nile. These images were never meant to be decorative, and yet the men who held the highest positions in the state employed master craftsmen to 'decorate' their tombs to provide for their continuing existence in the next world.

The most important spiritual aspect of an individual during the Old Kingdom was the *ka*, or the life-force, which remained with the body at death. To sustain the *ka* throughout eternity, the chapel walls abounded with images associated with food and drink: scenes from the annual agricultural cycle (ploughing, sowing, tending crops, harvesting, threshing and storing); animal breeding and herding; hunting in the papyrus marshes and adjacent deserts; fishing; catching and fattening fowl; growing grapes; as well as the production of bread, beer and wine. The Egyptians believed that with the pronouncement of the offering formula for the deceased, the images magically came into being providing endless quantities of food and drink.

Artists, guided by religious principles, were not expected to produce imaginative and original ideas, but rather adhere to a strict set of rules with regard to the themes and their arrangement into registers (horizontal strips, like a cartoon); the size, proportion and form of the chief figures; and the use of colour. Although there was some experimentation with lesser individuals (farmers, tradesmen) who were often shown in natural and relaxed poses, it was in their treatment of animals, birds, fish and vegetation that Old Kingdom artists showed their best work. They were great observers of nature, and skilfully captured the markings of the flora and fauna found along the Nile and in the adjacent deserts.

Because birds
and animals played
an important part in both secular and sacred life, they were
integral elements in Old Kingdom masterpieces. Livestock and bird breeding
represented the main wealth of the senior officials in charge of the administration and
many species of bird and animal were associated with Egyptian gods and goddesses. They also
featured prominently in the hieroglyphic script, a superb example of which is the slab stela of
Prince Wep-em-Nefret.

The Egyptians knew the annual cycles of the natural world around them and were aware of
the seasonal migrations of birds in their country and could distinguish between resident and
passage varieties. 'The rich bird life of ancient Egypt throngs the houses of the dead. Wild and
domesticated birds appear in scenes of everyday life and hunting, adding to the rich symbolism
of Egyptian art and helping to bring to life the valley of the Nile in ancient times' (Patrick
Houlihan, 'Bird Life Along the Ancient Nile', *Ancient Egypt*). Trapping birds was a recurring
tomb motif with fowlers depicted using large hexagonal-shaped clapnets to capture enormous
numbers of migratory duck, geese and cranes. Many were kept with domestic varieties in
poultry yards and aviaries, being force-fed until consumed or sacrificed.

The most dazzling of all bird images are the 'Meidum Geese' found in the combined tomb
of Nefer-maat (son of King Sneferu, founder of the fourth dynasty) and his wife, Itet. This
magnificent panel of painted plaster, in near pristine condition, features three pairs of strikingly
realistic geese feeding along the Nile. This masterpiece, now in the Cairo Museum, reveals the
technical ability and observational skills of the leading artists of the day.

OPPOSITE: Part of a painted low-raised wall relief from the Tomb of Ti at Saqqara depicting cattle fording a
canal in which a crocodile lurks. ABOVE: A fragment from a scene in the tomb chapel of Nofret at Meidum
depicting men trapping waterfowl with a clap net.

LEFT: A pair of geese from of the tomb painting known as the Meidum Geese. RIGHT: Animal hieroglyphs on a slab stela from the tomb of Prince Wep-em-nefret.

The geese have been identified, by their brilliant colouring and individual feathering, as bean geese, white-fronted geese and red-breasted geese, and according to Professor Patrick Houlihan this panel is the 'earliest ornithological record in history'. The painting was originally part of a scene showing four men trapping birds in the marshes with a clap net. When Luigi Vassali cut the 'Meidum Geese' panel from the wall of the chapel in 1872, however, he destroyed much that was above and below it. Only fragments survived. One magnificent piece in the British Museum shows a fowler holding a bird in one hand. The detailed plumage of the bird reveals the ancient artist's mastery of colour and texture.

Depictions of plenty

In the tomb of the fifth dynasty noble, Ptahhotep, there is a representation of a farmyard in which the species of waterfowl are named. In another register, Ptahhotep's supervisor of the corn store, Kahap, leads a flock of cranes, three sorts of geese, a group of swans, ducks, pigeons and finally chicks. The number of each of these birds is given, totalling more than 600,000. In the tomb of Ti, another fifth dynasty noble, attendants bring troops of demoiselle and common cranes from the villages of Ti's estates.

Recurring themes in the tombs are the breeding—mating, birthing, suckling, and caring of calves by herders—and census of livestock, as well as exquisite representations of hunting in the desert.

Hunting was a pastime enjoyed by the privileged classes, and was a way of rounding up wild animals to be tamed (mainly herbivores such as antelopes) and kept in their estate menageries. It also had an important symbolic purpose; the desert was the domain of Seth, the god of destruction and chaos, and scenes featuring wild animals being overthrown represented the overthrow of the forces of evil.

The artists' sharp sense of observation of the desert landscape, its wild fauna and the sleek and swift hunting dog (*basenji*), have produced realistic images of the chase and kill which are of exceptional quality. The *basenji* almost always wore a collar so they could be leashed once they had caught their prey. There is a scene in the tomb of Ptahhotep showing men drawing a sled containing a lion and a leopard and others carrying bound animals on a yoke or over their shoulders.

Tomb scenes showing the deceased hunting among the papyrus growing along the Nile are usually a reference to the next life. The papyrus thickets of the Delta were the mythical birthplace of the god Horus, and where his mother, Isis, protected him from Seth, his uncle, who tried to kill him. So, not only is the papyrus thicket a place of rebirth and revitalisation, but it can conceal dangers. The hostile forces of Seth, who sometimes took the form of a hippopotamus, could threaten the rebirth of the deceased and so had to be killed or mercilessly driven away.

Because birds and animals played an important part in both secular and sacred life, they were integral elements in Old Kingdom masterpieces.

Other exquisite images depicted in detail in these Old Kingdom tombs include the tomb owner and his family enjoying leisure time, often with their pets, or inspecting the activities of his farmers, herders, boat builders and craftsmen, and collecting taxes. All of these themes formed a basic part of the repertoire of Egyptian funerary art which remained remarkably stable for millennia.

13

'PRIAM'S TREASURE'

A cache of gold and jewellery from ancient Troy

It would have been impossible for me to have removed the treasure without the help of my dear wife, who stood at my side, ready to pack the things I cut out in her shawl and carry them away.

—Heinrich Schliemann, *Trojan Antiquities*

In 1873, the entrepreneur and amateur archaeologist, Heinrich Schliemann, rediscovered an Early Bronze Age city dated ca. 2450 BCE, at the site of ancient Troy in modern Turkey. He firmly believed it was the city of Priam the king of Troy mentioned in Homer's great epic poem *The Iliad*, which tells of the war between the Greeks and the Trojans. Schliemann dubbed the artefacts of gold, silver, copper, bronze, jadeite and lapis lazuli that he unearthed there, 'Priam's treasure'. Schliemann, a literalist who believed in the historical accuracy of Homer, was mistaken. The city and treasure he excavated have been dated to ca. 1250 BCE, over 1000 years older than the Troy of the Trojan War.

Heinrich Schliemann was an enigmatic character, an incurable dreamer and brilliant linguist, but unscrupulous in getting what he wanted: fame and treasure. He at times resorted to lying, cheating and smuggling to meet these ends. In his book *Schliemann of Troy: Treasure and*

OPPOSITE: An engraving made in 1877 of Heinrich Schliemann's wife Sophia, wearing some of the jewellery excavated from the remains of Bronze Age Troy.

Deceit, David Traill uses previously unpublished sources to accuse Schliemann of being a pathological liar who created a personal fiction and whose 'fieldwork' and journals were doctored to prove his theories.

According to Schliemann's own story, his interest in Troy began as an eight-year-old when he first saw a picture of Troy in flames, in a book given to him by his father. He became obsessed with Homer and was determined to find the Homeric city. His career included an apprenticeship as a grocer, a position as a clerk in Amsterdam, and a lucrative stint in Russia's St Petersburg as an indigo merchant. During this time he became fluent in many languages, including modern and ancient Greek. At age 41, and with a fortune behind him, he set off to travel, and in Greece married a young girl, Sophia, who apparently shared his passion for Homer.

In 1870, fuelled by an unwavering faith and determination, he and Sophia arrived in Turkey to prove the historicity of Homer's Ilium (Troy), despite the doubts and ridicule of many in the academic world. Those who like Schliemann believed that Troy had once existed pointed to a hill named Bunarbashi as the most likely site, but Schliemann was not convinced. Using *The Iliad* as his guide, he followed the poet's geographic clues and decided another hill named Hissarlick, commanding the western approach to the Dardanelles, fitted the Homeric site more closely.

With no archaeological background and without permission from the Turkish government, Schliemann dug two long trenches into the hill which immediately provided evidence of settlement. He was eventually forced to seek permission to dig, and from 1871 began a process that can only be referred to as 'strip-mining'. Other terms like 'bulldozing' have been used to describe his unethical and unprofessional methods of excavation, driven as he was by an impatience to locate Priam's city and treasure. Believing that they would be found at the bottom of the mound, he ruthlessly cut through layers of successive Troys, destroying much of the site, and losing valuable data forever. He himself admitted, 'I

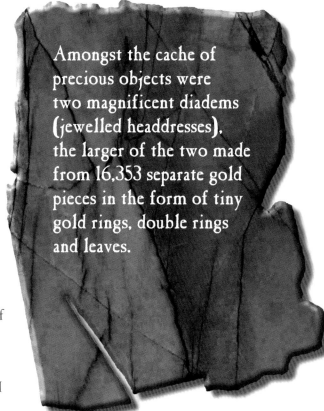

Amongst the cache of precious objects were two magnificent diadems (jewelled headdresses), the larger of the two made from 16,353 separate gold pieces in the form of tiny gold rings, double rings and leaves.

was forced to demolish many interesting ruins in the upper stratas'.

Towards the bottom of the mound was a settlement layer (later referred to as Troy II-g) that appeared to have been destroyed by a ferocious conflagration. Schliemann unearthed the remains of a fortress-city with towered gateways in brick and timber and outer walls with powerfully buttressed substructures. Surely, he thought, this must be the Scaean Gate and the tower in which Homer's old counsellors sat 'like cicadas perched in a tree'. He also found a central enclosure with a megaron hall, with what appeared to be residential quarters clustered around, and a paved road over five metres wide.

Everywhere he found signs of the destruction that he believed was caused by the Greeks, the fire seen in the book of his childhood. In places there were 2–3 metres of ash and 'partly vitrified fragments of bricks and stones' (Schliemann, *Trojan Antiquities*). However, after three years of excavation, he had not found 'Priam's treasure', 'the ten talents of gold' and the 'two shining tripods, four cauldrons and a very lovely cup' mentioned in *The Iliad*.

Just as he was about to give up, he saw the glint of gold in the soil. To prevent the Turkish workmen learning of his discovery, he used the pretext of his birthday to give them time off. He and Sophia dug beneath the fortified wall and he described how 'this involved great risk since the wall of fortification, beneath which I had to dig, threatened every moment to fall down upon me. But the sight of so many objects, every one of which is of inestimable value to archaeology, made me restless, and I never thought of any danger'.

Amongst the cache of precious objects were two magnificent diadems (jewelled headdresses), the larger of the two made from 16,353 separate gold pieces in the form of tiny gold rings, double rings and leaves. It comprised a gold chain from which hung seventy-four short chains of heart-shaped gold plates which rested on the wearer's forehead like a fringe, and sixteen longer chains that hung to the shoulders. There is an engraving of Sophia wearing what Schliemann said could have been the jewellery of Helen of Troy. The second diadem had a narrow band of gold and chains that hung to the temples. The hoard also included six gold bracelets; sixty earrings; a gold goblet weighing 601 grams; a large vessel of silver; ritual axes of jadeite and lapis lazuli, and 8700 gold trinkets.

Schliemann believed this treasure was hurriedly buried as the Mycenaean Greeks attacked Troy. However, David Traill questions the authenticity of the hoard, believing that many of the artefacts had been collected from outside the walls and that Schliemann planted objects to appear as if they came from the same location.

Later, Heinrich and Sophia smuggled the finds out of Turkey to Athens where they hid them 'in baskets and chests, in barns and stables, in the homes and on the farms of Sophia's many relatives' (Leonard Cottrell, *The Bull of Minos*). When the Turkish government discovered the situation, Schliemann paid them off for a fraction of what the treasures were worth. In 1881 he donated them to the Berlin Museum of Prehistory and Early History.

A plunderer's legacy

Excavations during the twentieth century revealed that Schliemann's Troy was only one of nine cities built on the site from ca. 3000 BCE to 600 CE. It appears that Troy VII 1250–1000, destroyed by war, is the most likely city of Homer. The great conflagration that burnt Troy II was part of a widespread catastrophe throughout the eastern Mediterranean and the Middle East. This catastrosphe brought an end to the Early Bronze Age settlements of Alaca Huyuk, Tarsus, Ugarit and Byblos, and may have contributed to the termination of the Old Kingdom in Egypt. The geologist Dr Robert Schoch believes that 'something big was going on then', perhaps meteor swarms produced when a comet broke up as it crossed earth's orbit (*Voices of the Rocks*).

Mortimer Wheeler, a giant in archaeology in the 1940s and 50s, wrote, 'We may be grateful to Schliemann because he showed us what a splendid book had in fact been buried there (Troy): but he tore it to pieces in snatching it from the earth, and it took us upwards of three-quarters of a century to stick it more or less together again and to read it right.'

The Trojan treasure remained in Germany until the last days of World War II when the Nazis moved it to a Berlin bunker for safekeeping. After their defeat, rumours abounded of its destruction, but it had been looted by members of the Russian army in 1945 during its occupation of Berlin. The treasure was spirited away to the Soviet Union where it lay for decades with thousands of other works of art in the bowels of the Pushkin Museum of Fine Arts in Moscow. Only a handful of Soviet officials, sworn to secrecy, knew of its existence.

When the museum's curator found out about the treasure by chance in 1975, he was not permitted to see it until 1993 when Russian authorities finally acknowledged its theft from Germany. The artefacts were authenticated, and in 1996, after more than half a century of intense mystery about their whereabouts, 260 pieces, in mint condition, went on display in the Pushkin Museum. There is now political bickering between Germany, Russia and Turkey over the ownership of 'Priam's Treasure'.

MINIATURE TOTEMS AND A MYSTERIOUS SCRIPT

Animal seals from Harappa and Mohenjo-daro

Many of the most exquisite objects are extremely small and ... made from raw materials that were transformed through complex techniques of manufacture. — Jonathan Mark Kenoyer, *Ancient Cities of the Indus Valley Civilization*

The Indus Valley civilisation, often referred to as the Harappan culture, arose from the earliest farming communities along the banks of the Indus River between ca. 2600–1900 BCE. This unique and highly developed culture covered a vast geographical area (680,000 square kilometres); from Baluchistan on the Persian border in the west, to the vast deserts of Cholistan and Thar that form the border between Pakistan and India in the east, and from the foothills of the Himalayas to the coastal regions of Pakistan (Gujurat) in the south.

This culture was far more widespread than both Mesopotamia and Egypt. In its heyday there were five major cities: Harappa, Mohenjo-daro, Ganweriwala, Rakhigarhi and Dholavira, each one the focus of an extensive hinterland and vast trading network.

Associated with the rise of these early cities was the appearance of the craft technology of seal carving, and perhaps the earliest form of writing: a pictographic script of 400 signs. The Indus Valley seals are distinctive in kind and unique in quality. The craftsmanship 'demonstrates a total control of the medium and the ability to capture the essence of a symbol or figure with a few delicate strokes' (*Ancient Cities of the Indus Valley Civilization*). However, the seals were more than just art objects; they were used for trade and to designate ownership, and so came to be symbols of status and power in the Indus Valley.

The two most remarkable archaeological sites so far excavated are in present-day Pakistan: Mohenjo-daro ('Mound of the Dead') in Sindh, and Harappa in Punjab, almost 600 kilometres apart. Discovered in the early 1920s, they are among the world's oldest urban centres and appear to have been sophisticated civic communities. It has been estimated that Mohenjo-daro and Harappa covered areas of 250 and 150 square hectares respectively, with populations possibly over 50,000 each. They were built on immense platforms high above the surrounding plain and fortified with lofty baked-brick walls, towers and gateways.

Each city had a citadel with imposing public buildings which functioned as administrative, assembly, market and ritual centres; wide roads arranged in a grid pattern; multilevel houses, some with up to thirty rooms; workshops; well-developed drainage and sewage systems; public baths; and private and public wells. At Mohenjo-daro, a 'great bath' (12 metres by 7.5 metres and 2.4 metres deep), possibly for ritual bathing, is the oldest public water tank in the ancient world.

Seal manufacturing workshops have been discovered in very restricted locations, pointing to a strong control of production, and the variety of raw materials at the sites demonstrate the vast trading links with distant resource centres. A large collection of these seals were found in a single house in Harappa, indicating that distinct social and economic classes used these specific artefacts to distinguish themselves.

The finest craftsmanship is found on the tiny animal seals (2–5 centimetres in diameter) cut out of grey/brown and tan steatite, a stone which is easily carved but becomes hard on firing. The motif was cut into the stone with a small chisel and drill, then coated with an alkali and heated to produce a white lustrous surface; some were unfired. The seals were normally square with a perforated boss on the back for handling and hanging around the neck or from the waist.

OPPOSITE: Square steatite seals with Indus script and buffalo, rhinoceros, elephant and horned tiger motifs.

They featured detailed images of domestic animals (the Zebu bull), wild animals that lived in the jungles and swampy grasslands on the edge of the Indus plain (rhinoceros, water buffalo, the gharial or crocodile, and tiger), and mythical animals (the unicorn). Several seals showed composite and multiple-headed animals. A famous example from Mohenjo-daro depicts a male deity sitting in a yogic position on a throne with legs in the shape of bulls' hooves, surrounded by an elephant, tiger, rhinoceros and water buffalo with two antelopes seated below the throne.

These totemic animal motifs are believed to have represented the clans to which the small, powerful merchant segment of the population belonged. At least ten clans have been identified. Combination animal seals may have symbolised the joining together of several clans in some kind of commercial venture or political treaty. Perhaps certain individuals had several affiliations.

Status and power

Above the animal motif was a short line of script. Although the Indus Valley script has never been deciphered, some scholars believe that it gives the owner's name. Iravatham Mahadevan, India's script pioneer and scholar of early Tamil, thinks that the terminal signs on the seals indicate a person's status or duties; for example priest, warrior, or civil office holder.

The most impressive motif found on the Indus seals is the majestically rendered humped Zebu or Brahman bull, with its heavy dewlap and wide curving horns. Although the bull, noted for its strength and virility, was a recurring theme on pottery and in figurines, its rarity on seals found in Mohenjo-daro and Harappa may indicate that it represented the most powerful clan or individual in the city, the leader of the herd.

The intriguing 'unicorn' seals are the most common (at least 388 found between 1927–31), indicating that the people who belonged to this clan

The craftsmanship 'demonstrates a total control of the medium and the ability to capture the essence of a symbol or figure with a few delicate strokes'.

were the most widespread. There has been much argument about the ox-like animal with its single ribbed or spiralling horn, bovine hooves, bushy-ended tail, elongated body and arching neck. In most of the seal depictions, the 'unicorn' has a carved collar or garland, and stands in front of some kind of sacred or ritual object. Was it the mythical animal that ancient Greek and Roman sources traced back to the subcontinent of India?

Greek writers of natural history were convinced of the existence of the magical unicorn that lived in the distant and fabulous realm of India. The earliest references were by Ctesias who, in his *Indica* (fourth century BCE) spoke of a wild white ass having on its forehead a horn a cubit and a half in length, from which the

ABOVE: Seal with Zebu or Brahman bull.

Indians made drinking cups that detoxified poisons. The Roman natural historian, Pliny the Elder, in his *Natural History* written in the first century CE mentions a very ferocious Indian ass with a body similar to a horse, the head of a deer, feet of an elephant, tail of a boar, a huge bellowing voice and a single black horn, two cubits in length, standing in the middle of its forehead.

The Chinese and Japanese had their own form of the unicorn, while Alexander the Great, Julius Caesar and Marco Polo each claimed to have seen a unicorn. Ghengis Khan's troops were supposedly turned away from India by a unicorn. It has been suggested that a huge extinct Eurasian rhinoceros with a large single horn in its forehead, known to scientists as *Elasmotherium*, may have been the basis of the unicorn myth. Perhaps it survived long enough to be remembered in legends.

Whatever the meaning of both totem animal and script, these small, perfectly rendered seals 'are among the world's greatest examples of an artist's ability to embody the essentials of a given form in artistic shape' (B. Rowland, *The Arts and Architecture of India*, 1967).

15

A RITUAL LANDSCAPE

Golden artefacts from Early Bronze Age Britain

The ghost would emerge from a nearby barrow and offer passers-by a golden cup which contained a magic potion ... —Richard Hobbs, *Treasure: Finding our Past*

Stories of ghostly apparitions, fairies and gold have been told for centuries by people living in the area of southern Britain associated with Neolithic ceremonial structures such as stone circles and mounds—Stonehenge, Avebury and Silbury Hill—and along the 'sacred' line that runs right across southern Britain, from the far west of Cornwall to a point on the east coast of Norfolk. This is a ritual landscape cloaked in mystery even to this day and is also associated with some of the richest barrow burials and deposition sites of the Early Bronze Age ca. 2150 BCE.

Early Britons were buried in long communal barrows (large mounds of earth or stone with surrounding ditches), but ca. 2000 BCE these were replaced with 'personal' burials in round barrows. The richest were associated with what is called the Wessex Culture (ca. 2000–1600 BCE) a name given to the archaeological finds from southern England in the vicinity of Stonehenge, Avebury and Silbury. The sophisticated grave goods from these barrows, and other sites in Cornwall and Wales, include metal daggers with richly decorated hilts; precious ornaments of gold and amber; amulets; gold cups; a sceptre with a polished mace head, and a ceremonial cape. The metal grave goods were probably not associated with everyday life but were ritual offerings.

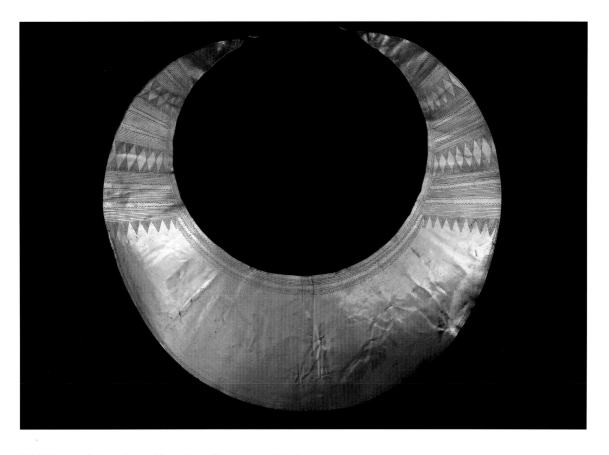

ABOVE: A gold lunula necklace from Bronze Age Britain.

The quote at the beginning of this chapter refers to continuing reports over hundreds of years that Bodman Moor was haunted by the ghost of a Druid who would offer travellers a drink from a cup that was impossible to drain dry. In 1837, a gold Early Bronze Age cup, known as the Rillaton Cup, was discovered in the area. This was not the only case where a major discovery of Bronze Age gold coincided with a local ghost legend.

In 1825 in Wales, at a place called Bryn-yr-Ellyllon (Goblin's Hill) a woman walking home late at night from the town of Mold skirted the Goblin's Hill and was confronted by a figure 'of unusual size and clothed in a coat of gold, which shone like the sun' (C.R. Beard and R. A. Coates, *The Romance of Treasure Trove*). The gold-covered figure crossed the road and disappeared as it reached Goblin's Hill. Eight years later, in 1833, a magnificent and unique gold cape was discovered on the site.

Many British Bronze Age treasures have been discovered by chance: during agricultural activities, quarrying, road building and repair. Amateur archaeologists with metal detectors have found others. In 1833, the Mold Gold Cape, 'an object of unparalleled beauty and craftsmanship, one of the true treasures of Wales' past' (The British Museum, *Compass* Online), was discovered, in an ancient burial mound, by workmen quarrying for stone. It was found in a crushed condition together with bronze strips and amber beads, close to skeletal remains. Unfortunately it came apart during recovery and some pieces 'disappeared'. The British Museum held on to the greater part of the treasure, and over the years, many of the missing pieces reappeared which allowed it to be repaired.

Initially it was believed to be a chest ornament for a horse, but in the 1960s it was recognised as some form of cape. Weighing 560 grams and dated ca. 1900 BCE, it is not only unique in form and design, but the largest artefact of gold from the Early Bronze Age. It was made from a single ingot of gold, hammered out to a sheet and then embossed with a design 'of ribs and bosses' that resemble multiple strings of beads. The perforations along its edges suggest that it was once attached to a backing, perhaps of leather. Because the cape would have restricted arm movements, it was probably a ceremonial garment that symbolised religious authority.

> The discoveries of two rare gold cups are further testimony to the incredible skill of the Early Bronze Age craftsmen.

Gold: a precious material

Gold, due to its rarity, ease of working, incorruptibility and association with the sun, was a most desirable metal amongst Bronze Age craftsmen. Some of the oldest finds come from Wales, possibly because it was the entry point of the river-washed gold from Ireland. A small sun disc (40 millimetres in diameter), which may have adorned a piece of clothing, was excavated from Banc Tyndaol, and a crescent-shaped neck ornament called a lunula (*luna* is Latin for moon) was discovered in 1869 at Llanllyfni when a farm worker, out shooting, saw what he thought was a yellow laurel leaf sticking out of some peat. The stunning lunula which weighs 185 grams is one of the oldest gold artefacts found in Wales.

Another hoard of treasures, including two stunning gold armlets and a bronze and copper dagger still in its leather scabbard, were found during the construction of a road in Leicestershire in 1994. They had been placed in a pit with some fragments of pottery, on the edge of a funerary complex. The ribs of one bracelet, decorated with finely punched dots, 'swell at intervals to form lozenge bosses which are thought to mimic contemporary strings of beads of jet and amber' (The British Museum, *Compass* Online). The other bracelet is composed of a series of five ribs.

The discoveries of two rare gold cups are further testimony to the incredible skill of the Early Bronze Age craftsmen. They are the only stylistically similar gold vessels found in Britain so far, although several others have been found in continental Europe. The Rillaton gold cup was found—and plundered—from a burial vault by workmen engaged in construction on Rillaton Manor in Cornwall in 1837. The other was located by an amateur archaeologist near the village of Ringlemere in Kent in 2001.

The Rillaton cup found its way into the private collection of royalty (King William IV) where it remained until it was loaned to the British Museum after the death of King George IV in 1936. In contrast, the discoverer of the Ringlemere cup immediately notified the relevant authorities so that an archaeological team could carefully examine the site and context of the cup. At the time, very few barrow burials were known in Kent because of centuries of erosion connected with ploughing.

The craftsmanship of both vessels is superb, although the Ringlemere cup had been crushed. The bodies of both cups were beaten out of a single lump of gold of very high quality. Both feature multiple horizontal corrugations which strengthened the sheet gold, but also added to the aesthetic appeal. The grooved handles, made of separate wide gold strips, were riveted to the body with lozenge-shaped (diamond-shaped) washers. The Ringlemere cup has what is called a sub-conical base, and could not have stood up on its own. This suggests that cups such as these were placed in a container of some perishable material, or were never meant to be put down until drained, possibly passed around during a ceremonial feast.

The daily and religious life of the owners of the gold and bronze treasures found in the barrows and deposition sites is a matter of conjecture. It is interesting to speculate on the ritual significance of these items, since the immediate forebears of the owners were responsible for the rebuilding of the original Stonehenge. Around 2550 BCE, they had added an inner circle of blue stones weighing on average five tonnes each, from the Prescelli mountains in Wales, and several hundred years later, added an outer circle of even more massive Sarcen stones weighing 45–50 tonnes.

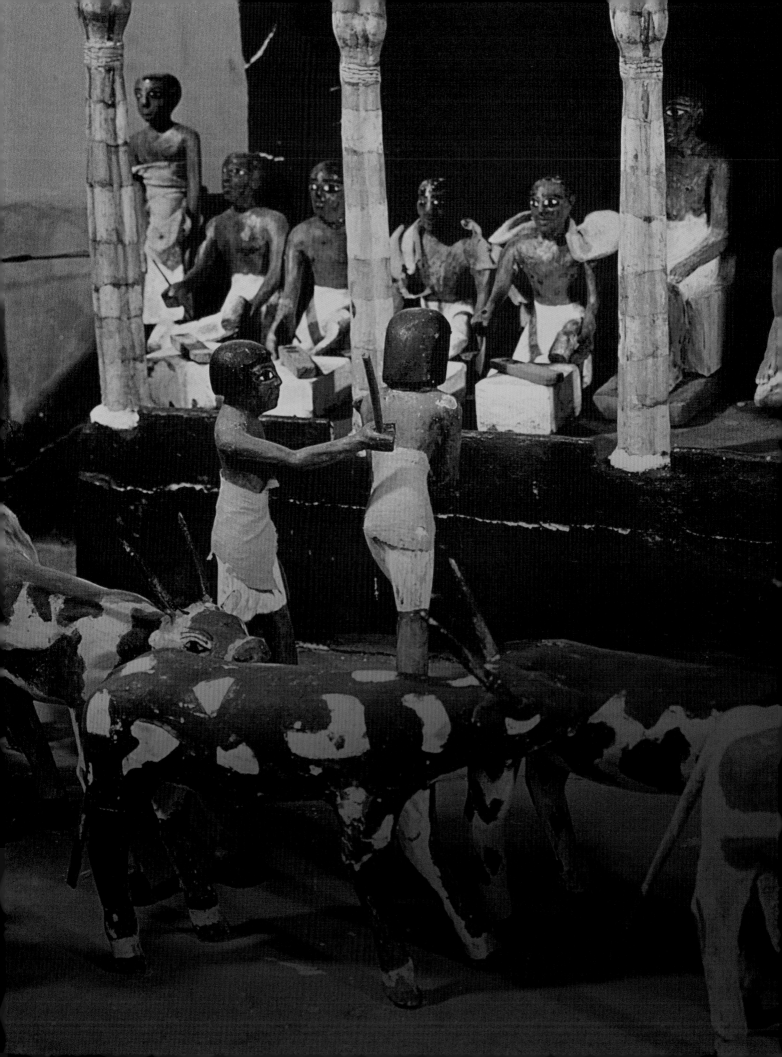

Part III

2nd Millennium BCE

Funerals, cults and the supernatural

16

A NOBLE EGYPTIAN ESTATE

Painted wooden models from the tomb of Meketre

I have become an equipped (blessed spirit),
I have furnished my place in the graveyard.
I have what I need in all things . . .

—From the *Prayers of Paheri*, trans. M. Lichtheim

In 1920, Herbert Winlock of the New York Metropolitan Museum found an extraordinary collection of twenty-five almost perfectly preserved, painted wooden models of a complete noble household. They were discovered in the tomb of Meketre on the western bank of the Nile at Luxor.

Meketre lived during what is called the Middle Kingdom of Egyptian history (ca. 2040–1783 BCE), serving under a number of kings as Chancellor and Steward of the royal palace. The king granted him estates throughout Egypt, and it is the activities on these estates that were replicated in the twenty-five superb models which are shared between the Egyptian and Metropolitan Museums.

Tomb models were believed to magically come to life with the right formulaic expression and serve the needs of the deceased in the hereafter. Meketre's models are unique in the exceptional quality of their craftsmanship, astonishing attention to detail and size. The figures and their immediate surroundings, arranged in tableaux, provide an intimate three- dimensional view of how Egyptians lived and worked.

The models of individual buildings, which have not survived in the real world, provide the only examples of such structures, while some of the manufacturing activities featured, such as weaving, provide a greater understanding of the processes and equipment used. The model depicting the brewing of beer is the best surviving documentation of ancient brewing practices.

With the exception of a pair of magnificent female offering bearers, the models range from 15.5–55.5 centimetres in height. They feature Meketre's house and gardens, granaries, bakeries and breweries, the counting and recording of his livestock, the fattening and slaughtering of his cattle, fishing, his workshops (carpenters and weavers) and his fleet of ships. Each is a work of art.

Although the models depict life on Meketre's estates while he was alive, there are many details which point to these being created for the afterlife. For example, Meketre sits in the shade of the cabin on a boat smelling a blue lotus, the symbol of rebirth; the sycamore tree shown in his garden was regarded as a celestial tree sacred to the goddess Hathor; beer was a link between gods and men, and the slaughtering of cattle was an integral part of the resurrection rites, particularly the removal of the heart and the cutting off of the shank.

The most stunning models are the two half-life-size female offering bearers. The Cairo Museum and the Metropolitan Museum each have one of these graceful pieces of art which symbolise the estates belonging to Meketre that were dedicated to providing his funerary offerings. Because wood is a more flexible medium than stone, the ancient craftsman had more freedom to create a statue in the round. Each offering bearer holds a live duck by the wing and supports a basket on her

ABOVE: An offering bearer.

head. In one, the basket contains bread and beer in stoppered vessels, in the other, cuts of meat. Their tight-fitting garments are beautifully rendered, one decorated with what appears as a net of various coloured beads, and the other with the feather pattern often associated with the goddesses Isis and Nephthys who protected the spirit of the deceased in the afterlife.

A 'snapshot' of a life long vanished

The Egyptians loved colour, gardens and pools and this is shown in the model of the facade of Meketre's house with its brightly painted columns supporting the roof of a portico which opens onto a copper-lined reflecting pool surrounded on three sides by sycamore trees in fruit. The minute detail in these models is shown in the copper spouts on the roof.

Scribes played an extremely important role in Egyptian life. They can be seen in the granary model recording, on papyrus rolls and a whitewashed board, the quantity of grain harvested and deposited in Meketre's storerooms. Other activities in this model show men pouring grain from sacks into large bins, women grinding flour and men cracking the grain with pestles. A combined bakery and brewing model reveals the importance of bread and beer in Egyptian daily life; the hieroglyph for 'meal' was a compound of those for 'bread' and 'beer'.

There were supposedly eight types of beer although beer made from barley and emmer (a form of wheat) was the most common. Everyone from the highest to the lowest, even slaves, were entitled to a ration of beer and bread. Beer was the sacrificial drink in temples and the dead were also supplied with crocks of beer. In Meketre's model, an overseer with a baton sits inside the door, while two women grind flour, a man works it into dough, and another treads the dough into a mash in a tall vat. It is then placed in crocks to ferment after which it is poured off into round jugs with black clay stoppers.

In the counting-of-cattle model, four scribes holding open papyrus scrolls take the census for tax purposes while

ABOVE: A wooden model, from the Tomb of Meketre, showing the deceased and his son inspecting a census of his cattle for tax purposes. OPPOSITE: Models of Meketre's fishing boats.

Meketre and his son, sitting under a portico, watch on. Large herds of cattle formed the basis of a noble's wealth and power. A supervisor, with an upraised staff, maintains decorum, and herdsmen, with sticks, keep the piebald cattle under control. A model with two compartments and a connecting door shows four animals in one section feeding from troughs, and others being fattened up for slaughter. Cattle were the chief sacrificial animals and the slaughter ritual was carried out with great care. The model of the slaughterhouse is grimly realistic, showing the trussed animal and the vigorous actions of a butcher with his flint knife at the throat of the animal. A stairway at the right side leads to a second floor where two butchers stand, cleavers

> Meketre's models are unique in the exceptional quality of their craftsmanship, astonishing attention to detail and size. The figures and their immediate surroundings, arranged in tableaux, provide an intimate three-dimensional view of how Egyptians lived and worked.

raised, perhaps ready to receive the meat for carving.

In antiquity, Egypt was known as the land of linen, made from flax. The most accurate picture of weaving and working horizontal looms is found in Meketre's model of a weaving workshop. Two seated and three standing female spinners are drawing unspun thread from pots on the ground and spinning flax on distaffs. Spindles, with threads still attached, lie on the floor. There are two horizontal looms. On the one to the back, the warp is being adjusted before the weaving can begin, while at the front loom, two women squat at the cloth beam. This loom still has woven cloth on it.

The model of a well-equipped and busy carpentry workshop is filled with incredible details like the chest containing stocks of miniature adzes, axes, reserve blades, chisels, drills and saws. Men, crouching around a fire at the back, reforge their metal tools while others are engaged in cutting planks, finishing a board with adzes, and polishing. A workman, using a mallet and chisel, cuts out the mortice holes to assemble the timbers.

The large number and range of boats found in the tomb indicate the importance of this form of transport. There are sailing and rowing boats, papyrus fishing rafts, a leisure boat for Meketre and his family, and even a kitchen tender used to convey provisions. Every figure in every boat is in its correct place: captain amidships giving orders; officers standing to attention; steersman working the steering paddle; the lookout at the rear taking the soundings with a long pole or weighted line; others ready to raise the sail; rowers sitting looking forward; fishermen manipulating their nets, and Meketre and his son installed in a light timber cabin with rolled up hangings to let in the breeze, being entertained by a singer and harpist. The details in these model boats are incredible: fishing nets with wooden floats, filled with fish, bits of linen cloth and twine and wooden shields, covered in bull's hides, painted on the side of a cabin.

With their realistic figures and lifelike activities, these models are 'like a modern-day snapshot' of a life long vanished (R. Schulz and M. Seidel, *Egypt, the World of the Pharaohs*).

17

SYMBOLISM AND MAGICAL PROTECTION

The jewellery of six royal Egyptian women

He rules the plains of the Silent Land, even he the golden of body, blue of head, on whose arms is turquoise. —*The Book of the Dead*

In a period spanning one hundred years from 1894–1994, four spectacular caches of royal jewellery were found in the mortuary complexes of Egypt's twelfth dynasty kings (1991-1797 BCE). The stunning jewellery belonged to six royal women: Weret II, chief queen of Senwosret III, and the princesses Khnumit, Sit-Hathor, Mereret, Sit-Hathor-Yunet and Neferuptah. These women, and the pharaohs to whom they were related, lived in a period of 'renaissance' in Egyptian culture during which 'the quality of artistic production reached a high point that, although equalled at other periods, was never surpassed' (Gay Robins, *The Art of Ancient Egypt*).

In these magnificent necklaces, pendants, pectorals, bracelets, anklets, girdles, *wesekh*-collars and diadems (jewelled headbands), the royal goldsmiths combined beauty and technical precision with amuletic protection. The colours of materials such as gold, silver, lapis lazuli, turquoise, carnelian, amethyst and feldspar were used to produce forms which gave the jewellery symbolic and magical qualities. These pieces, along with the princesses' toilet articles—a gold and silver Hathor mirror, black obsidian perfume containers, kohl pots, alabaster unguent vases

ABOVE: Part of the necklace of Princess Khnumit with gold falcon clasps.

and copper razors with gold handles—are only surpassed by the treasures of Tutankhamun.

Not long after Amenemhet I ascended the throne in 1991 BCE, he moved the Egyptian capital from Memphis to Ity-tawy near the entrance to the lush oasis of the Faiyum region. He and his successors, who built their pyramids nearby at Lisht, Lahun, Hawara and Dahshur, initiated vast irrigation and reclamation schemes in the Faiyum. Amenemhet III supposedly constructed a massive labyrinth of over 28,000 square metres which the Greek historian, Herodotus, who visited Egypt in the fifth century, said was almost beyond his power to describe. Such was the power and wealth of the kings whose wives, sisters and daughters were buried with such finery in their mortuary complexes.

The Egyptians believed that an amulet, by its shape, material and colour, could impart powers, capabilities and protection to the wearer. The hieroglyph *iwen*, translated as 'colour', could also be interpreted as 'nature', 'character' or 'disposition', which meant that the juxtaposition of particular colours with their own innate character, created an important symbolic picture.

Gold was associated with the sun god, Re, and symbolised eternal life. Silver, imported from Asia Minor, was never as common as gold, but was no less symbolic; it was associated with the moon. Semiprecious stones were highly valued for their colour. Lapis lazuli, which was imported into Egypt via the international trade routes from Afghanistan, was the most highly prized of all because its dark blue colouring with gold star-like flecks was the colour of the night sky; it represented the heavens.

Turquoise, mined in the Sinai, came in pale blue or blue green. It was the greener variety that the Egyptians valued most; green was the colour of new life and resurrection. Turquoise was, along with lapis lazuli, on the most valuable material list. Carnelian, with its rich red colour, was also considered precious. 'Symbolically carnelian reflects the curious dichotomy which the Egyptians felt to be embodied in the colour red' (Carol Andrews, *Amulets of Ancient Egypt*). Red was associated with blood, and therefore with energy and power, but on the other hand it was the colour of the bad-tempered Seth, god of chaos, and murderer of his brother Osiris.

Protective powers

During the Middle Kingdom there was a much larger repertoire of amuletic forms than in previous ages. Some of these are classified as protective or phylactic (protective against disease), and include vultures; cowrie shells; oyster shells; acacia seeds; the fish or *nekhau* and the hieroglyphic sign for protection, *sa*. Other amulets, like lions, leopards, falcon heads, bird and animal claws and tilapia fish, helped the wearer to assimilate their qualities and characteristic behaviour. The tilapia fish, which sheltered its eggs in its mouth, was symbolic of new life. Some charms were imbued with power and authority, while others helped in regeneration and rebirth (the vulture *Nekhbet* and cobra *Wadjyt* attached to the front of the royal headgear; the *Shen*-sign or magical knot that symbolised the universe; the *djed*-pillar for strength, stability and endurance; the *ankh* for life, and *heh* for infinity).

In these magnificent necklaces, pendants, pectorals, bracelets, anklets, girdles, wesekh-collars and diadems (jewelled headbands), the royal goldsmiths combined beauty and technical precision with amuletic protection.

Gold cowrie shells were used in elaborate girdles as they resembled the female genitalia and were therefore believed to protect the relevant body parts. Sometimes the hollow shells contained metal pellets which tinkled as the women moved. In these magnificent items, the shells were combined with rows of coloured semiprecious stone 'acacia seeds' and occasionally the fish amulet (*nekhau*) was added to protect a woman or child from drowning. A beautiful girdle, belonging to Mereret, featured amethyst beads joined by gold feline heads which are excellent examples of repoussé work (relief hammered into metal from the reverse side). Worn with this girdle was a matching amethyst anklet hung with gold leopard claws.

There were beautiful necklaces and bracelets of delicate gold chains with clasps in gold cloisonné (different colours separated by strips of metal). The inlays of lapis lazuli, carnelian, and turquoise are in the form of hieroglyphs for 'protection', 'joy' and 'birth'. Two broad beaded collars (*wesekh*) were found in the tombs of princesses Khnumit and Neferuptah. The former was composed predominantly of amulets of power arranged in pairs around a central *ankh*, the symbol for life. The latter featured six rows of tubular carnelian and feldspar beads alternating with tiny beads of gold. Both collars had clasps of falcon heads. Gold and silver oyster-shell amulets, found among the treasures of Mereret, Sit-Hathor and Khnumit, were placed over the throat to bring health to the wearer.

Three magnificent openwork pectorals, once belonging to Sit-Hathor and Mereret, were worn on the chest. They depict various images of the kings: as the incarnation of the falcon god Horus, as a falcon-headed griffin or sphinx trampling his foes, and in human form about to smite the chieftains of his foreign enemies. These would have been given to the royal women as gifts from their fathers, brothers or husbands and worn as a symbol of potent royal power.

Pendants in the form of hollow gold and amethyst cylinders with removable caps once held small rolls of papyrus written with a spell to protect women and children. The diadem of Sit-Hathor-Yunet, with its solid gold band ornamented with the sacred cobra, and inlaid with lapis lazuli, carnelian and green faience (a type of glazed earthenware), was designed to be worn over a wig.

In death, as in life, the heads, necks, chests, arms, hips and ankles of Middle Kingdom princesses and queens were adorned with symbolic and magical images of great beauty and richness.

OPPOSITE ABOVE: An open-work pectoral of Princess Sit-Hathor-yunet full of kingly symbols and with 370 small inlays. OPPOSITE BELOW: An open-work pectoral of Princess Mereret featuring the vulture goddess and the king in the form of griffins.

18
THE LABYRINTH OF THE MINOTAUR

Minoan treasures from Knossos

... Crete, a rich and lovely land, washed by the waves on every side, densely peopled and boasting ninety cities ... One of the ninety towns is a great city called Knossos, and there, for nine years, King Minos ruled and enjoyed the friendship of almighty Zeus. —Homer, *The Odyssey*

There are times when history, tradition and legend intertwine. Such was the case on the Mediterranean island of Crete. Greek tradition spoke of a legendary Cretan king and lawgiver named Minos who controlled a mighty fleet by which he ruled a large part of the eastern Mediterranean. Minos was mentioned in the works of the Greek poet Homer, in the work of the classical historian Thucydides, and in the well-known legend of the Minotaur, a monstrous half-bull, half-human who lived in a labyrinth of twisting passages beneath the palace of Minos. According to the legend, every nine years, seven youths and seven maidens from Athens were sent as tribute to Minos to be fed to the Minotaur.

When the English scholar/archaeologist, Sir Arthur Evans, who knew of these traditions, first began excavating the mound of Kephala at Knossos in 1900, he unearthed what appeared to be a great labyrinth of buildings. He began to see the image of the bull repeated over and over again: frescoes of the practice of bull leaping; a remarkable bull-headed rhyton or drinking cup in black

ABOVE: Fresco of bull leaping from the palace/temple of Knossos. This practice was part of ritual celebrations, possibly initiation rites.

steatite, crystal and gilt wood; 'horns of consecration'; depictions on sealstones; an ivory statuette once embellished with gold, and a solid bronze bull (the finest extant Cretan bronze). 'What a part these creatures play here!' Evans wrote. Perhaps it was from the numerous images of bulls that the ancient Greeks wove the legend of the Minotaur.

Evans was first led to Crete in 1893 by a desire to find the tiny engraved seal stones which he believed provided evidence of the earliest form of European writing. What he found all over Crete was not only hundreds of seal stones, but the remains of palaces and cities and evidence of 'a mature, sophisticated art, a skill in engineering and an architecture of such splendour, subtlety and refinement as could only have been produced by a civilization of great age' (L. Cottrell, *The Bull of Minos*). He called this previously unknown culture 'Minoan' after the legendary King Minos.

Over the years, Evans identified the buildings as a palace complex. Covering 20,000 square metres, and three storeys high, it was built around a large rectangular courtyard, 45 x 23 metres which was probably set aside for special ceremonies. A larger western court may have been used by the people who lived in the town and neighbouring countryside. The foundations of over three hundred chambers were found within the complex, but with the destroyed upper storeys taken into account, there may have been as many as one thousand rooms.

Some of these seem to have been arranged as 'apartments' for dignitaries. There was a sophisticated drainage system servicing the 'palace', a Grand Staircase in the East Wing, and light wells for ventilation and light. Perhaps the later Greek tradition of a labyrinth grew out of reports from ancient visitors of the sprawling maze of seemingly endless corridors and suites of subterranean rooms.

Evans found what he described as 'the noble throne of Minos'. The high-backed throne of gypsum, set on a square base, is partly embedded in a stucco wall painted with russet griffins (lion-like creatures with the heads of birds). It is the oldest throne in Europe by 2000 years and remains to this day in situ. On either side of the throne were stone benches and broad steps leading down to a ceremonial purification area (*adyton*). The Sanctuary of the Throne served a religious purpose and if such an individual as Minos existed, he may have been a priest/king. As Evans' excavation expanded, he found what he believed were cult areas. Double flights of stairs led downward to sunken and secluded rectangular ceremonial areas, none of which had been built to hold water. Small rooms, that he called pillar crypts, had central pillars, incised with the sacred double-axe (*labrys*). The pillars were not necessary to support the roof, and Evans surmised that they were symbolic, possibly a representation of the sacred tree. Judging by the ashes of animals found under the floors and by the depressions in the floor to collect liquid, these areas were intended for sacrifices.

He dated the complex at Knossos to ca. 1700–1450 BCE. This was the height of Minoan culture and is often referred to as the Second Palace Period. The earlier Cretan palaces, built at Knossos, Phaistos, Malia and Zakro between ca. 2000–1700, had been destroyed by earthquake, and rebuilt on a more elaborate plan. Around 1600 BCE, Crete was a world power and the palace of Knossos was the centre of a highly centralised bureaucratic system. However, it is now believed that the so-called 'Palace of Minos' was a temple complex, or at least that a very large part of it was devoted to cult activities.

It was the discovery of the first fresco of an ancient Cretan male carrying a rhyton or libation vessel in what appeared to be a ceremonial procession of young men that created a world sensation. More and more original, and 'intensely sensual' fresco fragments came to light, some depicting slim, muscular, lithe and scantily-clad males and graceful females in tight-waisted flounced skirts with bodices which could be arranged to cover or expose the breasts (Rodney Castleden, *Minoans: Life in Bronze Age Crete*). Both sexes had long flowing hair and wore jewellery.

There were miniature frescoes of large crowds watching cult ceremonies, the women sitting comfortably side by side in lively conversation. Other frescoes featured decorative motifs taken

OPPOSITE: A faience figurine representing a Minoan snake goddess or her priestess found in the palace/temple of Knossos.

from nature, mythical creatures and sacred symbols (the double axe and figure-of-eight shield), but the most remarkable was a painting depicting bull leaping, found in the cellars of the labyrinth's East Wing.

In the fresco, a slim agile figure is shown somersaulting over the back of a bull with two other figures ready to assist. A great deal of argument surrounds the spectacular and dangerous activity of bull leaping. It is generally thought that the person in the foregound of the fresco represented a group of people who grappled the bull, pulling its head low or protecting the leaper from the horns, while the individual at the back represented another group who waited to catch the leaper. Were the young men and women featured in this fresco the Athenian hostages supposedly sacrificed to the Minotaur of legend? More likely they were young people undergoing some form of initiation.

The bull was almost certainly associated with an earth deity, in the form of a Snake Goddess. A rare faience statuette of a bare-breasted goddess (or priestess) holding a snake was found in the underground treasury of the central sanctuary at Knossos. This, and other similar figures, reveal the high level of technical ability of the Cretan faience artists and 'are among the earliest examples in the round of the naturalism which was to be a characteristic feature of the art of the second palace/temples (Reynold Higgins, *Minoan and Mycenaean Art*).

Snakes are often linked with the underworld, and bulls associated with earthquakes. Homer declared in Book 20 of his *Iliad* that 'In Bulls does the Earth-Shaker delight'. Throughout ancient and modern times, Crete has been subjected to the destructive force of earthquakes, and Sir Arthur Evans gained some insights into the cultic objects and structures he unearthed when he experienced an earthquake himself. 'At 9.45 in the evening of a calm warm day, the shocks began. It is something to have heard with one's own ears the bellowing of the bull beneath the earth who, according to a primitive belief tosses it on his horns. It was doubtless the constant need of protection against these petulant bursts of the infernal powers that explains the Minoan tendency to concentrate their worship on the chthonic aspect of their Great Goddess wreathed with serpents as Lady of the Underworld' (Sir Arthur Evans, *Palace of Minos*).

After the destruction of the Cretan palace/temple complexes ca.1425 by earthquakes and then fire, possibly the result of an invasion by the Mycenaeans from the mainland, only Knossos was rebuilt. It became the centre of Mycenaean rule on the island until ca. 1050 BCE.

Sir Arthur Evans had gone to Crete to find an early form of writing. Instead, he had done what no other man had been able to achieve. 'He had written alone, a new chapter in the history of civilization' (*The Bull of Minos*).

19

A SPLENDID VISUAL LEGACY

The murals of Akrotiri

There came a sound as if from the Earth, Zeus' hollow thunder boomed, awful to hear . . . To the sea-beaten shore we looked, and saw a monstrous wave that soared into the sky . . . —Euripides, *Hippolytus*

According to the latest scientific findings, sometime in the late seventeeth century BCE, a volcano on the island of Thera in the Aegean Sea erupted with a magnitude five to six times that of the Indonesian volcano of Krakatoa in 1883. No specific date can be given for this Bronze Age cataclysm although radiocarbon dating puts it somewhere around 1628 BCE, much earlier than previously thought.

The explosion that tore Thera apart sent a column of ash and pumice 36 kilometres into the air and created a crater 83 square kilometres in area and extending 480 metres below sea level. Eighty metres of ash were deposited on the seabed for a distance of 20–30 kilometres in all directions and ash and pumice fell as far away as eastern Crete and Anatolia (modern Turkey). Whether the eruption and collapse of the magma chamber resulted in a massive tsunami is still debated. Thera, or what remained of it, was buried so deeply in ash that it was uninhabitable for 100–200 years.

Workmen quarrying for pumice on Thera to make cement for the construction of the Suez Canal in the mid-nineteenth century came upon a series of walls in the middle of the quarry, but

it was not until 1967 that Professor Spyridon Marinatos began systematic excavations on the site. What he found, preserved under metres of volcanic debris, was the once prosperous Bronze Age port city of Akrotiri buried 1700 years before Pompeii. It covered an area of approximately 0.2 square kilometres with two and three-storey houses and an elaborate drainage system.

Unlike Pompeii, Akrotiri was devoid of human remains and portable treasures; it appears that the people had sufficient warning and time to escape. What survived was a series of remarkable wall paintings. Each house, or complex of houses, in Akrotiri had at least one, maybe two, painted rooms. The preservation of these murals, their colours, excellent draughtsmanship and religious iconography, make Akrotiri one of the most important Bronze Age sites in the Aegean area along with Knossos and Mycenae. These artistically superb wall paintings 'provide a virtually inexhaustible source of information on the art, economy, environment, technology, manners and customs—indeed life in general—in the first half of the 2nd millennium BCE'.

Akrotiri, 120 kilometres north of Crete, is believed to have been a Minoan colony. Whether or not this is the case, it was certainly under Minoan influence as revealed in its architecture, pottery, cooking vessels, weight system and religious iconography. However, the artists of Akrotiri developed a distinctive Theran style and repertoire of scenes which focused on cultic activities such as presentation ceremonies (saffron and robes), adolescent initiation and nautical processions.

In most decorated spaces, there were related sequences, and a human activity was usually juxtaposed with something from the natural world: monkeys with the collection and presentation of saffron crocuses; gazelles with a pair of youthful boxers; dolphins with ships, and papyrus or maritime lilies with a robing scene. It is thought that although many of the animals were featured because of their own particular qualities, there were also mythic and divine associations. Some of the plants, such as saffron, had medicinal properties used in a cultic setting. The natural world was not always portrayed realistically as 'the artists were depicting another world than the everyday one; a symbolic world where general concepts of fecundity were more important than accuracy of detail' (Rodney Castleden, *Minoans: Life in Bronze Age Crete*).

The murals are in two styles: miniatures and large-scale. The most outstanding of the miniatures have a maritime theme. The 'Parade of Ships' or 'Nautical Procession' features a coastal landscape and two towns between which a flotilla of seven decorated ships is sailing. The 'arrival town' appears to be a representation of Akrotiri. This is the most complex single work of art of the Aegean Bronze

OPPOSITE: A fresco of a young fisherman from a house in the ancient town of Akrotiri on the island of Thera (Santorini).

> The preservation of these murals, their colours, excellent draughtsmanship and religious iconography, make Akrotiri one of the most important Bronze Age sites in the Aegean area along with Knossos and Mycenae.

Age so far recovered. The hulls and rigging of each ship are decorated with images such as lions, griffins, dolphins, flowers, birds and butterflies which may be some form of individual heraldry or symbols of deities. At the back of each ship is a decorated shrine-like cabin (*ikarion*) which may at first glance appear to be for the protection of the ship's captain. However, large-scale images of *ikaria* on adjoining walls suggest that they are more likely to have been a portable shrine for the statue of a goddess or the figure of a priestess and part of some form of seashore cult. In the same house, and continuing the maritime theme, are two images of fishermen. The nude youths with shaved and blue-painted heads hold their catches strung up by the gills.

Colour and symbolism

Blue and saffron (yellow/orange) are recurring colours in these paintings. Blue seems to be associated with special occasions, possibly rites of passage for adolescent males and females. Saffron, made from the red stamens of the *Crocus Satirus* flower, was valued in the ancient world as a dye, used for the robes of priestesses and people of great status. It was also effective for menstrual and gynaecological problems. The red stamens of the crocus were always associated in myth with blood. In one of several myths, a fertility demon, named Krokos, became the lover of Hermes who accidentally killed him. Wherever the blood of Krokos fell, a saffron flower grew. The three stamens retained forever the colour of his blood. It is easy to see the association of the plant with a girl's metamorphosis into a woman.

On the ground level of a complex known as Xeste 3, is a lustration, or purification, basin and paintings of three women; one young with a shaved, blue-painted head; one with a bodice decorated in red crocus stamens and holding a necklace; and the central figure sitting down with one hand on an injured foot and the other held to her head. The elaborate dresses, and an altar at one end with horns of consecration dripping with blood, indicate that this is a cultic activity of great importance, perhaps to do with menstruation, childbirth and coming of age. Also at ground level are three nude youths with blue painted heads looking towards an adult male in a loincloth.

One of the youths holds a striped cloth, perhaps a sacral robe. This series of paintings may represent male initiation during which ritual boxing took place.

On the first floor of this complex, well-dressed women of various ages collect saffron crocuses in baskets. The younger girl seems to be in a pupil-teacher relationship with the older woman. A blue monkey presents the saffron to a goddess, or her representative priestess dressed in a garment covered in crocuses and seated on a podium.

Blue monkeys are a recurring theme in these paintings, although monkeys were not native to the islands. They were probably introduced from Egypt where they were kept as pets, or in the case of the cynocephalus baboon, worshipped as deities. The symbolism of the blue monkey is not clear although it has been suggested that it introduced a mythic element into the wall images. On both Crete and Thera, they are associated with the saffron crocus.

Although there has been an enormous amount of literature written about the destruction of Thera and the paintings of Akrotiri, in which a broad spectrum of opinion is expressed, the symbolism of these superb murals and the cultic activities to which they relate, can only be inferred.

BELOW: Part of the excavated ancient Theran town of Akrotiri.

20

THE MASK OF AGAMEMNON

Treasures from the shaft graves of 'golden Mycenae'

' …King Agamemnon … was a proud man as he took his stand with his people, armed in gleaming bronze, the greatest captain of all …

—Homer, *The Iliad*

In the National Archaeological Museum of Athens, the gold death mask, labelled the 'Mask of Agamemnon', discovered by Heinrich Schliemann at Mycenae in 1876, has pride of place. It is 'an extraordinarily charismatic artefact, its combination of precious metal, startling naturalism and great antiquity, together with its mythic name' make it 'one of the most powerfully compelling archaeological discoveries of all time' (Cathy Gere, *The Tomb of Agamemnon: Mycenae and the Search for a Hero*).

Schliemann had always believed in the historicity of the world of Homer's heroes, so immediately after unearthing what he mistakenly believed was the treasure of Priam at Troy (see Chapter 13), he turned his attention to 'golden' Mycenae. This was an epithet given by Homer to the kingdom of Agamemnon, 'King of Men'. To guide him in searching for evidence of the

OPPOSITE: The gold funeral mask misnamed the 'Mask of Agamemnon' found in a shaft burial of Grave Circle A at Mycenae.

existence of Homer's hero, Schliemann relied on a passage in Pausanius' *Description of Greece*, a travelogue written in the second century CE, when Greece was a province of Rome and Mycenae was an abandoned ruin. According to Pausanius, all those who were murdered with Agamemnon on their return from Troy after an absence of ten years, were buried 'within the wall'.

Mycenae had once been the greatest of the 'Mycenaean' centres in Greece. The Greek-speaking people who occupied these cities and towns had entered Greece from the northeast, possibly ca.1900 BCE, but did not become powerful until ca.1600. They were a warlike people, governed by a warrior king or *wanax* supported by warrior companions of the king known as *eqetai*. It is thought that the leader of the people, known as a *lawagetas*, was responsible for mobilising the army for combat. The kings, like Homer's Agamemnon, built their fortress palaces on hills and only the highest-ranking people lived within the palace walls.

> With the same single-minded approach he had employed at Troy, he located a circle of five shaft graves referred to as Grave Circle A, the richest Bronze Age burials ever discovered.

Mycenae, perched on an outcrop of limestone above the Argive Plain, was little changed from the time of Pausanius when Schliemann arrived. The remains on its citadel were surrounded by massive walls from four to seven metres high with its famous Lion Gate, the earliest piece of monumental sculpture in the whole of Europe. Schliemann, following Pausanius' description, immediately began to dig just inside the Lion Gate.

With the same single-minded approach he had employed at Troy, he located a circle of five shaft graves referred to as Grave Circle A, the richest Bronze Age burials ever discovered. He sent a telegram to the King of Greece stating, 'With great joy I announce to Your majesty that I have discovered the tombs which the tradition proclaimed by Pausanius indicates to be the graves of Agamemnon, Cassandra, Eurymedon and their companions, all slain at a banquet by Clytemnestra and her lover Aegisthos'.

Schliemann recovered five golden death masks; golden shrouds wrapped around two children; gold funeral pectorals or breastplates, and five gold plate diadems, or crowns. Amongst the hoard of treasures were bronze swords with gold handles and five exquisite daggers inlaid with gold, silver, and alloys of gold, silver and copper on a black background of niello (a compound of copper, lead and sulphur). One dagger depicts a lion hunt and the other, a river scene reminiscent of the Nile. The artist or artists have shown amazing skill in fitting the superb designs into such a narrow space. These inlaid decorations 'represent one of the highlights of Mycenaean art'.

Also excavated from the graves was jewellery, including magnificent signet rings in gold, silver, agate, amethyst, crystal and amber; two magnificent libation vessels (*rhyta*) in the shape of a lion and bull's head; gold, silver and electrum (an alloy of gold and silver) cups, and hundreds of gold flat disc 'sequins' of repoussé work featuring butterflies, leaves, fish, flowers, stars and spirals. These are believed to have been ornaments sewn onto garments. The funeral ornaments in the third shaft grave containing the bodies of three women and two children took Schliemann forty-six pages to describe in his final excavation report. 'The sheer quantity of precious artefacts, combined with the strangeness and sophistication of their artistry put even Priam's Treasure in the shade' (*The Tomb of Agamemnon: Mycenae and the Search for a Hero*).

ABOVE: A gold diadem from Grave Circle A at Mycenae.

Is the mask genuine?

The so-called 'Mask of Agamemnon' with its handsome face, high cheekbones, trim beard, upturned moustache and tuft of hair beneath the lower lip certainly seems to be the face of a Homeric hero. However, this is not the mask that Schliemann originally designated as belonging to the 'King of Men'. It was in fact the rather comical round mask with the little crumpled mouth found in the same grave that he decided belonged to Agamemnon because the face beneath that mask was well-preserved. At some point the comical mask was usurped by its finer companion as belonging to Agamemnon, perhaps because it resembled the facial features of fashionable European princes of Schliemann's day.

Schliemann left Mycenae after only four months on the site. Unfortunately, in his determination to prove the historicity of Homer's heroes, and without careful analysis, Schliemann misinterpreted what he found. Between 1884–1902, Christos Tsuntas proved that all of Schliemann's interpretations were false. The burials in the shaft graves were dated at ca.1600–1500 BCE, 400 years too early to be associated with the 'heroes' of the Trojan War, if in fact they existed at all, and 200–300 years before Mycenae reached is peak.

Schliemann had a history of telling lies, 'salting' sites with artefacts from other sources, and writing deliberately vague excavation reports. For these reasons, and the fact that he discovered two of the greatest Bronze Age treasure hoards within years of each other, led some well-known archaeologists and historians to question the authenticity of the 'Mask of Agamemnon' with all its stylistic anomalies.

Leading the charge in the debate has been William Calder, Professor of Classics at Illinois University, who suggests that due to Schliemann's obsession to find evidence of Homer's 'King of men', he had a modern forgery made. In a 1999 issue of the prestigious publication *Archaeology*, the case for and against a hoax was presented, some scholars adamant that the mask is the genuine article, some suggesting it might be a pastiche (an ancient piece reworked in modern times), and others that it could be a forgery. The debate seems to centre on details of the eyes, ears and facial hair, particularly the handlebar moustache, which set it apart from all other contemporary masks.

According to David Traill, another of Schliemann's fiercest critics, the moustache appears to be a carelessly rendered modern addition. Neither Schliemann, nor other eyewitnesses, ever remarked on the moustache when first sighting the mask, and a journalist on the site reported that the mask was in the likeness of a young man with an engraved beard, but no moustache. The Museum of Archaeology in Athens has consistently refused to have it tested although there are several modern methods which, while not damaging the mask, could prove that it is not a fake.

The majority of scholars believe the mask is a genuine Mycenaean artefact, but according to David Traill, 'if asked to say whether I think the Agamemnon mask is an authentic piece found just as Schliemann reports, an authentic piece that has been altered, an authentic piece from a later burial, or a modern fake, I would have to say I simply do not know. It is easiest just to believe Schliemann, but that leaves many questions unanswered, and his credibility, even in his archaeological work, is steadily eroding' (David Traill, 'Behind the Mask of Agamemnon: Insistent Questions', *Archaeology*, Vol.52, No.4, July/August 1999).

A SUN-KING, A HERETIC AND A GREAT BEAUTY

Portraits of an Egyptian royal family

Amenhotep, ruler of Thebes, is the name of this child I have placed in your body . . . he shall rule the Two Lands like Ra forever.

—From an inscription in the Birth Chamber of Luxor Temple

In 1989, due to concerns that the magnificent columns in the main court of Luxor Temple in Upper Egypt were moving, and that the whole edifice was in danger of cracking, scientists began taking soil samples. As they dug down through the floor of the courtyard, they discovered an incredible cache of statues of gods and kings, possibly buried during a time of upheaval or perhaps when Egypt was under Roman rule.

Many were still in tact, but by far the most magnificent was a 2.5 metre red quartzite statue of Amenhotep III, the pharaoh responsible for the construction of Luxor Temple, itself one of the treasures of ancient Egypt. That glowing, serene statue now has pride of place in the Luxor Museum and has been described as 'a sculpture without equal in any collection of Egyptian art anywhere in the world' (N. Reeves, *Ancient Egypt: The Great Discoveries*).

Despite the idealised youthfulness of this superb statue, the iconography reveals a king who for nearly four decades presided over Egypt and its empire at the height of its power (ca. 1391–1354 BCE) and who 'embodied the sun god in opulent earthly form' (George Hart in the foreword to Joann Fletcher, *Egypt's Sun King*). It appears that parts of the statue were once

covered in gold, in keeping with an epithet sometimes used to describe Amenhotep III: *Aten-tjehun*, the dazzling sun disc.

This statue epitomises the great artistic flowering that occurred during his reign, one 'which was never again equalled in the 1500 years Pharaonic culture survived' (Donald Redford, *Akhenaten: The Heretic King*). The beauty, elegance, imagination, naturalism and novelty of the art of this period can be seen not only in the tombs of Amenhotep's nobles and high officials, but in the dazzling array of treasures from the tomb of Tutankhamun, believed to be his grandson.

Amenhotep ascended the throne when still a boy (about 12 years old), and soon after his coronation, he married Tiye, a girl of his own age, the daughter of provincial nobles from Akhmin, north of Thebes (modern Luxor). Amenhotep issued the so-called Marriage Scarab, a form of royal bulletin. For the first time, a queen's name was inserted with the titles of a pharaoh, and even more unusual, her father's and mother's names, Yuya and Thuya, were also included.

Amenhotep had reaped the benefits of the conquests of his predecessors. Peaceful conditions prevailed and incredible wealth poured into Egypt from the empire which extended from the Sudan to the upper Euphrates. The presence of master craftsmen, both local and foreign, and talented administrators, allowed Amenhotep to embark on a massive building program which earned him a reputation for excellence. Monumental statues of the king were erected in every temple, and Amenhotep's face shone 'down on the faces of the people like Aten when he shines at dawn'. Following in his father's footsteps, Amenhotep associated royalty with the worship of the sun god, in its form of the Aten or sun disc. Later in his reign, he officially identified himself as the sun god.

OPPOSITE: A stunning unfinished quartzite head of Queen Nefertiti found in a craftsman's workshop in Tell el-Amarna. ABOVE: Part of a colossus of Amenhotep III.

The 'Great Royal Wife', Tiye, is one of the best-documented figures in ancient Egypt. One excellent portrait of her, carved from green steatite, reveals 'a determined and serious woman with noble spirit, despite her apparent youth' (Official Catalogue of the Egyptian Museum, Cairo). Tiye appeared to have had the king's affection throughout their life together, even though he made diplomatic marriages with foreign princesses and had a harem full of concubines. Tiye's influence on the government was considerable and unquestioned, and she was respected for her diplomatic skills. Amenhotep included her name with his in inscriptions and she was depicted on an equal level in terms of size in statuary.

A massive statue pair of the king and queen dominates the atrium on the ground level of the Cairo Museum. Tiye was often depicted wearing the regalia of various goddesses. A stunning statuette in the Louvre shows her clothed in the feathered garb and headdress of the vulture goddess, Nekhbet, protector of the king. There is another unique head of Tiye found in the Berlin Museum, made of yew wood which features ebony, obsidian and alabaster inlays for the eyes, and earrings of gold and lapis-lazuli. It shows an older Tiye, after the death of her husband.

The 'heretic' king and his beautiful queen

Amenhotep IV (the later Akhenaten), who had been kept out of the public eye succeeded his father. He was already married to Nefertiti when he came to the throne at sixteen or seventeen. There are more images of Nefertiti as queen, wife and mother than any other woman in the New Kingdom and she is often shown in the traditional pose of a king.

Once on the throne, Amenhotep IV/Akhenaten took the worship of the Aten to a further stage. He built an open-air solar temple at Thebes featuring himself and Nefertiti, officiating as equals, in the worship of the sun disc (adorned with the uraeus, a spitting cobra used as a symbol of royalty, and with rays ending in small hands each holding an *ankh*, the symbol for life). The temple's court contained colossal statues of the king, exceptional in their break from the prevailing artistic tradition.

Nothing could be further from the idealised perfection of the red quartzite statue of his father than the grossly exaggerated, and asexual, images of Amenhotep IV in the early years of his reign. Even the beautiful Nefertiti was represented in this new deformed and controversial style. The king was depicted with a large head, long neck, narrow

ABOVE LEFT: The grossly exaggerated head of the heretic pharaoh Akhenaten, who introduced a new controversial form of art. RIGHT: A magnificent bust of Queen Nefertiti wearing the tall straight-edged blue headdress she initiated for herself.

face and greatly extended chin, with pouting lips and small, slanting eyes. His upper torso was narrow while his lower torso was of feminine proportions with prominent buttocks, swelling thighs, a drooping belly and no evidence of genitals. This image should not be considered as 'realistic', rather as a religious statement. Akhenaten regarded himself as the living image of the Aten, and as such was depicted in an androgynous form to incorporate both male and female aspects of the creator.

Between years 5 and 9 of his reign, Amenhotep IV changed his name to Akhenaten (*He who is serviceable to the Aten*) and built a new cult centre in central Egypt at Tell el-Amarna called Akhetaten or *Horizon of the Aten*. He moved the court there, ordered the closure of all the temples of the other gods and the erasure of their names from temple walls. Nefertiti continued

> The beauty, elegance, imagination, naturalism and novelty of the art of this period can be seen not only in the tombs of Amenhotep's nobles and high officials, but in the dazzling array of treasures from the tomb of Tutankhamun, believed to be his grandson.

to support her husband's new doctrine at Akhetaten and she was constantly by his side, whether shown in intimate family scenes with some of their six daughters, or playing a vital political and religious role.

That the 'Great Royal Wife' was beautiful and regal can be seen in a magnificent painted limestone bust found in a sculptor's workshop in Amarna in 1912, and now in the Egyptian Museum in Berlin. It shows her with her enigmatic smile, wearing the elegant and distinctive blue headdress that became her trademark. This image seems to confirm a text inscribed on one of Akhenaten's stelae which described her as 'fair of face'. However, in September 2006, the Director of Berlin's Museum, Dietrich Wildung, reported that on close examination the bust revealed an ageing Nefertiti as there are definite wrinkles running down her slender neck and puffy bags under her eyes, which made her even more fascinating.

The sculptors' workshops in Akhetaten continued to produce statues of the royal family. Two stunning heads in brown quartzite—an unfinished one of Nefertiti and another of a princess, possibly her eldest daughter Meritaten—are of the highest artistic quality. The revolutionary art of the 'heretic's' early reign 'eventually came to acquire a harmony and elegance of its own. An impression of serenity gradually replaced the rather tormented forms of the earlier portraits'.

While the name of the great sun-king Amenhotep III was listed in all the later King Lists, that of his controversial son Akhenaten and his immediate successors were wiped from the record, as if they and their sun cult had never existed.

22

A UNIQUE FUNERARY ENSEMBLE

The treasures of Tutankhamun

... details of the room within emerged from the mist: strange animals, statues and gold—everywhere the glint of gold.

—Sir Howard Carter's own account of the discovery of Tutankhamun's tomb

Never in the history of archaeology has there been such a dazzling discovery as that of the tomb of the Egyptian king, Tutankhamun, in the remote and desolate Valley of the Kings in 1922. The British archaeologist, Howard Carter, excavated approximately five thousand treasures, comprising the king's funerary ensemble, over a ten-year period. These breathtaking works of art, displayed in the Egyptian Museum in Cairo and visited by tens of thousands of visitors a year, are the most recognisable treasures in the world.

The story starts with Howard Carter's belief in the existence of a previously unknown king called Tutankhamun. After five futile seasons of digging in the Valley of the Kings between 1917–1921 his sponsor, Lord Carnarvon, granted him one more season only. This led to the discovery of a limestone step in the rubble under the tomb of Ramesses IX, and the disappointment at finding the tomb had been entered and resealed twice.

Then came his first peek into the antechamber by the light of a candle. When asked if he could see anything, all he could reply was, 'Yes, wonderful things'. Surely this is the greatest

understatement in archaeology. Not long after, when he revealed the illuminated antechamber to the brilliant American Egyptologist, Professor James Henry Breasted, the effect was overwhelming. 'To Breasted, it was … a totally impossible sight. It wasn't real; it was a fairytale, a peculiar combination of fantasy and truth. He felt as if he had, without warning, stumbled upon the vast and wholly enchanted property room of a theatre packed with opulent sets made for a wildly imaginative opera' (Thomas Hoving, *Tutankhamun the Untold Story*).

The most famous of all the artefacts are Tutankhamun's solid 22-carat gold coffin, his stunning gold mummy mask inlaid with lapis lazuli, obsidian, quartz and feldspar, and the complete canopic assemblage. The solid gold coffin, the innermost in a nest of three, weighed 110.4 kilograms. Unlike the face of the king on the two gilded outer coffins which show him to be a little weary of the world, the face on the inner coffin is more youthful, and the face mask shows the king as renewed and eternally young.

Also of singular beauty, and showing remarkable workmanship, are the containers holding the king's liver, stomach, lungs and intestines. The gold canopic shrine, magnificent alabaster canopic chest, and individual miniature coffins in gold repouss for the vital organs, are as finely made as the group of coffins for the mummy. The four gilded statuettes of the protective goddesses, Selket, Isis, Nephthys and Neith are breathtaking in their beauty.

Tutankhamun was nine when he succeeded to the throne in the mid-fourteenth century BCE, after the death of Akhenaten and his shadowy co-regent, Smenkhkare. Tutankhamun's parentage has been a source of intense speculation. Some academics believe he was the last son of Amenhotep III either by Tiye or another wife, while others are convinced he was the son of Akhenaten by his secondary queen Kiya. A painted stuccoed head of Tutankhamun as a child was found at the entrance to the tomb. His skull is elongated, a feature of the Amarnan style, and is emerging from the lotus flower which symbolises the sun god and rebirth.

Originally named Tutankhaten, he was brought up at Amarna under the Aten ('sun-disc') cult and was married to Ankhesenpaaten, the daughter of Akhenaten and Nefertiti. On his accession, the young couple were taken to Thebes where their names were changed to Tutankhamun and Ankhesenamun as an indication that Amun was reinstated as the chief god of Egypt. They ruled together, under the guidance of a former Amarna official named Ay, until Tutankhamun was old enough to rule alone.

OPPOSITE: The gold life-size death mask of King Tutankhamun decorated with lapis lazuli, carnelian, turquoise and coloured glass.

One of the most magnificent objects in the tomb is the king's throne on which are two wholly different cartouches, one containing the name 'Tutankhamun' and the other 'Tutankhaten'. Howard Carter saw this as the closest thing in the tomb to a historical document. It pointed to a period of religious and political transition. Even more surprising was the back of the throne where the Aten sun disc, with its rays terminating in the form of hands, shines down on the royal couple, in a rather intimate pose reminiscent of the court in Amarna. Maybe the young king and queen still adhered to the worship of the Aten.

Howard Carter described the throne, of gilded wood, silver sheet, opaque glass and semiprecious stones, 'as the most beautiful thing that has ever been found in Egypt'. It takes the traditional form with its lion head decoration, clawed feet and winged serpent armrests, but it is the back of the throne that reveals the incredible virtuosity of the craftsmen. In the king's kilt alone there are five hundred minute pieces of material, each of which had to be cut with precision.

Another masterpiece featuring the young couple is the small gold-plated shrine standing on a silver sled which once held a statue of the king. The sides, adorned with scenes in relief, depict the king and queen in various poses: Tutankhamun seated on a thick cushion on a stool with Ankhesenamun anointing him with an unguent; placing a double necklace on his neck; the king pouring unguent into his wife's hand; and another of the king accompanied by his wife, shooting ducks in the marshes. It should be remembered that all the elements in these scenes have a symbolic significance and may not represent actual activities carried out by the young king and queen.

According to Howard Carter, an exquisitely painted casket holding some of Tutankhamun's sandals and garments, 'will probably rank as one of the great artistic treasures of the tomb'. On his first visit to the tomb, he found it difficult to tear himself away from it. 'Descriptions give but a faint idea of the delicacy of the painting, which far surpasses anything of the kind that Egypt has yet produced. No photograph could do it justice, for even in the original a magnifying glass is essential to a due appreciation of the smaller details, such as the stippling of the lion's coats, or the decoration of the horses' trappings' (Howard Carter, *The Tomb of Tutankhamun*).

OPPOSITE TOP: An elaborately decorated chest of red wood inlaid, gilded and veneered with ebony, ivory and gilt. OPPOSITE BELOW: Detail from another casket with curved lid, a masterpiece of painting, depicting Tutankhamun battling Nubians. ABOVE: Detail of gilded background.

Mystery surrounds the young king

Tutankhamun died unexpectedly at the age of 18 or 19. Evidence from his mummy indicates a blow to the head but like everything about him and the period in which he lived, nothing can be said with certainty about his life and death except 'that the one outstanding feature of his life was that he died and was buried'. One of Carter's greatest disappointments was that he found no written evidence, no papyrus that could have solved the many questions about Tutankhamun's parentage, short life and mysterious death.

Despite the overwhelming nature of this treasure by which 'Tutankhamun, the unknown, became world famous overnight, his burial treasure, testifying to a refined culture, to funerary rituals and practices which had to be pieced together and understood, revealed little or nothing of his own life and personality. The king . . . remained shrouded in mystery' (Christiane Desroches- Noblecourt, *Tutankhamun: Life and Death of a Pharaoh*).

When standing in front of Tutankhamun's treasures in the Archaeological Museum in Cairo, it is easy to ignore the ten years of intense labour involved in the excavation, preservation and restoration of these objects. They were so haphazardly 'arranged' in the chambers that it was like playing a game of fiddlesticks, where to carelessly move one might have brought others crashing down. Also, many of the objects were very fragile and could have crumbled at the first touch.

Sometimes preservation treatment had to be done on the spot before an object could be transported to the laboratory, and each object presented a unique problem requiring a special form of conservation. However, these were challenges Carter enjoyed. What he did not enjoy were the constant frustrations caused by the demands of the international press, the tens of thousands of visitors who flocked to the site, including VIP's with government passes, and the hostility of Pierre Lacau, Director General of the Egyptian Antiquities Service, who wanted to have more control over the supervision of the site.

From the moment on 26 November 1922, when Howard Carter made a tiny hole in the door that led into the antechamber of the tomb, to a spring day one decade later when work on the tomb was finally completed, the excavation was at the centre of an unfolding archaeological drama that captured the attention of the world. Thomas Hoving, in his book *Tutankhamun The Untold Story*, describes this drama as 'full of intrigue, secret deals and private arrangements, covert political activities, skulduggery, self interest, arrogance, lies, dashed hopes, poignance and sorrow'.

23

THE TRANSFIGURATION OF AN EGYPTIAN QUEEN

Wall paintings in the tomb of Nefertari

King's great wife, mistress of the Two Lands, possessor of charm, sweetness, and love, lady of Upper and Lower Egypt . . . justified before Osiris who resides in the West. —From *The Book of the Dead* in the descending corridor of the tomb of Nefertari

The brilliant 3250-year-old tomb images depicting the journey of Queen Nefertari to the hereafter rank among 'the most precious and most fragile of Egyptian treasures, indeed of humanity' (Miguel Angel Corzo, Director of the Getty Conservation Institute). The tomb's painted reliefs, which cover 520 square metres, glow with a multitude of original colours, and are exceptional for the finely executed details on garments, headdresses and hieroglyphs.

The wall paintings are not only visually stunning, but by following them from the upper chambers, through a descending corridor to the burial chamber and back once again to the entrance, the viewer can accompany Nefertari as she makes her symbolic way to the realms of the underworld, meets all the challenges along the way, and is transformed into a blessed soul in the hereafter.

For over two decades Nefertari was the chief wife of the great nineteenth dynasty king, Ramesses II, whose reign (ca 1279–1213 BCE) marked a peak in Egyptian power. It is believed that he married her in a shrewd political move, when they were both teenagers. Ramesses was from a military family from the delta region and had no connection with the kings of the previous dynasty who came originally from Thebes. Although Nefertari was not a king's daughter, her epithet, 'Beloved of Mut', indicates that she came from Thebes, while her name suggests that she may have been a descendant of one of the illustrious queen's of the eighteenth dynasty, Ahmose-Nefertari.

> The design of her tomb, the orientation of the images and their iconographical grouping represent the underworld domain that Nefertari had to journey through on her way to eternal life.

Whatever the motivation behind the marriage, Ramesses always honoured his beloved consort above all other women in his life. His high regard is seen in the temple at Abu Simbel that he dedicated, not only to the goddess Hathor, but to Nefertari, so bestowing on her the status of a god. She appeared beside him on important state and religious occasions and by year 3 of his reign, she was shown in monumental scale on the interior face of the new pylon at Luxor.

Although there is no reference to her that can be dated for the next eighteen years, she is known to have communicated with the Hittite queen, Padukhepa, in year 21 expressing wishes for peace between their two kingdoms. She died about year 24 of Ramesses' reign; her husband ruled for another 43 years. It is believed that he produced as many as fifty sons and forty daughters from his eight principal wives, secondary wives and concubines. Despite Nefertari's esteem, none of her children succeeded their father; he outlived thirteen of his heirs.

Her tomb is located in what is now referred to as the Valley of the Queens. Unlike the isolated and rugged Valley of the Kings, this burial ground for nineteenth dynasty wives,

OPPOSITE: An image of Queen Nefertari with the cartouche containing her titles and epithets on the wall of Chamber G in her tomb in the Valley of the Queens.

126

princes and princesses, is not a secret, hidden place. It is a broad, sweeping, and easily accessible wadi, or dry watercourse. Ramesses buried four other wives there, and built a unique communal tomb for the majority of his fifty or so sons. Most of the tombs in the valley are unfinished and unpainted.

The design of her tomb, the orientation of the images and their iconographical grouping represent the underworld domain that Nefertari had to journey through on her way to eternal life. The ceiling is painted to represent the night sky in deep blue over black, with superimposed five-pointed yellow stars to symbolically represent the underworld. The wall paintings are arranged along two symbolic axes: one representing the nocturnal underworld of Osiris in the west, and the other, the solar or daytime world of Re in the east.

On the underside of the door lintel to the entrance to the first room in the tomb, there is an

BELOW: A view of recess E depicting the scarab-headed god Khepre, the goddess Hathor and falcon-headed Re-Horakhty with the vulture Nekhbet on the lintel. OPPOSITE: Nefertari being led by the goddess Isis.

image of the sun on the desert horizon. It is oriented in such a way that the top of the sun is nearest the outside of the tomb. The queen starts and finishes her journey of transformation here. As she enters the tomb, she and the sun sink together into the west and proceed into the night realm of Osiris. As she descends further, she must overcome many negative forces and successfully pass through a series of portals each with its keeper, guardian and announcer. She must know their names and secrets before being allowed to pass. The queen's solar rebirth is represented by the mummiform, ram-headed god, implying the union of Osiris and Re. Her journey ends as she passes once again under the door lintel at the entrance/exit of the tomb, emerging transfigured and triumphant from the eastern horizon in the likeness of a solar disc.

Except for when Nefertari is depicted as a mummy or a *ba* (soul) bird, she is dressed in a fine pleated linen garment and wears the conventional wig and vulture headdress topped by the double ostrich feather plumes and sun disc. Her earrings are in the form of the lotus (symbol of rebirth) or the protective cobra of royalty.

The unnamed craftsmen who cut, plastered, carved and painted her tomb came from the closed village of Deir el-Medina which was a community devoted solely to the preparation of the tombs of royalty. Unlike the limestone in the Valley of the Kings, the stone in the Valley of the Queens was of poor consistency and could not be carved satisfactorily. The workmen were forced to apply layers of plaster over the limestone, then prime it with a gypsum wash before carving the low reliefs and painting the images in vivid shades of red, blue, green, yellow, white and black. One unusual feature of the tomb is the colour of Nefertari's skin. Throughout Egyptian history women were depicted with a creamy yellow skin, but in Nefertari's case it was a pinkish red. Perhaps the colour was meant to indicate that she had a special status in the religious and political affairs of the state.

Precious pigments crumbling to dust

Ernesto Schiaparelli, the Italian archaeologist who discovered the tomb in 1904, recognised the exquisite nature of the paintings, but also saw that they were in a fragile state. Over the millennia, moisture had seeped into the tomb through fissures in the rock above or via flash floods, and humidity from the breath of the ancient workmen also added to the moisture content in the tomb. The salts in the limestone and mud plaster walls had absorbed the moisture, and when it evaporated, the salt was drawn to the surface forming salt crystals. These formed between the limestone and plaster causing layers of plaster to dislodge and also eroded the pigments, turning them to coloured dust.

So, from the moment Nefertari was sealed within her 'house of eternity' the sacred wall paintings began to deteriorate. In the decades after the tomb's discovery, the damage accelerated at a greater rate, much of it due to human carelessness and vandalism. In 1954, Arpag Mekhitarian, in his book *Egyptian Painting*, wrote that the superb paintings were already in a precarious state and that it would only be a matter of years before they would crumble to dust.

Despite desperate attempts to save the paintings, including the closure of the tomb, the authorities realised that these cultural treasures were continuing to deteriorate. By the 1980s over 20 per cent had been lost forever. In 1986, an extensive collaborative conservation project between the Egyptian Antiquities Department and the Getty Conservation Institute was initiated. Scientists and conservators from all over the world, led by Miguel Angel Corzo, Director of Special Projects for the Getty Institute 'addressed the hydraulic, climatologic, microbial and microfloral status of the tomb. Chemical, spectrographic and X-ray diffraction tests of all material, especially plaster, pigments, and salts were also performed' (Jeffrey Levin, *Nefertari: Saving the Queen*). For six years, this team applied about 10,000 small strips of fine-grained Japanese mulberry bark paper to cracks and loose plaster, securing the paintings. Apart from cleaning, nothing was done to restore the colour of the images which remain the authentic products of the ancient artists from Deir el-Medina. The conservators kept the tomb closed until 1995 to monitor the moisture content, and only reopened it to a limited number of tourists a day. No one was permitted to remain in the tomb for more than ten minutes. The tomb was closed again in 2003, for an indefinite period, to investigate signs of deterioration because the problem of the salt remains.

'Today Queen Nefertari's final resting place has been resurrected not by divine intervention, but through human skill and concern. Its place in eternity will depend upon human wisdom' (Levin, *Nefertari: Saving the Queen*).

DIVINATION AND ANCESTOR WORSHIP

Oracle bones and ritual bronzes from Anyang

When first Cangjie observed the patterns of the bird tracks and then created writing, deceit and artifice sprouted to life.

—Chinese traditional account of the invention of writing

The Shang dynasty, ca.1600–1050 BCE, particularly the late Shang, is often called the golden age of Chinese archaeology. This is due to the discovery of caches of the earliest shell and bone writings ('oracle' bones) in the foundations of a large temple/palace complex near Anyang in Henan province, and the excavation of magnificent ritual bronzes from the graves of Shang royalty in the same area. This site provides 90 per cent of all the written and archaeological data on the Shang civilization.

Evidence of writing from the Shang dynasty was first discovered in the shops of Chinese apothecaries in the nineteenth century. The so-called 'dragon bones' they were selling as cures for illnesses were found to be animal bones and turtle shells covered with an early form of writing. By the 1920s, they were traced to the location of Anyang where the last Shang dynasty capital was rediscovered and excavated. In the 1950s an earlier Shang capital was found at Zhengzhou, where thousands of inscribed bones were stored and buried in what appears to have been an ancient document archive. These 'oracle' bones are the earliest historical writings that

have survived from China. If the legendary Cangjie had indeed invented writing by imitating bird tracks, by the time of the Shang dynasty, the early pictographs had already begun to evolve into the square characters of modern Chinese.

In 1976, the elaborate and untouched grave of a female member of Shang royalty, the lady Fu Hao, was found in the vicinity of Anyang. She was one of the three principal consorts of King Wu-Ding, during whose reign (ca.1250 BCE) the Shang reached its zenith. Sixteen men, women and children had been

ABOVE: A taotie design.

sacrificed with Fu Hao and 460 bronze objects weighing 1.6 metric tonnes surrounded her body. These included 200 bronze wine and food vessels of twenty different ceremonial types, the largest and most complete set of ritual vessels unearthed from a Shang grave. Also, among her funerary items was a magnificent ivory goblet inlaid with turquoise and made from a single hollow elephant tusk, as well as more than 130 weapons, 23 bells, 27 knives, 4 mirrors, 750 jade objects, 70 stone sculptures, and nearly 500 bone hairpins.

It appears that Fu Hao commanded great respect from her husband, courtiers and people. There are over 200 references to her in the oracle bones, some concerning her pregnancies; her active life at court; her involvement in ritual ceremonies; an estate outside the capital given to her by Wu-Ding; and surprisingly, her involvement in military affairs. The oracle bones speak of Lady Fu Hao raising and leading a force of 13,000 troops in military campaigns against the neighbouring Tu, Ba, Yi and Quiang tribes.

Because the Shang was a feudal society, the king, who had power of life and death over those under him, was able to raise large forces from his retainers for warfare and for the construction of fortifications. Despite massive walls, such as those at Zhengzhou which were 18 metres wide, 9 metres high and 727 metres long, the Shang rulers moved their capital five times due to power struggles and wars with hostile neighbours. Yin, in the area of Anyang, was the last capital, where the court remained for 250 years. The Shang rulers also needed huge workforces for the mass production of bronze, and for digging their enormous tombs. Of the eleven excavated at Anyang, the largest is 91 metres in length and 18 metres deep. It contained the

OPPOSITE: A bronze ritual wine vessel from the Shang period in the form of two rams back to back.

remains of a king, ninety followers who joined him in death, seventy-four human sacrifices and twenty-three animal sacrifices.

The king's role was predominantly religious and the two most significant achievements of this period, writing and magnificent bronze work, were associated with religious ritual. The king performed priestly duties associated with the ancestor cult and the worship of the high god Di, which, when carried out properly, confirmed his legitimacy to rule. One of his major roles was to communicate with his ancestors through divination (predicting the future) and sacrifice (animal and sometimes human).

The royal ancestors were believed to be able to intervene with Di, to avoid danger and calamities such as epidemics, flood, famine, succession issues, and war; to ward off curses; to assist the king in battle; to help in producing an heir, and even to prevent personal health problems such as toothache. When there was trouble, it was important to find out which disaffected ancestor was responsible and carry out the appropriate rites to placate him or her. To ensure their efficacy, the rites had to be scheduled at the correct time. When a person died, he or she was given a temple name corresponding to one of the days of the week, and it was on this day that the rites were conducted.

The king used ox bones (scapula and shin bone) and tortoise shells to determine the will of the ancestors. Professional diviners prepared the shells and carved them with a series of grooves. A question was written on the oracle bones in black or red, and heat was applied to the grooves causing small heat-stress cracks to appear. These were then interpreted for an auspicious or inauspicious response, and the answer and eventual outcome were also recorded on the oracle bones. A 40.5 centimetre scapula bone, now in the Institute of Archaeology, Chinese Academy of Social Sciences, Beijing, appears to have been used to discover if the ancestors found the sacrificial rites performed in their honour to be satisfactory. Part of it reads, 'to ancestress Yi offer a fine pig, to ancestress Gui a boar, to ancestress Ding a pig, to ancestress Yi a pig'.

Unique methods, sophisticated design

Associated with divination were the sacrificial rites conducted by the living for their dead ancestors. Bronze was the metal of ritual and objects made from it were highly esteemed. The great bulk of surviving Shang bronze objects are wine and water containers, cauldrons, steamers, cups, goblets and jugs. They were kept in ancestral halls for use during important feasts and sacrifices. Because of their symbolic value, there were strict guidelines as to how many and what type could be displayed and used. The two most important were the *ding* or cauldron for cooking food and the *zun* for holding wine. The ritual books of old China specify that a king could use 9 *dings* (symbolising his authority over the 9 regions of China) and numbers were prescribed for other nobles in order of rank.

Bronze vessels containing food and wine were also buried with the dead. Some weighed over 90 kilograms, with the largest known bronze—the Simuwu Quadripod—a tribute to the mother of a Shang king, weighing 732.84 kilograms.

Metallurgy originated in Anatolia (modern Turkey), but when knowledge of bronze manufacture reached China, the Chinese developed unique processes and sophisticated shapes and styles. Not only did bronze have a functional and symbolic role in Shang society, it also reflected the latest technical and artistic developments, reaching a peak around the thirteenth century BCE. Unlike the method used to manufacture bronze in the Mediterranean and Near East, called the lost wax method, the Chinese metallurgists used a piece-mould casting method. A pottery model was made first and any desired pattern, no matter how intricate, could be incised into the outside. Then two or more pieces of clay were placed around the model and once the impression was registered on the clay, they were taken off and fired. They were then held in place and molten bronze was poured into the mould which was removed once the bronze had cooled.

> The king's role was predominantly religious and the two most significant achievements of this period, writing and magnificent bronze work, were associated with religious ritual.

Although some Shang vessels were in the shape of animals and birds (elephants, tigers and owls), it is the designs rather than their shapes that are recognised as being unique in the world. The *taotie*, a voracious animal or monster mask, with its symmetry and focus on the two eyes, was especially adapted to the piece-mould method of casting bronze and became one of China's most popular motifs.

In 2001, the Academy of Social Sciences and the Institute of Cultural Relics and Archaeology announced that Shang finds, particularly near Anyang, had been ranked first in the top one hundred significant archaeological discoveries made in China in the twentieth century.

25

A SUPERNATURAL WORLD

The ritual art of the Olmecs of Mexico

Olmec artisans created some of ancient America's most striking and beautiful objects ...—Richard A. Diehl, *The Olmecs: America's First Civilization*

Somewhere around 1500 BCE, the antecedent of all Mesoamerican cultures, the Olmec, developed in the steamy and swampy tropical lowlands of Mexico's southern Gulf Coast. It has been described as one of the few pristine cultures of the world and is the first tropical lowland civilisation so far discovered. However it was not until the 1930s and 1940s that the occasional pieces of Olmec art appearing on the Mexican antiquities markets, and the first of the mysterious colossal heads discovered at Tres Zapotes, were attributed to the Olmecs. Previously, these works were assumed to be Mayan or, more imaginatively, the work of seafaring people from as far away as Africa, Phoenicia and China.

The heartland of the Olmecs was a fertile landscape of upland ridges surrounded by a mosaic of rivers, large streams, springs, lagoons, swamps and levees. The Tuxtla Mountains and four volcanoes formed the backdrop of this watery landscape. Archaeologists have identified two chief politico-religious centres both situated on ridges: one in the vicinity of San Lorenzo, 60

OPPOSITE: A jade votive axe representing a supernatural being with a combination of human and animal (jaguar, eagle and toad) traits.

kilometres from the Gulf of Mexico, and the other at La Venta, 15 kilometres from the coast.

In ancient times both sites stood like islands, safe from the floods that frequently occurred in the regions. These urban, ceremonial centres reached their peaks at different times, although there may have been a period of overlap. San Lorenzo developed into a full blown city ca.1200 BCE and flourished until the 10th century BCE when it was replaced by La Venta which became the most advanced society in Mesoamerica, until about the fifth–fourth centuries BCE.

The Olmecs' stunning sculptural artefacts ranged from monumental basalt heads to exquisite small ritual objects (figurines, masks and celts, or ceremonial axes) carved out of greenstone, a material highly valued by the Olmecs in all periods, possibly because 'its colour served as a metaphor for maize, the staff of life, and fertility in general' (*The Olmecs: America's First Civilization*).

Many Olmec artefacts were found by accident. In 1946, archaeologists Matthew and Marion Stirling heard rumours of a giant stone eye staring out from an eroded dirt track near the village of Tenochtitlan. The following year they began excavation and unearthed over twenty stone monuments including the five largest and best-preserved heads known. These colossal Olmec heads were carved from massive basalt boulders quarried in the Tuxtla Mountains. The labour and organisation needed to transport them long distances across waterways and over ridges to the ritual sites indicates the power of the rulers of San Lorenzo and La Venta.

These mysterious heads, between 1.5–3.5 metres high with some weighing around 20 tonnes, are believed to have represented rulers or ancestors. Although they have similar facial features — jowly cheeks, flat noses and slightly crossed eyes — there are enough differences to indicate particular individuals. Each one features a distinctive headdress, probably copied from originals made of cloth and decorated with feathers, skins, claws or talons. Large plugs were inserted into their ear lobes. Some remnants of a reddish paint suggest that the stone heads may have been brightly coloured.

Another accidental find was the statue referred to as the 'Lord of Las Limas'. Two children from Las Limas, searching for a stone to crack open palm nuts, found a masterpiece of Olmec

OPPOSITE AND ABOVE: Mysterious monumental basalt heads thought to be part of a ruler or ancestor cult.

138

sculpture featuring a seated male holding a half-jaguar, half-human baby. The local Christian Indians venerated the statue as an apparition of the Virgin Mary until authorities from the provincial capital of Xalapa realised its presence and significance. This 55-centimetre high sculptured piece, with five supernatural images carved into its surface, provided a key to understanding Olmec deities.

To the Olmecs, mist-shrouded mountains, water (rivers, springs, ponds), and caves, were imbued with sacred qualities, and they worshipped and deposited cultic objects to their various deities at these sites.

A spectacular sculpture of a life-sized kneeling man, wearing a feathered headdress and mask, was found on the summit of the almost inaccessible volcano, San Martin Pajapan, in the Tuxtla Mountains. Until it was removed to the Museum of Anthropology in Xalapa in 1967 it was still venerated by the locals, who like their forebears, made the trek up the volcano's steep slopes and through its almost impenetrable forests.

Two remarkable caches of Olmec treasures were found in water. In 1969, fishermen discovered an immense cache of over one thousand jadeite and serpentine celts, figurines of deities and dozens of life-sized masks. Unfortunately, most of these artefacts were smuggled out of Mexico and sold to overseas collectors. In 1989, at El Manati in the realm of San Lorenzo, where permanent springs came to the surface creating a bog, archaeologists found beautifully polished jadeite celts and forty rare wooden busts.

Numerous outstanding Olmec-style artefacts and paintings have been found in caves. In the Juxtlahuaca and Oxtotitlan caves in the western Mexican state of Guerrero, are the 'most sophisticated and complex cave paintings known in America' (*The Olmecs: America's First Civilization*). Painted in vivid colours, the best preserved is 10 metres above the base of the cliff face and features an Olmec ruler in a bird costume with elaborate feathered headdress and cape, sitting on a flat-topped throne in the form of an earth monster.

> The Olmecs' stunning sculptural artefacts ranged from monumental basalt heads to exquisite small ritual objects—figurines, masks and celts, or ceremonial axes—carved out of greenstone, a material highly valued by the Olmecs in all periods.

ABOVE: Restored sections from an Olmec painting.

Depictions of the supernatural

It is the supernatural world of the Olmecs that has created the most controversy. Olmec deities 'combine human, reptilian, avian and feline attributes in bewildering arrays' (*The Olmecs: America's First Civilization*). One of the strangest is the were-jaguar, carved on figurines, ritual axes and thrones. These human babies with jaguar-like faces have a cleft in the top of the head. One theory is that the Olmecs believed that a mating between a human and a jaguar had resulted in a race of were-jaguars.

There is no doubt that the jaguar, the largest and most powerful cat in the Americas, was probably a symbol of authority and prowess, as well as a spirit companion to the shamans in their journeys to the spirit world. Because jaguars were just as much at home in trees, water and caves, and because of their ability to hunt at night just as easily as in the day, they were seen as moving between worlds. Shamans are believed to have shape-shifted, taking the form of the jaguar, to move from the earthly to the supernatural world. There are many Olmec images of humans in the process of transformation into a jaguar.

Other scholars have suggested that these images actually represented a toad, a species of which, commonly found in Mesoamerica, has a cleft in its head, a fleshy toothless mouth, sheds its skin (a sign of death and rebirth) and has hallucinogenic properties.

Whether the Olmecs were one unified ethnic group or not, they shared a similar culture, in which the supernatural world of deities and forces was as real to them as the physical world.

The exact reasons for the demise of the Olmecs are not known, but environmental changes have been suggested. Perhaps tectonic upheavals and a change in river courses may have triggered other social and economic factors. Their beautifully made objects, however, continue to fascinate.

Part IV

1st Millennium BCE

Technological genius and artistic creativity

26
QUEENS OF KALHU

The 'Nimrud Treasures' of Assyria

The Assyrian came down like a wolf on the fold,
And his cohorts were gleaming in purple and gold;
And the sheen of their spears was like stars on the sea,
When the blue wave rolls nightly on deep Galilee.

—Lord Byron, *The Destruction of Sennacherib*

In 1988, Muzahem Hussein, working for the Iraqi Department of Antiquities and Heritage on the palace of the Assyrian King Ashurnasirpal II at Nimrud (ancient Kalhu) in northern Iraq, noticed a number of floor bricks out of place. While repositioning them he found that they actually covered a vault, a vertical shaft and stairway. Once the debris was removed, he found the first of three tombs that together comprised the most spectacular archaeological discovery since the days of Sir Leonard Woolley at Ur and Howard Carter in the Valley of the Kings.

They proved to be the tombs of the consorts to some of the most powerful Assyrian kings. The relatively intact burials were rare in Iraq, as most tombs had been plundered in antiquity. In the sarcophagus of one consort were 157 items of gold, silver and precious stones weighing fourteen kilograms while the antechamber of another tomb delivered up 450 objects, with the gold and silver alone weighing over 22 kilograms.

OPPOSITE: Gold necklace and bracelets from the tombs of the Queens of Kalhu that form part of the magnificent Nimrud Treasures.

For millennia the ancient Assyrians received bad press. Their contemporaries, particularly the biblical prophets, described them as cruel, arrogant warmongers who 'exterminated all the nations' (*The Bible*: Kings II), and initially, this claim seemed to be confirmed when nineteenth century archaeologists discovered repetitive carvings of military activities: sieges, war chariots trampling the bodies of enemy soldiers and gory scenes of impaling, flaying and plunder.

However, according to the Assyriologist, Professor Nicholas Postgate of Cambridge University, the Assyrians were probably no more bloodthirsty than their contemporaries, and a careful study of the positioning of these brutal images—in reception and throne rooms—revealed that their real purpose was propaganda to intimidate foreigners visiting the courts of the Assyrian kings.

There is no doubt that the Assyrians were a great military power and at their height could assemble a large professional standing army. With the addition of conscripts they were able to put between 200,000 and 300,000 men in the field equipped with iron spears and swords, bows and arrows, metal armour, chariots, swift horses and battering rams. Paved roads enabled their armies to move rapidly throughout their empire which extended from the Mediterranean and southern Egypt to the Persian Gulf, and north beyond the Taurus Mountains of Turkey. Part of their military policy was the controversial large-scale deportations and relocations of people to prevent local uprisings: Jews and Israelites were sent to Assyria and Medea, Babylonians to Palestine, and Chaldeans to Armenia. However, these were not forced marches and the health and welfare of these deportees were of prime importance to the Assyrians.

It is often forgotten that they actually welcomed those who willingly accepted their rule, encouraged ethnic equality and encouraged intermarriage. Some of their leaders were scholars, like King Ashurbanipal, who built the first library of the ancient world at Ninevah, supposed to have contained between 20–30,000 tablets. The kings constructed royal cities like Ninevah with its 15-metre-high walls, 15 gates, temples, palaces, public squares, botanical and zoological garden irrigated with water carried by the oldest known aqueduct from 48 kilometres away.

Somewhere between 884–859 BCE, the capital of Assyria was moved from Ashur to the city of Kalhu, modern Nimrud, where it remained until ca. 710, when Ninevah superseded. Kahlu was a major centre and royal residence city until destroyed in 612 by the Medes and Babylonians. It became one of the best-known archaeological sites from the mid-nineteenth century when the British archaeologist Austen Henry Layard began excavation there. On its citadel were the remains of four palaces, featuring remarkable bas-reliefs of human-headed winged lions and bulls guarding the entrances to the king's court; three smaller palatial buildings; an arsenal; perhaps five temples; three gates and a ziggurat or temple tower of Ninurta, the city's patron god.

Recovered only to be endangered

The first tomb excavated by Muzahem Hussein at Kalhu held a sealed sarcophagus containing the remains of a woman about fifty years old with a silver bowl placed beneath her skull. She was covered in exquisite jewellery: finely crafted gold earrings, armlets and rings. On her left forefinger alone were five gold rings. The second tomb, only 92 metres away, was more spectacular. It included two female bodies in the same sarcophagus.

The original burial belonged to Queen Yab, wife of the powerful Tilgather Pileser III (ca. 744–727 BCE). Despite a curse, threatening any one who opened or disturbed her burial with eternal thirst and restlessness, another queen had been interred some time later. An inscribed golden bowl on her upper body identified her as Atalia, queen of Sargon (ca. 721–705). An inscribed crystal bowl mentions a third queen: Banitu, queen of Shalmaneser V (ca. 726–722), but there are no remains. The skeletons of Yaba and Atalia indicate that they died somewhere between the ages of 30–35. Both were covered in embroidered linen and the treasures of gold and semiprecious stones included a crown; a mesh diadem; 79 earrings; 30 rings; 14 armlets; 4 anklets; 15 vessels and many golden chains. Although the burial chamber of the third tomb that belonged to Mullissu-mukannisat Ninua, queen of Ashurnasirpal II, and mother of Shalmaneser III, had been robbed in antiquity, an antechamber with three bronze coffins had apparently been overlooked. One coffin contained the bones of a young adult, three children, a baby and a foetus. The second contained a young woman (probably a queen judging by the magnificent crown she wore) and a child. The third held five adults. It was in this antechamber that Hussein discovered the greatest quantity of gold treasures.

The treasures had only just been put on display in the Baghdad Museum when the Iraqi dictator, Saddam Hussein, invaded Kuwait in 1990. A few months later they were spirited away to an underground vault in the Central Bank of Baghdad where they remained for twelve years. The First Gulf War in 1991 interrupted excavation at Nimrud and for the next decade archaeologists worked under less than satisfactory conditions, always aware of the armed looters who roamed the deserts. Having survived the pillage of the Babylonians and Medes in the seventh century BCE, the Nimrud treasure faced another danger nearly 2800 years later. During the Second Gulf War of 2003, the Central Bank of Baghdad, where the treasure was supposedly stored, suffered severe damage from American attacks. Although the vaults were not damaged, they were flooded. On June 5, 2003, five waterlogged crates containing the treasure were discovered, but could only be recovered after three million litres of water were pumped from the bank's basement. The treasures were found intact and have remained in the bank vault since.

27

GEOMETRIC, ORIENTAL AND FIGURED MOTIFS

Masterpieces of Greek vase painting

... When old age shall this generation waste
Thou shalt remain ...

—John Keats, *Ode on a Grecian Urn*

Although nothing survives of the monumental Greek painting that was so famed in its day, painted Greek pottery features largely in the record of ancient Greece, because fired clay has proven almost indestructible. Even when pottery was shattered, the shards provided a valuable way of dating, and although generally utilitarian, painted pots and their fragments are the most abundant sources of images of Greek mythology and everyday life in the city-states (*poleis*) of ancient Greece.

Amongst the thousands of vessels scattered around the Mediterranean, and originally used for storage—mixing, pouring, and drinking wine; carrying water; cooking; holding perfumes and oils, and for ritual practices—there are a number considered true masterpieces. These include the Dipylon Vase (ca. 760–750 BCE); the Milesian Wild Goat Oinochoe (late seventh century); the Chigi Jug (ca. 629 BCE); the Francois Vase (ca. 570 BCE); Exekias' kylix based on the abduction

OPPOSITE: A stunning black-figured amphora by Exekias depicting Achilles slaying Penthesilea, Queen of the Amazons.

of Dionysus (ca. 550–525) and Euphronius' kylix kraters of Hercules wrestling the Libyan Titan Anteus, and the death of Sarpedon (ca. 525–480 BCE).

The eleventh–eighth century BCE, is known as the Geometric Period in Greek pottery decoration. Bands of geometric motifs (triangles, semicircles, lozenges and the famous Greek 'key' or *meander*) encircled the vases emphasising the curves of the pots. About the ninth century, some of the bands which had formerly contained geometrical patterns became filled with stylised figures of humans and animals. This style of ornamentation, which reached its peak in Attica (the city-state of Athens) in the eighth century, was distinguished by a 'remarkable blend and harmony of shape and decoration' (Helena Yatra, *Ancient Greek Pottery*).

A masterpiece of this late Geometric style was the 1.5-metre-high Dipylon Vase named for the Dipylon cemetery just outside Athens where it was discovered. It was used as a marker for the grave of an Athenian aristocrat. Its sophisticated ornamentation is a combination of multiple geometric friezes and a central scene featuring a 'lying in state' where the deceased is being mourned by family and friends. This is now housed in the Archaeological Museum of Athens.

From the eighth century, the Greeks began sending out colonies to all parts of the Mediterranean. This brought them into contact with other cultures, particularly those of the East, and as trade flourished, the closer communication with the 'orient' influenced Greek pottery. During this 'orientalising' period the city of Corinth, which had been a leading coloniser and was a prosperous trading centre, dominated Greek pottery production. Vases were adorned with bands of animals, both realistic and fantastic, as well as sphinxes and other motifs of an eastern origin.

The Milesian Wild Goat *oinochoe*, also known as the 'Levy Oinochoe' is possibly the best example of this type of decorated pot. Around the same time, a new form developed with the human figure as the main focus. With its scenes of hunting, horsemen and chariots, and the first example of a 'hoplite phalanx', the closely packed ranks of heavily armed Greek

LEFT: Detail of Exekias' vase showing Ajax and Achilles playing dice at Troy.

infantrymen, the Chigi Jug is the finest example of Corinthian pottery.

By the sixth century, the Greeks had 'consolidated their own cultural characteristics' (Furio Durando, *Splendours of Ancient Greece*) and they no longer borrowed from the East. Both Corinthian and Athenian potters adopted a different technique of decorating pots called the black-figured style. This involved leaving the deep reddish brown of the clay as a background and adding a diluted clay (slip) of the same material as the pot for the figures which turned black on firing. Details were incised into the pot and an occasional touch of white added variety. The artists of these black-figured pots drew on an almost unending supply of ancient myths and legends for decorative inspiration.

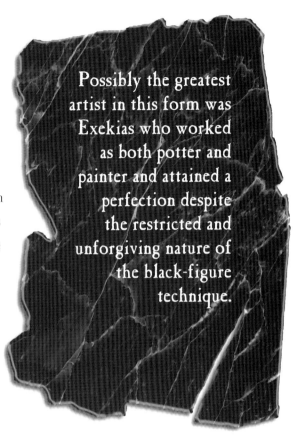

Possibly the greatest artist in this form was Exekias who worked as both potter and painter and attained a perfection despite the restricted and unforgiving nature of the black-figure technique.

The Francois Vase made by the potter Ergotimos and painted by Kleitas was a masterpiece of this form, showing gods, goddesses, heroes and monsters rendered in the finest detail. Kleitias was probably the best vase painter of mythological scenes of all time using a huge cast of characters. The vase depicted 271 mythological figures and 121 inscriptions. 'Both technical perfection and remarkable narrative power and movement' are a feature of Kleitias' work.

Because this kind of *krater* (a vase used to mix wine and water) was used at social gatherings, and the main theme seems to be the marriage of Peleus and Thetis (the parents of Achilles), it has been speculated that this vessel was made for an Athenian wedding. In 1900, a disgruntled museum guard threw a stool at the display case containing the *krater*, smashing it into 638 pieces. It was painstakingly restored first in 1904 and again in 1974 in order to incorporate previously missing fragments and can be now seen in the Archaeological Museum of Florence.

Fantastic legends and everyday life

Gradually the Athenians surpassed the Corinthians in both vase-making and pottery export. By the second half of the sixth century, the potters' workshops in the Kerameikos quarter of Athens were producing a variety of magnificent vessels. Possibly the greatest artist in this form was

Exekias who worked as both potter and painter and attained a perfection despite the restricted and unforgiving nature of the black-figure technique.

He used the shape of the vessel as a kind of terrain for his central compositions which, like the themes of tragedies, focused on the dramatic moments in life, death and religion: Ajax and Achilles playing dice at Troy as if trying to influence the outcome of the war; Achilles' slaying of Penthesilea, Queen of the Amazons, who is totally at his mercy; and Ajax preparing to fall on his sword knowing he can no longer win honour on the battlefield. Exekias always paid careful attention to the finest details, which being incised into the pot allowed no room for mistakes.

One of the last masterpieces of the black-figured form by Exekias is his famous *kylix* (drinking cup) based on the myth of the abduction of Dionysus by Tyrrhenian pirates. In the myth, Dionysus flooded the pirate ship with wine, made vines grow out of its mast and turned himself into a lion so that the terrified pirate crew jumped into the sea and were transformed into dolphins. John Boardman says of Exekias, 'the hallmark of his style is a near statuesque dignity which brings vase painting for the first time close to claiming a place as a major art' (*Athenian Black-figure Vases*).

Within half a century, a new technique in vase decoration appeared: red figures on a black background. Although this was the reverse of the more artificial black-figured form, it gave the artist greater freedom. The figures were left in the red of the clay against a black background, the details rendered with a brush instead of being incised, allowing for more subtle effects especially in the expressions of the face, the anatomy of the body and the folds of garments. For a while both forms were produced, but black-figured decoration continued only in the so-called

152

ABOVE: Detail from Exekias' kylix showing the god Dionysus.
OPPOSITE: The Wild Goat oinochoe from the early orientalising period in Greek pottery.

Panathenaic amphorae (food and wine storage vessels) offered as prizes for contests. Some of the most beautiful Attic ceramic art was produced between 525–480 BCE and is referred to as the austere style. Possibly the greatest potter and painter of this period was Euphronius who worked on large vases and drew his themes from mythology. It was his portrayal of the anatomical details and perfect proportion of the human body that set him apart.

After the Persian Wars (480 BCE), pottery images reflected greater realism and freedom of movement. Also, there was a change in subject matter in favour of everyday life, particularly the world of women. These later pots provide a unique source of information on the eating and drinking habits of Athenians, slavery, the collection of water from fountains, types of musical instruments; forms of entertainment, work and relaxation in the women's quarters of the home—in fact, nearly every aspect of life in fifth century Greece.

In the second half of the fifth century, when the quality of Attic red-figured vase painting declined, small, narrow-necked, one-handled jugs called *lekythoi*, used for the storage of precious unguents, were produced. These were luxury items placed on graves. The surface of the jug was covered in white and the scenes, usually associated with death, were in rich, varied colours, more in the style of the monumental paintings described by ancient sources. Unfortunately, not a single large-scale Greek painting has survived, and the only clues to the ancient artists' skills are the vase paintings, many of which are believed to be copies of larger paintings.

Over the centuries, Greek pottery became an invaluable record, the 'foster-child of Silence and slow Time', able to tell 'a flowery tale more sweetly than our rhyme: Of deities or mortals, or of both . . .' (John Keats, *Ode on a Grecian Urn*).

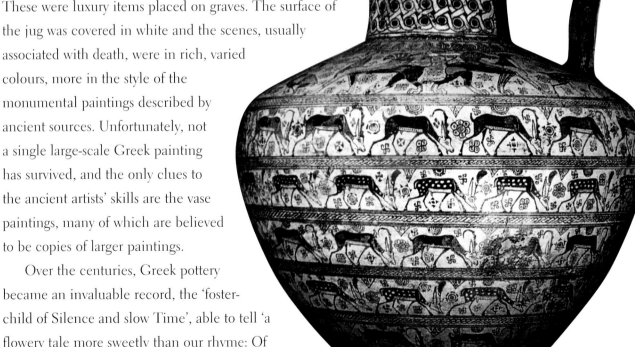

HORSEMEN OF THE EURASIAN STEPPES

Scythian gold and nomadic textiles

…various members of the king's household are buried beside him … all of them strangled. Horses are buried too, and gold cups … and a selection of his other treasures. —Herodotus, *Histories*, Bk.4.71

Between the seventh and third centuries BCE, nomadic warrior horsemen known as Scythians (Sacae), roamed the Eurasian steppes from China and Outer Mongolia in the east, across Siberia to the Black Sea and the Danube River in the west. While those in the remote Altai Mountains in the heart of Siberia (the Eastern Scythians) remained relatively isolated, those in the west, including the Royal Scythians, came into contact with the Greek colonists who had settled around the Black Sea area from the seventh century BCE. At various stages throughout their history these ferocious and skilled horsemen came into conflict with the Assyrians, Medes, Persians and Macedonians.

Archaeologists, excavating the Scythians' *kurgans*, or burial mounds, in present-day Ukraine and Siberia, found embalmed bodies of warrior men and women, some with elaborate tattoos, along with their sacrificed horses, wagons and weapons, and an abundance of gold. The Scythians covered themselves in gold in the form of pectorals, bracelets, belts and embossed

OPPOSITE: A magnificent gold comb featuring a battle scene found in a royal Scythian tomb at Solokha.

ABOVE: A gold panther that formed part of the decoration on a Scythian shield.

plaques sewn onto their garments. They used it to decorate their sword hilts and scabbards, shields, bow and arrow cases (*gortyos*), as well as the trappings of their horses and wagons.

In a rare untouched Scythian grave in the Siberian Altai Mountains discovered in 2001, 5000 decorative gold pieces, weighing 20 kilograms, adorned the royal male and female bodies. Dr Ellen Reeder of the Museum of Brooklyn and an expert on Scythian art says 'They created things that came alive with sound. They wore rustling gowns, tinkling earrings, robes awash with pendants that jingled. Even the finials on their wagon poles rattled to announce their coming' (*Scythian Treasures from the Ancient Ukraine*, Brooklyn Museum).

From the *kurgans* of Pazyryk, 1600 metres above sea level in the remote Altai Mountains— close to where Russia, Kazakhstan, China and Mongolia meet—unique articles made from wool, felt, fur, leather and silk have been excavated. Normally textiles and leather do not survive over time, but at Pazyryk, the climatic conditions were ideal for the preservation of perishable material for over 2500 years. The burial mounds were made from larch logs covered with stones and boulders which deflected the sun but allowed water to seep through into the chambers. This turned to ice during the winter and remained frozen, so preserving everything within the grave. Some of the organic articles preserved in the ice include the world's oldest surviving wool-pile rug, a 30-metre-square appliquéd carpet, felt appliquéd wall hangings, and saddlecloths.

The various Scythian tribes shared a common culture based on their nomadic way of life and the importance of their horses. The fifth century Greek historian, Herodotus, asked, 'having neither cities or forts, and carrying their dwellings with them wherever they go: accustomed moreover, one and all of them to shoot from horseback; and living not by agriculture but on their cattle, their wagons the only houses that they possess, how can they fail of being unconquerable, and unassailable even?'. These fierce fighters 'wore trousers and tall pointed hats set upright on their heads, and were armed with the bows of their country, daggers, and the *sagaris*, or battle axe'. Young, unmarried Scythian women, dressed and armed like the men, apparently fought alongside them in battle.

Herodotus also detailed some of the more unusual and bloody Scythian customs. Upon a king's death, 'the belly is slit open, cleaned out and filled with various aromatic substances, crushed galingale, parsley-seed and anise; it is then sewn up again and the whole body coated with wax'. The embalmed king was then taken on a wagon around to each tribe, the members of which cut pieces from their ears, shaved their heads, made incisions in their arms, gashed their noses and foreheads and pushed arrows through their left hands as part of their mourning for the king

The Scythians also used cannabis as part of their death rites. After a burial, they purified themselves, not with water, but by means of a vapour bath which took place in a small tent-like structure. Cannabis seeds and the resinous flower calyxes were thrown onto hot stones giving off a vapour which the Scythians enjoyed so much that, according to Herodotus, they howled with pleasure.

The art of the Scythians, like other ancient nomadic people is predominantly animal art, featuring motifs based on the horse, the animals of the steppes (stags, ibex, boars, bears, wolves, panthers and eagles), and mythical beasts like the griffin. These zoomorphic motifs served more than just a decorative purpose: they were amulets with magical powers. Some represented the cycle of life, death and transformation.

Although animal art goes back well into the past, the Scythians produced a style that was new and individual. Most pieces are small, but of exceptional workmanship, emphasising each animal's distinctive features. The Scythian craftsmen of the seventh and sixth centuries BCE combined basic representational art with a lively imagination to produce pieces that are both forceful and beautiful. The most outstanding examples are the reclining Kostromsky Stag with its legs tucked under its body, head raised and muscles taut, and the Kelermes Panther.

The gold plaques, necklaces and vessels from the fifth and fourth century royal graves of the Kul Oba, Solokha, Chertomlyk and Tovsta Mohyla sites are executed in a Greco-Scythian style. These were probably commissioned by Scythian chieftains from one of the Greek goldsmith workshops in the cities on the north coast of the Black Sea. One magnificent piece is the so-called

The Scythians covered themselves in gold in the form of pectorals, bracelets, belts and embossed plaques sewn onto their garments.

Solokha Comb showing a legendary battle between two Scythian groups. The skilled craftsmen obviously knew of Scythian dress, hairstyles and weaponry.

Two other unique artefacts are a gold vessel featuring Scythian warriors in typical pointed cap or hood, trousers, and jacket trimmed with fur or fleece, and a large crescent-shaped gold and blue enamel chestplate or necklace, divided into three registers. The top register shows two long-haired, bare-chested Scythians working on the fleece of a sheep and surrounded by domestic animals nursing their young, presenting a tranquil scene from Scythian daily life.

Preserved textiles a rarity

Some of the textiles from the *kurgans* of Pazyryk show Chinese influence, such as the appliquéd felt hanging featuring tethered swans, and the wall hanging of a leader sitting on a throne in a Chinese-style robe being approached by horsemen. The stunning 3.4 square metre woollen pile carpet features a central motif of plants, surrounded by a border of stags and an outer band of riders on horses with clipped manes and feathered headdresses. Although the Scythians had leather bridles, they did not have stirrups and rode with just a felt covering, relying on grip and balance. Some of the saddlecloths are as rich as the carpets.

Well-preserved articles of clothing were also found in the Pazyryk graves. In 1993, Russian archaeologist Natalia Polosmak discovered a larch coffin with stylised images of snow leopards and deer carved in leather, encased in a solid block of ice. It belonged to a blond-haired woman referred to as the 'Ice Maiden' who in death was accompanied by six of her horses, which appeared to have been struck down with an axe. She was between 20–30 years old when she died, and for her afterlife she was dressed in a unique metre-high felt headdress with fifteen birds sewn onto it.

According to Polosmak the headdress was 'literally a construction' and was probably associated with the tree of life which identified her as someone of high standing, possibly a spiritual leader such as a shaman. She wore thigh-high leather riding boots, still supple after nearly 2500 years, a crimson dress with bands of three colours, made from wool and camel hair, held together by a tasselled belt, and a blouse made from precious wild silk. 'This costume is one of the oldest pieces of female clothing ever found from a nomadic society. Nothing has to be reconstructed. We have a complete outfit right down to the belt. It's an amazingly rare find in the history of archaeology' (*The Siberian Ice Maiden*, BBC TV).

The State Hermitage Museum in St Petersburg, Russia, has by far the world's greatest collection of Scythian gold, animal art and ancient nomadic textiles.

29

A CULTURAL ENIGMA

Terracotta Nok sculptures from Nigeria

Masterful relics severed from their predecessors and successors by the passage of time, Nok terracottas currently occupy an important space in the history of African art.

—*Timeline of Art History*, The Metropolitan Museum of Art

In the early 1930s, eleven terracotta statues in perfect condition were discovered near the city of Sokoto, in northern Nigeria. A decade later, a British archaeologist named Bernard Fagg, an administrative officer of the Nigerian Colonial Service in the city of Jos, was shown the head of a statue by the director of a tin mine, near the village of Nok. The mine director had bought the head from one of his workers who had it in his yam garden as a scarecrow. It, and other pieces, had come to light accidentally during mining.

Bragg asked the miners to inform him whenever they discovered any more figures or fragments, and eventually he accumulated 150. He organised the search further afield. Many pieces were located in the alluvial mud of riverbeds having been washed from their original sites by the wet season floodwaters. The find sites are spread over an area of 153,600 square kilometres north of the confluence of the Niger and Benue Rivers, but it is not possible to say if the terracotta statues all come from one culture or two. Although the area to the north around Sokoto is often referred to as the Kwatakwashi culture area, and the area in the central Jos Plateau as the Nok culture, the mysterious figures are known as Nok terracottas.

The bulk of the terracottas are human effigies of both genders, some intact, others with their heads broken off. There are some depictions of animals. Those figures showing a person on a horse are the most valuable due to their rarity. They range in size from 10 centimetres to over a metre in height and some of the heads are life-sized. The figures are shown standing, sitting and in ritual postures. The pose of a 'thinker' was a particular favourite. They are both minimally naturalistic and abstract in form. It is the heads, and particularly the eyes, which fascinate.

The heads, with large overhanging foreheads, are elongated and out of proportion to the rest of the body, and the facial features distorted. This suggests that the head, as in other ancient cultures around the world, was regarded as significant. The eyes are stylised, often depicted as an arc or a triangle and the pupils, as well as the nostrils, lips and ears, are pierced. That personal adornment was taken seriously is indicated by the elaborate hairstyles and the abundance of jewellery around the neck, on the limbs and around the torso. Despite these stylistic similarities, each figure is unique.

The Nok terracottas featured are among the oldest witnesses of the artistic creativity of the people of Africa.

The ancient craftsmen used the course-grained clay of the area and worked by hand. Rather than building up the figure by adding sections, it appears that many of the pieces were sculpted more in the fashion of woodcarving. Many are hollow which means that the thickness of the clay had to be even throughout to avoid breaking when fired at temperatures of 300°C or higher, in the ashes of their open-hearth ovens. Originally covered in a slip which gave a smooth polished look, most now have a pocked appearance due to weathering. The large terracottas, which show incredible skill in modelling, suggest that these were not the beginnings of a style but were the result of a much longer artistic tradition.

Over a period ranging from ca. 600 BCE–200 CE, the Nok artists with their technical skill and inventiveness created works of great beauty and variety, and yet the culture from which they came is still a mystery. There are, however, some stylistic similarities with present-day Yoruba art.

OPPOSITE: A 49.5-centimetre high terracotta bust of a man with elaborate hair-do and jewellery.

Who these statues represented is not known. Perhaps they depicted dignitaries, ancestors, deities or mythical kings. That they served some ritual purpose is highly likely. The Nok was an agricultural society and they may have played some part in a fertility cult, but it is more likely that they were associated with the cult of royalty and ancestors such as in later Nigerian cultures like that of Benin. Those depicting physical deformities may have been used in healing and it is possible that some may have been placed on top of houses to indicate a sacred space, as occurs in some parts of West Africa today. The tiniest images were probably worn around the neck as ornaments or protective charms.

Black market in antiquities

Despite the Nigerian Government's attempts to prohibit the export of these fascinating terracotta pieces, they are found for sale in European and North American antique galleries, auction houses and on the internet. There is a worldwide black market industry in Nok statues. At the Nigerian end, this involves official corruption (granting of export licences, and mining permits which provide a cover for 'coming across' buried Nok treasures), looting of sites by organised teams of villagers, museum thefts and smuggling, even in diplomatic pouches.

Official apathy, greed and the poverty of many Nigerians has led to 'this organised and systematic rape of some of Nigeria's earliest material culture' (Patrick J. Darling, *The Rape of Nok and Kwatakwashi: the crisis in Nigerian Antiquities*). 'There is almost no record of what Nigeria has lost: almost two complete ancient cultures have been looted, (Nok and Kwatakwashi) and there are no photographs, no records of associated artefacts, no mapping of past settlement distribution, and no noting of stylistic comparisons or archaeological provenances'.

Some of those terracotta figures that escaped the looters have been destroyed as idols by Nigerian Muslims and there appears to be little interest by many community leaders in pre-Islamic history. Perhaps the material remains of the Nok culture are safer, at the moment, in the various collections around the world. In 1997, The Banque Generale du Luxembourg and the Musee Barbier-Mueller in Geneva promoted a major exhibition of Nok statuary from private collections called 'The Birth of Art in Africa'. The Nok terracottas featured are 'among the oldest witnesses of the artistic creativity of the people of Africa' (Bernard de Grunne, *The Birth of Art in Africa*).

30

ORIENTAL LUXURY

The 'Oxus Treasure' of ancient Persia

Treasure there was in plenty — tents full of gold and silver furniture; couches overlaid with the same precious metals; bowls, goblets, and cups, all of gold; and wagons loaded with sacks of gold and silver basins.

—Herodotus, *The Histories*

Ancient Greek sources—Herodotus, Xenophon and Plutarch—leave their readers in no doubt about the fabulous riches of the Persian Empire under the Achaemenid dynasty (kings with names like Cyrus, Cambyses, Darius, Xerxes and Artaxerxes) who ruled from the cities of Pasargadae, Susa and Persepolis from 550–323 BCE. The empire began with the conquests of Cyrus the Great. His successors, Cambyses and Darius I, added further territory, but neither Darius nor his son Xerxes managed to bring the Greek mainland under their control.

At the height of its power, the Persian Empire, a multi-ethnic and multicultural entity, extended from Egypt and the Aegean Sea to Afghanistan and the Indus Valley. In his gold and silver Foundation Tablets deposited at Persepolis, Darius I declared, 'Here is the kingdom that I possess, from the Sakas who are beyond Sogdiana to the Land of Kush (Nubia), from India to Sardis'. Tribute from subject rulers poured into the royal treasuries, and reliefs, depicting delegations of these tribute states, on the sides of the Apadana (audience hall) at Persepolis are among some of the finest in existence.

Under Darius I, the empire was divided into twenty satrapies (provinces) with satraps (governors) answerable to the 'King of Kings', although the distance of some of the provinces from the capital of Susa meant that these officials had a great deal of autonomy. The dynasty, marked by intrigues, conspiracies and assassinations, survived until the Macedonian king, Alexander the Great, crossed the Hellespont from Europe into Asia in 334 BCE. Over the next decade, until his death in Babylon in 323, Alexander made the Persian Empire his own.

The oriental luxury enjoyed by the Persian kings and their nobility was legendary. During the invasion of Greece by Xerxes in 480 BCE, part of the Persian fleet was wrecked off the north coast of Greece. A local inhabitant 'picked up a large number of gold and silver drinking cups which were washed ashore, and found Persian treasure chests containing more gold, beyond counting' (Herodotus, *The Histories*). The Persian elite used gold and silver in abundance at banquets, as gifts, and as ornaments for decorating their garments.

Herodotus recorded how overwhelmed Pausanius, the Spartan king, was when, after the Greek victory against the Persians at Plataea in 479, he entered the camp of the Persian commander, Mardonius. There he 'saw gold and silver couches all beautifully draped, and gold and silver tables, and everything prepared for the feast with great magnificence' (*The Histories*). In his *Anabasis*, Xenophon says that bracelets were highly esteemed as tokens of honour and, again, according to Herodotus, every one of the ten thousand-strong-body of elite Persian troops (the Immortals) 'glittered with gold which he carried about his person in unlimited quantities'.

Archaeological sites in modern Iran, and as far afield as Turkey, Iraq, Afghanistan and Uzbekistan, have confirmed what the sources recorded.

In 1877, a large number of gold and silver objects were found scattered in the sands of the Amu Darya River (the Oxus River of antiquity) in Central Asia. These stunning artefacts, in what is called the Achaemenid Court Style, are dated to the fifth and fourth centuries BCE. The hoard is referred to as the Oxus Treasure and is the most important collection of Achaemenid metal work ever found. The story of the Oxus Treasure's supposed discovery, filled with a strange cast of characters, in settings with exotic names like Buhkara, Kabul, Peshawar and Rawalpindi, is intriguing.

LEFT: A gold model chariot pulled by four small horses or ponies, part of the Oxus Treasure.

Theft and recovery

Near a former ferry crossing at Takht-i Kuwad on the north bank of the Oxus River are some ancient ruins, parts of which have been washed away. This area was once close to the border between the ancient Persian provinces of Bactria and Sogdiana. It is this site where the Oxus treasure is supposed to have been found by local villagers.

The objects may have once formed part of a temple deposit of votive offerings, or a currency hoard; precious metals, particularly silver, were commonly used as items of exchange, even after the introduction of coinage. Exactly when these items were deposited or hidden is unknown, although the end of the third century BCE has been suggested. The villagers supposedly sold the treasures to three merchants from Bukhara (in present day Uzbekistan), but as the merchants were travelling from Kabul (Afghanistan) to Peshawar (present day Pakistan), they were attacked, seized and robbed by a band of tribesmen.

A servant managed to escape and alerted the British authorities. Captain F. C. Burton, with only two soldiers, found the robbers in a cave at night dividing up the spoils. When he threatened to return with a large force of soldiers, most of the treasure was returned. In gratitude to Burton, the merchants allowed him to buy a magnificent gold armlet. The merchants later sold the treasure to various antiquities dealers in Rawalpindi. The British Director-General of the Archaeological Survey of India, Sir Alexander Cunningham, bought part of the treasure, then sold the pieces to Sir Augustus Franks who eventually bequeathed them to the British Museum in 1897.

It is difficult to know if the pieces of the Oxus Treasure all came from the same source or if other objects were added later in Rawalpindi. Although there were suggestions that some of them might be fakes, the treasures in the British Museum have been proven to be authentic Achaemenid artefacts. The Treasure includes about 180 magnificent pieces: gold and silver jugs and bowls, some embossed; a gold scabbard with a hunting scene; gold model chariots with horses and drivers; silver and gold votive figurines; jewellery, including two large gold armlets with lion-griffin terminals, and spiral bracelets or torcs; ornaments to be attached to clothes; gold votive plaques; and numerous coins. According to Darius' Foundation Tablets, the goldsmiths who made objects for the Achaemenid rulers were Medes and Egyptians.

A large part of the Oxus Treasure is made up of votive plaques and statues. Most of the fifty-one plaques feature embossed human figures in typical Median dress, carrying flowers and *barsoms* (bundles of sticks and twigs carried by a priest) as a sign of piety. The gold and silver figurines may have represented supplicants seeking a favour from, or giving thanks to, a god. Also, it is possible that the magnificent armlets with lion-griffin terminals might also have been votive offerings since the terminals 'standing up proud of the hoop would have made them very impractical' to wear (J. Curtis and N. Tallis, *Forgotten Empire: The Word of Ancient Persia*).

The magnificent model chariot pulled by four pony-sized horses, complete with driver and passenger is likely to have belonged to a child due to the presence of a Bes head on the front of the chariot. Bes was a grotesque Egyptian dwarf god who warded off evil and became popular throughout the Persian Empire as a protector of the young.

Satraps and other representatives of the king, far from the courts of Susa and Persepolis, copied the stunning workmanship of the Achaemenid Court Style in the fifth–fourth centuries. For this reason 'any enquiry into the material culture of the period must extend far beyond the borders of modern Iran' (J. Curtis, *Ancient Persia*, 2000).

> The treasure includes about 180 magnificent pieces: gold and silver jugs and bowls; a gold scabbard with a hunting scene; gold model chariots with horses and drivers; silver and gold votive figurines; jewellery; ornaments to be attached to clothes; gold votive plaques; and numerous coins.

OPPOSITE: Part of the reliefs from the Apadana of Persopolis showing tribute bearers.

31

CEREMONIAL MUSIC

Bronze bells and stone chimes from the tomb of Marquis Yi of Zeng

... Transforming ways and refining customs, music brings peace to all the world. — *Confucius*

According to an ancient myth, the founder of Chinese music—the scholar Ling Lun— travelled to the mountains of western China to cut a bamboo pipe in such a way that it produced a musical note of a specific pitch. This was the 'foundation tone' of Chinese music.

Although music was used as entertainment in the courts of ancient China, more significantly, it was associated with important court rituals. It also played an indispensable part in literature; characters in poetry and prose were chosen according to tones, and the earliest poetry was sung to music.

Chinese scholars like Confucius and Xunzi saw moral and healing qualities in music, which had implications for rulers; certain types of music could be used to produce harmony and restraint in the common people by channelling their desires into constructive effort, while other types could give rise to 'wanton and destructive thoughts' and cause a breakdown in society. Before the unification of China into one empire, each state had its own 'proper pitch' and style of musical notation.

OPPOSITE: The 64-piece bronze bell set from the Tomb of Marquis Yi found together with chimes, flutes, pipes, drums and zithers.

The most magnificent and largest collection of musical instruments ever found in China came from the rich and undisturbed fifth century BCE tomb of Marquis Yi of Zeng, discovered by a unit of the Chinese People's Liberation Army in Hubei province in 1977 when they were levelling a small hill to build a factory. The burial dates from 433 BCE, and the collection of 124 instruments found in its chambers included one of the greatest technological achievements of Chinese civilisation: a set of 65 ritual bronze bells (*bianzhongs*). Also found were 32 lithophones or chimed stones; bamboo flutes; reed pipes; a twenty-five stringed lute; zithers with five to twenty-five strings, and drums.

Until this discovery, the state of Zeng had never been recorded in any ancient documents and was unknown to Chinese scholars. It is believed that Zeng may have been a northern vassal of the great state of Chu, since the largest bell in the set of 65 bears an inscription which indicates that King Hui of Chu, in his fifty-sixth year, ordered the musical bells to be made so that they could be used for the mourning rituals of Marquis Yi. Perhaps they were a gift in gratitude for a previous favour. Despite the discovery, the ancient state of Zeng is still a mystery, but there is no doubt about the magnificence of Marquis Yi's tomb. Sunk 13 metres into the ground and covering 220 square metres, it was arranged as a re-creation of his worldly palace.

ABOVE: Inscribed bronze of women playing bells.

The 400 objects in bronze, jade, lacquer and bamboo indicate that he hoped to continue his life of pleasure ('wine, women and song') in the next world.

There were four chambers to the tomb: the eastern room contained the Marquis' body in a magnificent red and black lacquered double-coffin, together with the coffins of eight young women between the ages of 13–24, possibly concubines or musicians. In that chamber were the pan flutes and zithers, used to entertain the Marquis with singers and dancers. The western chamber contained the bodies of thirteen other women, probably slaves, and the northern chamber appears to have been an armoury and storeroom. These three rooms were built around a central chamber which was symbolic of Yi's ceremonial and ancestral hall. It was filled with an ensemble of ritual musical instruments—the set of 65 bells and 32 chime stones—which were used periodically for important court and ancestral ceremonies. The instruments appear to have been buried according to their social function.

Access to a lost musical culture

The bells range in size from 20 centimetres in height and around 2.25 kilograms in weight, to 1.52 metres, weighing 203 kilograms. Apart from the large middle one that hangs alone, they are arranged in eight groups on a magnificent wooden and copper frame with red and black lacquered details and exquisite bronze fittings. The structure is 7.48 metres by 3.35 metres with the whole assemblage about 2.75 metres high. This is the largest set of bells ever discovered. The shaft or *yong* helps suspend each bell so that it tilts towards the player, while the body of the bell or *zhiong* has nine raised bosses (a sacred cosmological number) to give greater resonance.

The bells have no clappers because they have an elliptical-shaped cross-section and, skilfully played, are able to produce the Chinese musical scale of five notes and 12 half tones. Each bell, when struck, gives off two tones: one when struck in the centre of the broader side and another when struck on the narrower side. Each is inscribed with musical theories, the bell's position in the set and its particular pitch/tone. It appears, from historical records and other archaeological finds, that the bells were played by five people, two in front to play the larger bells with long poles, and three behind playing the smaller bells with wooden mallet-type implements.

The subtle variations in the pitch of each bell must have required exceptional skill in casting the bronze, as modern craftsmen discovered when building a replica thousands of years later. Until these bells were discovered with their inscribed information, nothing much was known about the sound of Chinese ritual music. According to Angela M. H. Schuster (*Archaeology*) 'The bells' tonal range has been likened to that of a modern piano'.

On another smaller set of 26 bells discovered in Henan Province around the same time as those of Marquis Yi, an inscription reads: 'I Wangsun Gao, selected my auspicious metals and for myself made these harmonising bells. They are long vibrating and sonorous, and their fine sound is very loud. With them, sternly and in a dignified manner, I reverently serve the king of Chua . . .'

Found with Marquis Yi's bells, and played with them, was a set of lithophones or stone chimes. The thirty-two marble slabs, that produced a clearer and higher sound when struck, were suspended from supporting columns decorated with mythical animals.

The more languorous and lilting sounds created by wind and stringed instruments were used for dancing and singing. As Xunzi recorded, 'Music is joy, an emotion that human beings cannot help but feel at certain times. Unable to resist feeling joy, they must find an outlet through voice and movement'. However, it was the more important bells, chimes and percussion instruments, producing sterner and more majestic sounds, that were used in formal court ritual.

> The subtle variations in the pitch of each bell must have required exceptional skill in casting the bronze, as modern craftsmen discovered when building a replica thousands of years later.

32

MUMMY BUNDLES AND EMBROIDERED FUNERAL REGALIA

Rare textiles from the Paracas culture of southern Peru

The embroidered mantles and other garments from the Paracas Necropolis constitute one of the textile wonders of the world ...

—Mary Elizabeth King, *Latin American Antiquity*

In the 1920s, the Peruvian archaeologist Julio C. Tello excavated a necropolis on the remote, barren and windswept Paracas Peninsula of southern Peru. The elite burials, on the northern slope of Cerro Colorado, yielded some of the most magnificent creations of Andean art: embroidered textiles in the form of funeral mantles, tunics and ponchos, possibly the richest find of such artefacts ever found in the world.

Dated from ca. 500–200 BCE, these spectacular textiles made from alpaca, llama and vicuna wool and cotton have been well preserved in the arid climate of the coastal desert. They are outstanding for the quality of their weaving and embroidery, their brilliant colours, the complexity of the overall design and symbolism, and state of preservation. The weavers and embroiderers of Paracas were creative geniuses. What is unusual about these textile masterpieces is that they were

ABOVE: A conical mummy bundle from the necropolis on the Paracas Peninsula in southern Peru.

an integral part of conical mummy bundles (layers wrapped around a body before burial), which have been described by Jeffrey Quilter in *Treasures of the Andes* as 'elaborate art constructions'.

Throughout Andean history, textiles were more highly prized than gold and silver. Not only were they labour intensive and therefore an indication of the owner's wealth and power, they were a sacred form of communication and accompanied the dead to the afterlife.

Julio Tello and his associates found evidence of two successive and related groups in the area, identified by their burials. The earliest group buried their dead in underground tomb chambers, often with multiple burials around a central mummy bundle, perhaps clan or family burials. This is known as the *Cavean* Phase of the Paracas culture and is dated from ca. 700 BCE, but it is from the later, and more elaborate, pit graves found about 1.6 kilometres away, referred to as *Necropolis*, that the largest mummy bundles and most stunning textiles come.

Four hundred and twenty-nine mummy bundles of various sizes were excavated from both sites. It appears that the smaller and some medium-sized bundles were lower class burials, while the larger ones, some measuring 1.8 metres high and 1.2 metres wide, when unwrapped, contained the mummies of men of advanced years who had probably achieved a certain degree

ABOVE: Restoration of embroidered textile mantles from the Paracas culture. The mantles and other fancy cloth items were an integral part of the mummy bundles.

of status during their lifetimes. Ann Paul, in *Paracus Ritual Attire: Symbols of Authority in Ancient Peru*, suggests they were Shaman-priests and village leaders

The greatest number, and most beautiful, of the embroidered textiles were found in these mummy bundles, some of which might contain more than forty fancy cloths, some as large as 3.5 square metres. One bundle is known to have included ten embroidered and eight unembroidered mantles, thirteen head cloths, four headbands, five ponchos, two tunics and a loincloth. The embroidering of each mantle was labour intensive and it has been estimated that the women of the dignitary's household, using perforated cactus thorn needles, may have taken anywhere from six months to well over three years to create the mantles for the mummy bundle.

The bodies, unclothed except for perhaps a deerskin and headdress, were flexed and bound into a sitting position just as they would have been seen on public occasions when alive. They were then placed in a large shallow basket and sometimes a gourd was placed over their heads or between their legs. Fragments of sheet gold were inserted in their mouths and over their eyes. Gold or cotton was used to cover the other body orifices. Placed within the innermost layers of covering cloths were items of a personal nature such as needles, yarns, miniature garments, leather bags containing pigments, and various pieces of embroidered clothing that showed signs of use—tunics, shoulder ponchos, loin cloths and cotton head cloths.

Symbolic of fertility and life

Plain mantles were alternated with the embroidered shrouds which tended to predominate in the outer layers of the bundle as if the mummy was 'dressed' for display. Amongst the outer embroidered shrouds were a standard set of items such as a tunic with panels of feather work; yellow feathered panels that may have been wrist and ankle bands; feathered headdress ornaments; feathered fans; and a staff bound with sinew and feathers. The outer cloth was then sewn together, a headdress placed on its symbolic head, and a reed mat placed over the whole bundle.

Some scholars believe that the conical mummy bundles were shaped like mountains which were venerated in a barren landscape as a source of life-giving water. Perhaps there was some association between the mummy and the concern for water as a source of abundance and new life. On the other hand, 'the form of the whole mummy bundle appears to represent a huge seed with the kernel, the flexed body of an ancestor, waiting to be born again' (*Treasures of the Andes*). Some of the figures embroidered on the mantles sprout bean vines. Perhaps it was hoped the deceased would become one of these supernatural figures and bring fertility to the land and its people. In 1970 when Tello and his assistant Mejia unwrapped a bundle they found at its centre, not a mummy, but a bag of beans.

Camelid yarn, probably alpaca, which was very fine, durable and strong and could be dyed to

> Throughout Andean history, textiles were more highly prized than gold and silver. Not only were they labour intensive and therefore an indication of the owner's wealth and power, they were a sacred form of communication and accompanied the dead to the afterlife.

brilliant colours, was used for the embroidered textile mantles and shoulder ponchos. Some of the textiles were covered in solid blocks of embroidery while others had alternating strips leaving the bare red or dark blue background cloth as a contrast. The overall designs were executed in spaced patterns (checkerboard and diagonal), and colour was used to create these patterns. Although there were often repetitive motifs, the embroiderers attempted to make each image unique or to change the orientation of the image to add variety.

Motifs were symbolic rather than representational. Human-bird, human-feline and human-serpent combinations were associated with the spirit world and transformation. There was an amazing intermingling of shamanistic images: snake belts feathered wings, headdresses, monster heads with bands of nasal mucus (associated with the taking of psychotropic substances), trophy heads, staffs and semicircular knives, creating a superb visual effect.

The Paracas culture that produced the stunning embroidered textiles was superseded by another about the beginning of the Common Era. The Nazca culture that flourished in the Nazca Valley, about 160 kilometres further south, had its origins in the earlier Paracas culture. Although they are most renowned for their gigantic landscape designs (the Nazca Lines), they also continued the tradition of an 'exuberant use of a rich and varied coloured palette', particularly in their pottery and feathered garments.

BELOW: Textile details from Paracas funerary mantles.

33

THE NOBLEST OF IMAGES

The Parthenon Frieze

Mighty indeed are the marks and monuments of our empire which we have left. Future ages will wonder at us, as the present age wonders at us now.

—From the funeral oration of Pericles in Thucydides, *The Peloponnesian War*

I n the second half of the fifth century BCE, when Pericles was the dominant political figure in Athens, a massive building program was initiated which included the construction of a new Doric temple (the Parthenon) to house a colossal cult statue of the city's patron goddess, Athena. It seems that the architects, Iktinos and Kallicrates, plus the master sculptor, Pheidias, cooperated in the design of the temple and its sculptural elements.

These included a 160 metre-long sculpted frieze encircling the temple, 92 metopes in high relief, and larger-than-life sculptures in the triangular-shaped pediments at either end of the temple. Together these elements are referred to as the Parthenon marbles and are masterpieces of Classical Greek art. Although intended as an integral part of the Parthenon, most of the surviving marbles are in the British Museum and known as the Elgin Marbles after the Scottish aristocrat, Thomas Bruce, seventh Earl of Elgin, who had them removed in the early 1800s.

The theme of the Parthenon Frieze is believed to be a depiction of some aspects of the principal festival of Athens, the Great Panathenaea, dedicated to Athena. With its complex

ABOVE: Part of the cavalcade of horsemen on the northern side of the Parthenon frieze.

composition of 623 carved images of gods, humans and animals in low relief, its subtle iconography and dignified grandeur, it is a unique artistic creation.

The Great Panathenaea was held over a number of days in late July or early August and allowed all Athenians, except for slaves, to take part. It had three main elements: contests, a procession ending in the presentation of a new robe (*peplos*) to the goddess Athena, and sacrifices. The contests featured musical, rhapsodic (recitation of Homer's epic poems) and athletic competitions for men and boys; four and two-horse chariot races; exhibitions of equestrian prowess; boat races and a torch relay race. Winners in the contests were awarded black-figured amphorae (ceramic vases).

The religious procession assembled before dawn at the Dipylon gate in the northern part of the city and wound its way for one kilometre across the agora (the commercial, social and political centre of Athens) via the Panathenaic Way and up to the Acropolis. Taking part in the procession were priestesses of Athena; women and young girls carrying ritual paraphernalia; sacrificial animals; men carrying gold trays bearing cakes and honeycombs for offerings; youths with water jars for purification during the sacrifices; and musicians playing the *aulos* (a wind instrument) and *kithara* (a stringed instrument).

The colossal robe for the goddess, which hung on the mast of a ship on wheels, came next; then old men carrying olive branches; chariots with charioteers; craftswomen who had woven the sacred *peplos*; infantry and cavalry; victors in the games, and ordinary Athenians arranged in their *demes* (local areas). The procession culminated with the presentation of the *peplos* and ritual sacrifice of the one hundred heifers. After the sacrifice the flesh was roasted in the agora and distributed to the populace.

The Parthenon frieze was a tour de force of planning and carving from the initial decision about which elements of the procession to include. There were considerable design issues to be overcome, such as how to fill the 160-metre-long space with a procession of animals and humans without making it repetitious and boring. Different poses, as well as showing successive stages of an action, provided variety and movement. For example, in the section depicting the water carriers, one youth bends to pick up the jar from the ground, another stands and raises the jar to his shoulder, while another adjusts the jar with his hand. In the case of the horses, some are shown walking, others as racing with flaring manes and tails, or rearing out of control. Some cattle are docile and others are straining on their leads. Further variety was added with dynamic and energetic horse tamers attempting to

The Parthenon frieze was a tour de force of planning and carving from the initial decision about which elements of the procession to include. There were considerable design issues to be overcome.

keep their animals under control, and a young man with his cloak fluttering jumping off and on his chariot which appears to be travelling at a high speed.

Another problem to be addressed was how to fit the figures into a band only one metre high, and how to adjust the figures of gods (larger than mortals), and men on horseback and in chariots, to conform to the principle known as *isocephaly* where figures always stood on the same level and their heads uniformly reached the top of the frieze. The designers revealed their genius in the convincing manner they coped with this. 'The viewer is unaware of the fact that the horses are too small for the riders or that the gods, by being seated, are one third larger' (Jenifer Neils, *The Parthenon Frieze*).

Teams of stonemasons, sculptors, metal smiths and painters were employed and the blocks of marble cut and transported from Mt Pentelikon, 19 kilometres away. These were hoisted into place atop the architraves of the porches and long walls of the cella (a temple's inner chamber) because it was safer to carve the frieze in situ rather than risk damage by lifting a finished block and leveraging it into position.

The Greeks painted their statuary and architectural reliefs, which would have helped the low relief of the frieze, projecting only 5.6 centimetres from the background, to be seen more clearly from a distance.

> The poet Byron, who was in Greece during this time, wrote in his poem, 'Childe Harald':
>
> Dull is the eye that will not weep to see.
> Thy walls defaced, thy mouldering shrines removed.
> By British hands ...

180

The preliminaries to the procession are shown on the western end of the frieze, supposedly in the vicinity of the Dipylon Gate. There is an inspection of horses and a herald with either his staff or trumpet-like *salphinex* announces the start of the procession which moves off along the north and south sides of the frieze, presumably through the agora and up to the Acropolis. Cavalry escorts and sacrificial animals dominated the procession on both long sides of the frieze.

At the eastern end of the Parthenon, the procession converges from both sides on an assembly of twelve seated deities, six on each side of a ritual scene involving three women, and a man and a child folding a piece of cloth symbolising the *peplos*. The Greeks did not represent the most significant moment of a ritual for fear that something could go wrong. So the eastern end of the frieze merely suggests the sacrifice of the hundred cows and presentation of the *peplos*.

'Today, stripped of its colourful paint and gleaming metal attachments, the Parthenon frieze impresses by the uniform style of its carving, the virtuosity of its superimposed planes and the naturalism and idealisation of its figures. In this respect it is unique' (*The Parthenon Frieze*).

Cultural theft

In the early nineteenth century, when Greece was still part of the Turkish Ottoman Empire, Lord Elgin, British ambassador to the Ottoman court, was given a permit 'to take away any pieces of stone with inscriptions or figures'. For five years his agents removed over 100 pieces from the Parthenon using marble saws to cut off the backs of the blocks, weakening the structure in the process. For ease of transportation some of the blocks were sliced into smaller sections.

One shipload of marbles, on its way to England, was caught in a storm and sank near the Greek island of Kythera in 1802. It took Greek sponge divers two years to recover the marbles at a huge cost to Elgin. Even then they did not find their way to England for another ten years. Lord Nelson authorised a ship to go to Greece to transport them to Malta where they remained for the duration of the Napoleonic War. The last shipment of marbles arrived in England about 1811–12. By this time Elgin was in financial difficulties and was forced to sell them to the British Government who handed them over to the British Museum where they first went on display in 1816.

One hundred and sixty years later, the Greek government requested the repatriation of the marbles in time to be displayed in a new museum for the 2004 Olympics in Athens. The British Museum refused and the argument over custodianship of the 'Elgin Marbles' continues.

LEFT: Water carriers from the northern side of the Parthenon frieze.

34

RESCUED FROM THE SEA

Rare Greek bronze statuary

Marcus ... adorned the capital (Rome) with works of art which possessed the Hellenic grace and charm and truth to nature. He liked to claim that he had taught the ignorant Romans to admire and honour the glories of Greek art.

—Plutarch, *Marcellus*

Few large-scale Greek bronzes have survived from antiquity. Most of those in the world's museums were found in ancient shipwrecks around the Mediterranean in the twentieth century. They were originally plundered from Greek sanctuaries by Roman generals for the beautification of Roman public spaces, for their own villas and those of wealthy senators, and later, for members of the imperial family.

Many upper class Romans of the second and first centuries BCE were phil-Hellenes (admirers of Hellenic culture). When the Roman elite was unable to obtain a Greek original, they commissioned a copy, and today our knowledge of Greek sculptural masterpieces comes predominantly from Roman copies, as well as the bronzes that disappeared beneath the sea, such as The Zeus/Poseidon; the Riace Bronzes; the Antikythera Youth; The Boy from Marathon, and the Victorious Youth.

OPPOSITE: Upper portion of the bronze statue of Zeus/Poseidon recovered from a shipwreck off Cape Artemiseum in Eastern Greece.

Removal of Greek art began on a massive scale when the Romans took control of the Greek cities of Sicily, such as Syracuse, after the first Punic War (264-241 BCE), followed by the sacking of Corinth in 146 BCE and again in 86 BCE when Greece became a Roman province. The two pan-Hellenic sanctuaries of Olympia and Delphi, with their rich display of large-scale statuary, were prime targets for theft.

It appears that many transports went down in storms off the rugged coasts of the Mediterranean where the Greek masterpieces lay for millennia corroded by the salt water and covered with thick layers of chalky deposits until discovered by fishermen, sponge collectors and scuba divers. Unfortunately, the men who sculpted these masterpieces and their original location remain unknown. Those bronzes that did manage to survive the downfall of the Roman Empire were often melted down during the Middle Ages, just as marble masterpieces were destroyed to be used as a source of lime.

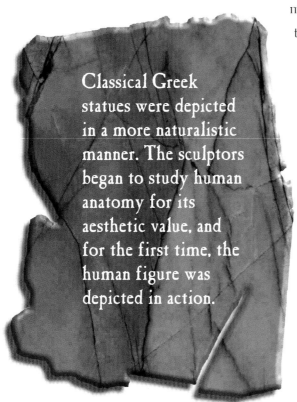

Classical Greek statues were depicted in a more naturalistic manner. The sculptors began to study human anatomy for its aesthetic value, and for the first time, the human figure was depicted in action.

About half of all Greek sculpture in the classical period was in bronze due to its strength, durability, versatility, brilliant sheen, and its lightness compared to the weight of a full-sized marble figure. Bronze allowed Greek sculptors to experiment. Unlike the stylised and stiff Archaic figures prior to the fifth century BCE. Art reflected other developments occurring in Greece at that time. Philosophers saw the world as a series of opposing forces which, when in balance, created a perfect entity. Sculptors incorporated this concept into their art, depicting the balance between tension and relaxation of different muscles.

Casting of large-scale bronzes developed around 550 BCE using the 'lost wax' method. Firstly the sculptor prepared a full-sized and detailed clay model which was covered with a thin layer of

184

OPPOSITE: Bronze statue of a youth recovered from the sea off the tiny island of Antikythera between Greece and Crete.

wax and a thicker
mould of clay. The
model, wax and mould
were then fired allowing the
wax to melt away through small
holes. The narrow space left by
the melted wax was filled with molten
bronze which cooled and solidified, after which
the outer mould was removed and the inner core scraped
away from a hole in the bottom of the statue. Finishing
touches included the addition of other metals and glass for
body details (nipples, lips, teeth and eyes), more detailed
carving (hair and beard), and polishing.

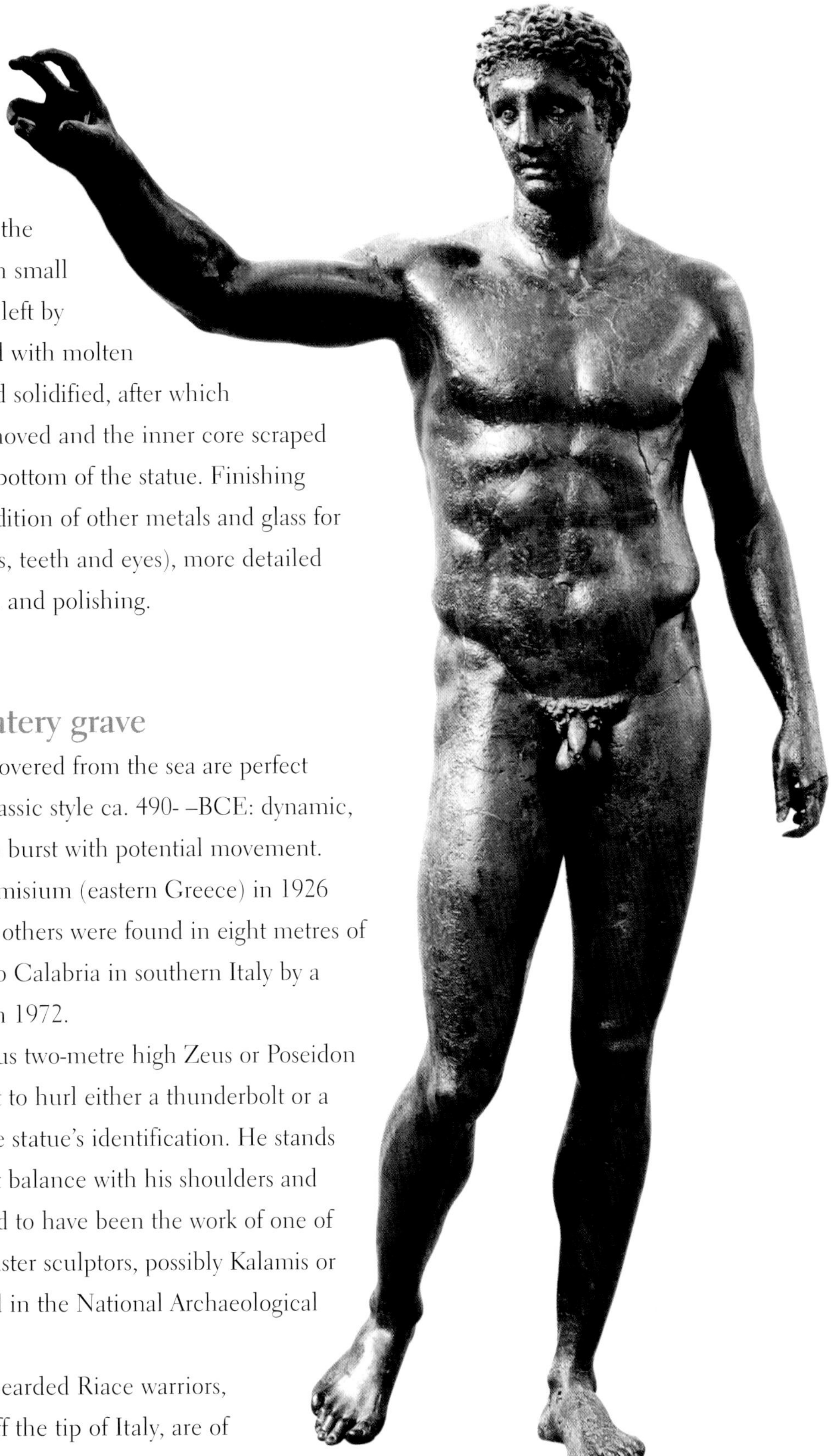

Preserved in a watery grave

Several masterpieces recovered from the sea are perfect
examples of the early Classic style ca. 490- –BCE: dynamic,
powerful and seeming to burst with potential movement.
Fishermen off Cape Atemisium (eastern Greece) in 1926
discovered one, and two others were found in eight metres of
water off Riace in Reggio Calabria in southern Italy by a
holidaying scuba diver in 1972.

The first is the famous two-metre high Zeus or Poseidon
whose right arm is about to hurl either a thunderbolt or a
trident depending on the statue's identification. He stands
with feet apart in perfect balance with his shoulders and
raised arms. It is believed to have been the work of one of
the mid-fifth century master sculptors, possibly Kalamis or
Polyklitus, and is housed in the National Archaeological
Museum in Athens.

The two nude and bearded Riace warriors,
preserved by the mud off the tip of Italy, are of

ABOVE: The full statue of Zeus/Poseidon.

outstanding artistic quality and have been associated with Pheidias, possibly the greatest sculptor of all time. However, some scholars have suggested that they may have been the product of a local Greek craftsman in southern Italy. They once held silver weapons. The anatomical details—powerful muscles, strong limbs, rich beards and thick hair, copper nipples and lips, silver teeth, and ivory and glass-paste eyes—make them two of the most admired of Greek statues. They have pride of place in the National Museum of Reggio Calabria.

Two more life-sized bronzes, one discovered by sponge divers in a shipwreck off the tiny island of Antikythera south of the Greek mainland in 1900, and another from the Bay of Marathon in 1925, are stunning examples of late Classical sculpture which incorporated new elements: the turning of the head towards the relaxed right leg which barely touches the ground with the toes. The Antikythera Youth has been dated to ca. 340 BCE and could be the work of the sculptor, Euphranor. The Boy from Marathon (ca. 325–300 BCE) may be the god Hermes. According to the label from the Athens Archaeological Museum, 'the dreamy expression and easy pose are characteristic of Praxiteles, the leading late classical sculptor'.

The Victorious Youth, now referred to as the Getty Bronze after the museum where it is housed (the J. Paul Getty Villa in Los Angeles), was dragged up in the net of a fishing trawler in the Adriatic Sea, north of Ancona, in 1964. A crewman, on first seeing the figure, believed it was a dead man, but the trawler's captain soon realised that it was a bronze statue. The fact that its ankles and feet are missing indicates that it was carelessly removed from its stone base for transportation to Italy. The pose of the figure with its right hand within centimetres of his head, crowned in a victor's olive wreath, required incredible technical skill and led Heinz Herzer, a Munich art dealer, on first seeing the statue to say that it sent shivers down his spine.

It is almost certain that the left hand held the palm branch of a Greek athletic winner. Flax fibres found in the core of the statue during conservation seem to point to Olympia as its original location since that was the only flax-growing area of Greece. Some scholars think that due to the more individual face and the less than humble gaze, this statue of a youth of about 15, does not belong to the Classical period.

The 'immediate conclusion suggests identification with a very young scion of one of the royal families that succeeded Alexander' (Jiri Frel, *The Getty Bronze*) possibly between the late fourth century to 200 BCE. Lysippos, Alexander the Great's personal sculptor, has been named as the possible creator of this statue. If this is the case, it is the only one of his 1500 works to have survived. His work is now only known through several Roman copies.

The ancient Roman's demands for Greek statuary and their ruthless plundering of sacred sites were little different to the trade today in ancient antiquities. Before finally coming to rest in the modern humidity-controlled Getty Museum, the Victorious Youth was subjected to the indignity of being transported from its watery grave on a fish cart and buried in a cabbage field; sold to the owners of a cement factory for a mere US $5600; stored in a church sacristy and under the stairs of a priest's house; spirited across borders; sold to an unnamed Brazilian; and owned by a European art consortium. It became the subject of numerous failed negotiations before finally being sold in 1977 to the Getty Museum for $US3.98 million.

35

RAIDING, FEASTING AND PROPITIATING THE GODS

Celtic metalwork from Western Europe

... the naked warriors in the front ranks made a terrifying spectacle.
They were all men of splendid physique ... and those in the leading
companies were richly adorned with gold necklaces and armlets.

—Polybius, *The Rise of the Roman Empire*, Bk. 2. 29

Celtic treasures have been found in elite burials from the Atlantic to Romania and in numerous ritual deposition sites such as British rivers, a Swiss lake, a Danish bog and a ditch sanctuary in the Czech Republic. Specially built structures (piers) or natural features (overhanging rocks) were used for launching the offerings. The great ritual deposits probably occurred at special times during the year, but may also have represented a tribe's need to propitiate the gods during a momentous event.

The stunning artefacts—shields, helmets, cups, cauldrons, and flagons made of iron and bronze, some heavily embossed in gold and inlaid with red enamel and coral, plus gold and

OPPOSITE: The Battersea Shield made of copper alloy sheeting and decorated with insets of red glass found in the river Thames at Battersea in London.

silver torcs or neck rings—reveal an originality and vitality that makes Celtic art one of the great artistic achievements of Europe. According to Paul Jacobstall, in his seminal 1944 work, *Early Celtic Art*, it 'is refined in thought and technique; elaborate and clever; full of paradoxes; restless; puzzlingly ambiguous; rational and irrational; dark and uncanny ...'

The Greeks referred to the Celts as *Keltoi*, the Romans as *Celtae*. Certain Celtic tribes were known to the Romans as Gauls. Throughout the first millennium BCE, there were Celtic-speaking groups spread across western and central Europe, but it was not until 450–200 BCE that a truly distinctive Celtic material culture and art style can be identified. It is this warrior culture, referred to as 'La Tene', that provided the Classical writers with their stereotypical views of the northern barbarians.

Like Polybius, quoted above, the ancient Greek and Roman sources on the Celts focused on their military prowess, appearance, wild feasting, hard drinking, boasting, competitiveness, and the strange religious beliefs that made them unafraid to die. Although biased, the sources provide valuable supplementary evidence to the wealth of the material remains.

Originally, La Tene art blended native motifs with Etruscan and eastern influences to create something distinctively Celtic, like the pair of flagons found in France. This was followed by an emphasis on plant motifs such as that found on the gold-covered helmet discovered in France, and gold open-work like that covering a wooden cup found in a barrow at Schwarzenbach in Germany. Other treasures combined the plant motifs with the heads of animals, fabulous beasts and humans, especially on the bosses of shields and in torcs and arm rings. Two other treasures, the Trichtingen Torc found in Germany and the Gunderstrup Cauldron located in Denmark, show influences from the lower Danube and reveal the mobility of valuable Celtic objects throughout Europe during the La Tene period.

These treasures must be understood within the Celtic social and religious context.

A culture of conquest and ritual

The central focus of Celtic society was the need to raid. Strabo, the Greek geographer of the first century BCE described them as a race 'madly fond of war, high-spirited and quick to battle . . .' (*Geography*). The warrior elites maintained their positions and status by exhibitions of military prowess, the ability to command large forces, and to collect booty to distribute publicly in the form of gifts. In time, raids on neighbours were replaced by extended military adventures further afield.

This imperative, plus overpopulation in the three original core La Tene territories of Marne, Moselle and Bohemia, led to migrations of the Celts in the fourth century BCE. They moved through the Alpine passes into northern Italy which became known as Cisalpine Gaul, thrusting towards the Etruscans and the city of Rome. In 390, Rome was sacked by the Celts, an event that remained in the Roman consciousness for centuries. By the third century they were on the move along the Danube corridor to the Balkans, attacking Macedonia and even the sacred site of Delphi in Greece. By 278 they had moved further east into Asia Minor to an area that became known as Galatia.

These ferocious warriors carried iron swords, often with a personalised form of decoration stamped into the blade, in elaborately decorated sheaths. The ritual haul recovered from Lake Neuchatel in what is modern-day Switzerland, between 1857–1917, indicated that spears came in a number of lethal designs: notched, serrated, flame-shaped, so that they penetrated easily, but they also tore the flesh and ripped open the wound when removed.

Wooden, leather and bronze shields covered the whole body, but usually only the highly decorative bronze boss (the protruding centre of the shield) has survived the passage of time. Several shields covered in bronze were recovered from deposition sites in the Thames and Witham Rivers and were probably manufactured for ceremonial rather than military activities. Horned helmets and others with bird and boar attachments have been found.

Diodorus Siculus writing in the first century BCE, claimed that the Celts were 'boasters and threateners and given to bombastic self-dramatisation' (*Hist*). Prior to battle, the bravest challenged one of the opposition to single combat which then involved listing the courageous acts of his ancestors and his own great deeds. What impressed the Romans was that some Celtic warriors fought naked except for a sword hanging from their waists and a gold torc (an ornamental necklace) around their necks. Both the nakedness and the wearing of the torc seem to have had some ritual significance. Images on the Gunderstrup Cauldron show Celtic deities wearing torcs, and since so many have been found in deposition sites, it seems that they may have been regarded as a form of divine protection.

The skilled men who were able to design and execute the timeless Celtic works of art, were clearly far more than just craftsmen. They carried with them a deep knowledge of mythology.

As important to the Celtic social system as the raid, was the feast. This was one of many ways, such as wearing the torc, and shaving the cheeks while leaving the moustache to grow long over the lips, that the rigid hierarchy in Celtic society was revealed. At a feast, the individual with the greatest status (either military skill, wealth or nobility) was given the central position in the circle, all others placed according to their status.

When the cooked beast was carved up, the greatest hero was entitled to the thigh from the hindquarters. If another claimed that portion, the two fought in single combat often leading to serious injuries and even death. Huge quantities of imported wine were served and the amount of wine imbibed and level of inebriation of those present also added to the status of the host. These feasts were places where young warriors could stake a claim to lead a future raid, and where gifts of gold, silver and wine might be distributed or pledged.

'The skilled men who were able to design and execute the timeless Celtic works of art, were clearly far more than just craftsmen. They carried with them a deep knowledge of mythology. The symbols that they used and the combinations in which they used them were a form of communication' (Barry Cunliffe, *The Ancient Celts*).

36

ASSASSINATIONS AND A ROYAL STYLE

Macedonian treasures from the tombs of Derveni and Vergina

Not only no Greek, nor related to the Greeks, but ... not even a barbarian from any place that can be named with honour, but a pestilent knave from Macedonia ... —Demosthenes, *Third Philippic*

The statement of the Athenian orator, Demosthenes, about King Philip II of Macedon, was sparked by the growing power and influence of Greece's northern neighbour under Philip's leadership in the fourth century BCE. The Greeks regarded all non-Greek-speaking people as 'barbarians' and considered them inferior. Demosthenes thought Philip a 'pestilent knave' because he was threatening the freedom of the quarrelsome Greek states that found it difficult to resolve their own problems and jealousies.

Despite the Greek view, the graves of Macedonian royalty and nobility, excavated at sites such as Derveni and Vergina, reveal the wealth and taste of the fourth century Macedonian elite, and the high level of the technical and artistic skills of the local craftsmen. The fourth century saw the emergence of 'personal opulence and its display, linked to the deliberate development of a royal style, selective blending of styles, and the admission of eastern influences into local traditions' (Lucilla Burn, *Hellenistic Art: From Alexander the Great to Augustus*).

In 1962, a cluster of six rich burials was discovered on a road from Thessaloniki, Greece's second largest city. In the most opulent of the plastered and painted tombs was the magnificent 'Derveni Krater', 91 centimetres high and dated to ca. 340 BCE. The burnt bones of a man and a woman, wrapped in a cloth, were found within the two-handled *krater* (wine bowl) which acted as a funerary urn. Even though the *krater* had a strainer to collect wine dregs, its interior shows no sign of it ever having been used for wine.

At first sight this bowl appears to be made of gold, but it is bronze, the illusion created by its high tin content. Some of the decoration (ivy leafs, a berry garland and vine wreath) is in silver, as is the inscription on the rim: 'Astion, son of Anaxagoras, native of Larisa'. Larisa was in Thessaly, an area south of Macedonia which Philip brought under his control. Whether Astion was the name of the craftsmen who made the *krater*, or the person for whom it was made, is unclear. Perhaps it belonged to one of the aristocratic hostages Philip took from Larisa in 344 BCE to ensure the city's loyalty. In the light of evidence from other Macedonian graves, it was probably produced locally and exemplifies the inventiveness and creativity of the Macedonian artist.

The spiral-scrolled handles incorporating bearded heads are unusual, and the four detailed figures sitting on the neck of the *krater* were made separately and added later. The main body of the urn features a Dionysiac scene which has been hammered from the back to create the detailed reliefs of Dionysus and Ariadne. Although Dionysus was a god of wine, he was also associated with the afterlife. In the same burial were two other stunning vessels: a silver and gilt jug and a fluted silver libation bowl.

Despite the magnificence of the Derveni Krater, it was the discoveries made in 1977–78 by Professor Manolis Andronikos at the site of ancient Aigai, near the modern village of Vergina, which confirmed the tradition of Macedonian opulence. Aigai was the capital of Macedonia from the seventh–fifth centuries BCE, and even after the court's removal to Pella, Aigai continued to be used for royal burials. Andronikos excavated four monumental tombs under the Great Mound, the largest of which he identified as belonging to Philip II, and another, as the final resting place of Alexander IV, the sixteen-year-old son of Alexander the Great by the Bactrian princess Roxanne. Both of these tombs were still intact.

> The graves of Macedonian royalty and nobility, excavated at sites such as Derveni and Vergina, reveal the wealth and taste of the fourth century Macedonian elite, and the high level of the technical and artistic skills of the local craftsmen.

The 'Philip' tomb

In the so-called 'Philip' tomb, Andronikos found a marble sarcophagus which contained what has come to be regarded as one of the greatest treasures of the ancient world: a golden burial casket (*larnax*) holding the cremated remains of a man wrapped in purple cloth. In the antechamber, a smaller gold chest contained the bones of the royal spouse wrapped in a gold and purple sheet. Philip's larnax contains 7820 grams of pure gold and on its lid is a sixteen-rayed star in the middle of which is a blue enamelled rosette. The sides of the casket are decorated with lotus buds and rosettes and the chest stands on legs in the form of lion's paws. The gold oak wreath crown with its 313 separate leaves and 68 acorns weighs 714 grams and is the heaviest and most impressive surviving from the Greek world.

OPPOSITE: A two-handled bronze and silver wine bowl, known as the Derveni Krater, decorated with Dionysian motifs.

The remains of all the deceased were accompanied by gold oak wreaths. During life, wreaths were worn at important religious ceremonies and banquets. At death, they were placed in the tomb as a symbol 'of the prize won by the deceased in the struggle of life' (Hellenic Ministry of Culture). Most took the form of oak, myrtle, olive and laurel leaves.

The tomb also contained the deceased's iron helmet, his cuirass (armour), his sword and a golden diadem (jewelled headband), symbols of military prowess and royal power. There was a ceremonial shield of gold and ivory, the only one of its kind to have survived from antiquity; the remains of a wooden couch decorated with gold, glass and ivory; and a large number of silver vessels all for serving or drinking wine.

Macedonian aristocracy, including Philip and Alexander, were noted for their excessive drinking. According to Plutarch, on the occasion of Philip's last marriage to a Macedonian girl named Cleopatra, Alexander became embroiled in a quarrel and hurled a drinking cup. At this Philip lurched to his feet and drew his sword, but was so overcome with drink that he tripped and fell. Alexander ridiculed his father. 'Here is the man who was making ready to cross from Europe to Asia, and who cannot even cross from one table to another without losing his balance.'

Manolis Andronikos was sure that the largest and most ornate of the royal tombs belonged to Philip II who was assassinated at the marriage of his daughter in the theatre of Aigai in 336. According to the ancient sources, the assassin was one of his bodyguards by the name of Pausanius who was angered at the King's failure to address a grievance he had against Philip's father-in-law, Attalus. Other sources indicate that the vindictive and ambitious Olympias, the mother of Alexander, used Pausanius for her own ends. She is supposed to have had Philip's last wife, Cleopatra, murdered. However, it is now generally accepted that the evidence points to a date later than the death of Philip II, and that the remains in the tomb are those of Philip Arrhidaeus and his wife Erydice.

Philip Arrhidaeus was the illegitimate son of Philip II. After the death of Alexander the Great in 323 BCE, a succession crisis occurred. His illegitimate half-brother, Arrhidaeus, who was supposedly mentally impaired, seemed the only candidate for the throne. It was decided that if Alexander the Great's child, being carried by Roxanne, turned out to be a male, he and Arrhidaeus would rule together with a regent.

In 317, Olympias and her allies invaded Macedon and brought the child Alexander (IV) with them. Philip Arrhidaeus and Erydice fled, but were later caught and confined. They were considered too much of a threat to be left alive and Olympias had Arrhidaeus murdered and

196

forced Erydice to commit suicide. It is believed that the regent Kassander buried them and equipped their tomb. Seven years later, Kassander killed the young Alexander IV and brought the ruling dynasty to an end.

No matter which Philip was interred in the tomb, its contents are among the ancient world's greatest treasures. While Macedon's kings were fighting off their neighbours, succumbing to assassinations, taking control of Greece and the Persian empire, its craftsmen, working in gold, silver and bronze, were giving free rein to their imaginations, creating beautifully made objects that combined delicacy and elegance.

ABOVE: A small heavy golden burial casket believed to have held the remains of either Philip II or Philip Arrhidaeus of Macedon.

MILITARY PROTECTION FOR ETERNITY

The terracotta army of Qin Shi Huang

The clever combatant looks to the effect of combined energy, and does not require too much from individuals. When he uses combined energy, his fighting men become like unto rolling logs or stones.

—Sun Tzu, *The Art of War*

A massive army served the first emperor of China, Qin Shi Huang (221-210 BCE), both in life and in death. Not only did Qin defeat the other states of China, gain an empire and personally control all aspects of it, 'he recreated the entire empire in microcosm for his afterlife' (Xiaoneng Yang, *Chinese Archaeology in the Twentieth Century: New Perspectives on China's Past*).

According to the great historian, Sima Qian (145–90 BCE), the emperor built a tomb that incorporated a scale replica of the universe. On the ceiling was a map of the heavens with pearls representing the stars and planets, on the floor was a panorama of China with flowing mercury depicting the rivers and seas. He also ordered an army of 7000 life-sized terracotta warriors, with horses and chariots, to guard his burial and thus protect him in the next world.

OPPOSITE: Part of the buried terracotta army guarding the tomb of Emperor Qin. No two figures are identical.

The emperor's mausoleum, constructed near Mount Lisham in Shaanxi province, 35 kilometres east of the city of Xi'an, was a walled compound around a massive earthen mound with structures such as administrative buildings, horse stables and cemeteries. It covered an area of 7.5 square kilometres. The burial mound has not yet been excavated, although the latest scientific analysis indicates the presence of mercury in the soil which may verify the traditional account of Qin Shi Huang's tomb.

In 1974, farmers drilling a well about 600 metres east of the mausoleum precinct discovered the site of the terracotta army. Due to the size of the find, it has taken archaeologists over 30 years to excavate the three pits and restore the figures. The largest pit, about 16, 000 square metres, held 6000 infantrymen, chariots and horses, and is believed to have represented the main Qin army. The second pit with 1400 figures of cavalry and infantry, 500 horses and 90 chariots of wood was probably a military guard, while the smallest pit, with only 68 figures and a war chariot, is thought to represent the Emperor's command unit. In 1980, two magnificent half-scale bronze chariots with gold and silver details, were found only 20 metres from the mausoleum. Perhaps these were intended for the emperor's tours of inspection in the afterlife.

The figures that made up Qin Shi Huang's magnificent eternal army were arranged in the massive pits according to rank and duty: superior officers, lesser officers, armoured and unarmoured soldiers, charioteers, cavalrymen and archers, each one given a real weapon (bronze spears, swords and wooden crossbows). The figures are identified by outfit and posture.

For example, the charioteers stand with their arms stretched out in front as if holding reins, while cavalrymen hold the reins of their horses in their right hand and their crossbows in their left. Archers are depicted either standing or kneeling. Despite the vast numbers, each figure is unique. The variety in the detail of facial features, hairstyles, headgear and uniforms is stunning and the use of real weapons adds realism to the whole military gathering.

> Due to the size of the find, it has taken archaeologists over 30 years to excavate the three pits and restore the figures.

The figures were made in several parts (solid terracotta lower torso, hollow upper torso) and assembled after firing. A clay slip was added to allow the moulding of details and then a lacquer applied for durability. The scant remains of pigments on the figures indicate that they were

ABOVE: Careful preservation of the terracotta army.

originally brightly coloured. Officers appear to have worn a double robe of purple and vermillion over green trousers with brown headgear and armour.

Who was the man behind this massive project?

From 480–222 BCE, the state of Qin was just one of a number of warring feudal states in China. During this period there was a change in the mode of warfare from chariot battles to massed infantry armies equipped with crossbows. The need to control these enormous armies gave rise to a number of manuals on the art of warfare, and enabled the generals to gain administrative skills. It was also a time of great intellectual development especially with regard to political theory, which in the western state of Qin, focused on what has been described as the Legalist view.

Whereas the Confucians stressed that strong government depended on the moral qualities of the ruler and his officials, the Legalists claimed that effective government depended on laws, finding practical ways to cope with disorder, and techniques for the accumulation of power of the ruler, resulting in an authoritarian form of government. Laws had to be made very clear and rewards and punishments had to be carried out immediately.

ABOVE: Life-sized horses and members of Emperor Qin's eternal army.

In 247 BCE, at the age of 12, a young boy named Zheng came to the throne of Qin and at 22 he staged a coup, got rid of his regents (his mother and a chief minister), assumed control, appointed another chief minister, Li Si, and began a series of military conquests. By 221, he had incorporated the states of Han, Zhao, Wei, Chu, Yan and Qi into the first Chinese empire. He adopted a new name—Qin Shi Huang—to signify that the king of Qin was now 'august' and 'lord' of 'All Under Heaven' (Emperor), and established the centralised bureaucratic monarchy that characterised Chinese history until the twentieth century.

An authoritarian obssessed with immortality

Qin Shi Huang banished feudalism throughout the empire and brought many of the former state rulers and members of influential families to his capital Xianyang to prevent acts of treason. He divided the empire into thirty-six new administrative areas and appointed two governors, one civilian and one military, responsible only to him. He instituted strict punishments for those whose performance was less than adequate. Uniformity was introduced throughout the empire by standardising all writing scripts, currency, weights and measures.

He conscripted hundreds of thousands of workers to demolish the walls dividing former states, to build canals, roads and great palaces and begin construction on his massive mausoleum. On the northern border of the empire he ordered a force of 300,000 soldiers and conscripts to build a great wall to keep out the nomadic horsemen who dominated the steppes beyond. Some of the previous states had already built ramparts along much of this frontier. These were incorporated into a new defensive wall of rammed earth with towers and barracks that extended for more than 6000 kilometres. It was called 'The Wall of Ten Thousand Li'.

The emperor would tolerate no opposition, and the tradition describes him as cruel, arbitrary and suspicious. He is believed to have put to death—by burying alive—over 400 recalcitrant scholars who spoke out against some of his policies, and to have proscribed all books except technical manuals.

His authoritarianism led to three attempts on his life and he became obsessed with finding the secrets of immortality, even sending a group of young men and women out to sea to search for the mythical island of immortality, Peng Lai. It is ironic that he died at the age of 50 by supposedly swallowing mercury pills which were meant to make him immortal.

According to tradition, he was on one of his inspection tours of the realm, about two months by road from his capital, when he died in 210 BCE. The Chief Minister, Li Si, fearing an uprising by those who had suffered under his brutal policies and monumental building projects, kept the Emperor's death a secret until their return to Xianyang. On the journey home, Li Si continued to enter the wagon carrying the emperor's body as if discussing state affairs. His entourage had no suspicions because they were used to Qin Shi Huang's secretive nature, but Li Si was forced to order two wagons full of fish to travel before and after the state wagon to hide the smell of the emperor's decomposing body.

With the announcement of his death, the Qin imperial structure began to fall apart. His eighteenth son killed the legitimate heir as well as Li Si, and assumed control. Disgruntled peasants rebelled and the new Chief Minister killed the Emperor, then he in turn was murdered by the successor he put on the throne. Within seven years of the death of Qin Shi Huang, his glorious empire had passed to the Han Dynasty (202 BCE–220 CE).

According to the Chinese, Heaven supposedly only conferred its blessings and legitimacy to rule on the virtuous. Had Qin Shi Huang lost the 'Mandate of Heaven'?

38

ECHOES OF A DISTANT DRUM

Dong Son kettledrums from Vietnam and South-East Asia

The drum embodied a frog spirit—that is a spirit of water and rain—and its voice was the booming rumble of a bullfrog.

—Edward Schafer, *The Vermilion Bird*

For millennia, the various ethnic groups of South-East Asia (from Southern China to Indonesia) used elaborately decorated bronze drums for ritual purposes. These ancient drums were probably produced somewhere between 600 BCE and the third century CE, although the earliest surviving ones known at the present are about 2000 years old.

In the late seventeeth century, a Dutch naturalist named G. E. Rumphius discovered a drum in Indonesia. He sent it as a gift to the Duke of Tuscany, and for the next two centuries, European travellers to Indochina discovered others, most kept in villages and temples. However, it was from an ancient burial and habitation site, Dong Son, on the edge of the Hong or Red River delta south of Hanoi, in northern Vietnam, that drums were first found in an archaeological context with other bronze artefacts such as tools, weapons, ornaments and statuettes.

This site, excavated in the 1920s, is the best-documented find of this culture and has given its name to the eastern branch of the South-Eastern Asian Bronze Age. However, as recently as 2006, a Vietnamese man named Nguyen Van Luan, looking for scrap metal to sell, found the pieces of an ancient drum buried in a central Vietnamese province. Since archaeology is still in its early days in this region, it is possible that other large sites may be found.

The Dong Son culture is believed to have existed towards the end of the Bronze Age in the first millennium BCE, following a series of other Hong River cultures. Vietnamese historians see the Dong Son as the formative culture of Vietnam and identify it with Vietnam's first ruling dynasty, the Van Lang/Au Lac. It is thought that it was contemporary with the Ban Chiang and Non Nok Tha cultures of Thailand, and it may have been from these sites, rather than from China as suggested by some (Chinese) scholars, that the Dong Son received their knowledge of bronze manufacturing.

BELOW: A moulded bronze Vietnamese Dong Son drum with concentric decoration in low relief and central star.

> Although the complex bronze technology (the lost wax method) employed by the Dong Son may have originated elsewhere, the decorations on the drums feature aspects of local life and traditions.

The Dong Son culture may have reached its peak in the last centuries BCE, although by then immigrants from southern China, under pressure from the expanding Han Dynasty, were settling in the area. In 208 BCE, the Han general, Trieu, conquered the Dong Son area and in 111 BCE it was absorbed into China's Han Dynasty. According to the *Book of Later Han*, written in the fifth century CE and attributed to Fan Ye, the Vietnamese rebelled between 40–43 CE and the Chinese general Ma Yuan, in the process of subduing the local chieftains, confiscated their bronze drums and had them melted down. Perhaps he had reason to believe they were insignias of leadership.

The fertile delta of the Hong River supported a dense population of rice growers who kept buffaloes and pigs and lived in houses (close to the river or sea) that were built on bamboo stilts with overhanging saddle-shaped roofs. The Dong Son people were skilled sailors, going to sea in a type of long dugout canoe and developing trading networks and transferring technology with their southern and eastern neighbours. Although the complex bronze technology (the lost wax method) employed by the Dong Son may have originated elsewhere, the decorations on the drums feature aspects of local life and traditions.

Bronze kettledrums are known in some places as 'rain drums'. They vary in size from the miniature to examples with a tympanum more than a metre in diameter. The largest drum still in use can be found in a Balinese temple. Known as the 'Moon of Pejeng' and around 2000 years old, it is the height of a man and 1.6 metres in diameter. Amongst the Muong people, a highland group in Vietnam's western mountains, these drums are still used in some form of shamanistic rituals, perhaps for rainmaking or to call the ancestors. Miniature forms, known as Moho drums, are used on the eastern Indonesian island of Alor for buying a bride.

Debated symbolism

Dong Son drums reflect great artistic and technological skill, but their precise uses, and the meaning of their symbolic decoration, are a matter of conjecture. They consist of three major elements: a tympanum or membrane, a convex area, and an inverted truncated cone, and are decorated with incised geometrical patterns and scenes, low reliefs and three-dimensional carvings.

The most outstanding feature is the central starburst with eight, twelve or sixteen points, enclosed in a circle. Some scholars believe this motif represents the sun and its rays. The spaces between the points or rays are usually filled with stylised human faces. Outside the centre is a series of concentric circles of decoration with geometric designs alternating with figures in feathered ceremonial robes engaged in cultic activities, as well as birds such as the heron, and animals, particularly the deer. There is a commonly held belief that the spirits of the dead were expected to appear in the form of birds.

On the outer plain zone of the tympanum there are usually four carvings of frogs or toads believed to be associated with rain and water. The Chinese see them as frogs while the Vietnamese interpret them as toads because there is an old saying that the rains will fall when the toad raises its head and croaks (Pham Huy Thong, *Dong Son Drums in Vietnam*). The convex zone usually features boats, decorated with the head and tail of a bird, carrying a helmsman, paddlers and feathered warriors. There is a belief in South-East Asia that the souls of the dead were carried to the underworld by boat, and that the boats are shown moving counter-clockwise because the next world was believed to lie downstream or across the sea. Some scholars think the boats are associated with boat racing, perhaps as part of a celebration of the role of water in agriculture. Many drums were buried in rice fields.

Perhaps the drums were used at funerals to communicate with the souls of the ancestors, and at rainmaking ceremonies. As well as revealing some of the rituals of these Bronze Age people, the drums provide pictorial evidence of Dong Son society in their depiction of houses, canoes, weapons, dancing, musical instruments and even rice grinding.

These ancient bronze drums are considered the most important archaeological artefacts found in South-East Asia. Unfortunately, during the twentieth century, nationalistic attempts by China and Vietnam to each claim the invention of the bronze drum, to take credit for the earliest bronze-making, and to interpret the drums' motifs in the light of their own cultures, has led to a considerable amount of biased literature. At the time and in the culture that the bronze drum was created, the boundaries we know today did not exist.

39

A SEARCH FOR IMMORTALITY

Jade suits, silk and lacquerware from Ma-wang-dui and Man-ch'eng

The soul was conceived to have two aspects. The lighter, more heavenly part would ascend to the clouds and might possibly enter the realm of the immortals. The more earthly part of the soul stayed in or near the grave ...

—Patricia Buckley Ebrey, *China*

The search for immortality was of great concern to the nobles of the Han Dynasty of China (ca. 206 BCE–220 CE) and many hoped to find it in the paradise of the Great Mother of the West, the Kunlun Mountains, whose constant companions were strange mythical beasts and birds, such as a three-legged crow, a dancing toad and a nine-tailed fox.

A belief from this time held that the individual had two 'souls', the *Hun* and the *Po*. When these two elements converged, life was created and when they diverged, the result was death. The *Hun* was light and airy and was believed to leave the body through the head, hopefully ascending to the heavenly realms at death. The *Po* had a semi-fluid, corporeal quality and was supposed to stay with the body, discouraged from leaving by the *mingqi*, the 'spirit objects' in the grave. For these reasons many of the burials from this period had inventories of the contents addressed to the Lord Master of the Dead.

Between 1968–1974, two of the most archaeologically significant tomb groups from the Han

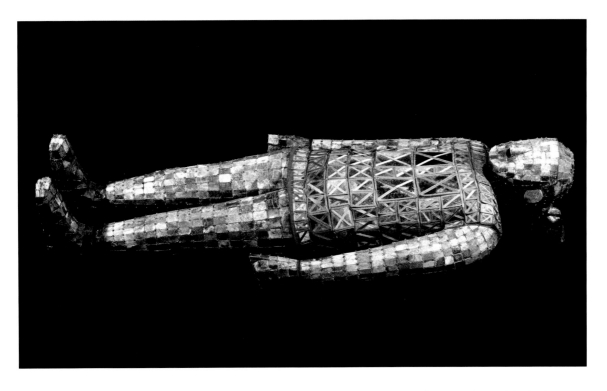

ABOVE: The jade burial suit of Princess Don Wan. Jade was believed to prevent decomposition of the body.

period were excavated in Hebei and Hunan Provinces. They contained stunning funerary objects made from the most prized of Chinese materials: jade, silk and lacquer. All three have been synonymous with China since Neolithic times. Jade was believed to have magical properties which would prevent the decay of the body; silk was a symbol of a person's virtue, wealth and status in life, and lacquer, made from the sap of the lac tree, was valued for its protective qualities (impervious to water, and resistant to heat and acids) and for the brilliance of its lustre.

Magnificent jade burial 'suits' (*pinyin*), like the two complete ones found in the tombs of Prince Liu Sheng and his consort Dou Wan in Man-ch'eng (late second century BCE), were designed to keep the *Po* happy and to preserve the body. They were composed of thousands of small jade plaques, sewn together with wire thread of gold, silver or copper, the type used depending on rank.

Until the discovery of the Man-ch'eng tombs, Chinese archaeologists thought that jade burial suits were simply objects of myth, even though they were mentioned in documents such as the *The Book of Later Han* written in the fifth century CE. The bodies of Prince Liu Sheng and Princess Dou Wan were totally encased in jade except for the *pi* disc opening left in the head

The two Man-ch'eng jade burial suits are the earliest and most complete ever found. The 1.88 metre-long suit belonging to the prince was made of 2498 jade pieces sewn together with one kilogram of gold wire.

section to allow for the easy exit of the *Hun*. Jade plugs filled all the openings of the body so that the *Hun* would not inadvertently leave via one of these, and so become confused. The plugs also removed the temptation for the *Po* to escape.

The two Man-ch'eng jade burial suits are the earliest and most complete ever found. The 1.88 metre-long suit belonging to the prince was made of 2498 jade pieces sewn together with one kilogram of gold wire. It has been estimated that it would have taken ten years to make. Liu Sheng and Dou Wan lay with their heads resting on gilt bronze headrests inlaid with jade, and they each held jade crescents in their hands. However, despite these massive precautions, their bodies did not survive; even their bones had turned to dust.

In contrast, the body of Xin-Zhui, wife of Li Cang, the Marquis of Dai, found in her tomb at Ma-wang-dui, was almost perfectly preserved. She is thought to have died ca. 150 BCE, outliving her husband and son who were buried in the two adjacent graves. She did not wear a jade suit and neither had she been mummified in the traditional sense, and yet when removed from her innermost coffin, after nearly 2100 years underground, her body was still supple, and her organs still soft.

The remarkable preservation of her body is believed to have been the result of a number of factors: her tomb was surrounded with a layer of charcoal 1.5 metres thick and a layer of white clay a metre thick which kept out moisture and oxygen, and she rested within four lacquered coffins, sealed so tightly that they lacked oxygen as fuel for bacteria.

According to Wang Yeh-chiu of the Chinese Institute of the Academy of Science, the presence of large sachets of aromatic herbs found in the storage area of the tomb, and a silk bag filled with herbs, held in one of Xin-Zhui hands, contributed to the preservation. These factors also helped preserve the amazing collection of perishable items, notably those of silk.

OPPOSITE: Part of the T-shaped silk funerary banner found in the tomb of Lady Dai at Ma-wang-dui.

Mastery of materials

There were forty-nine changes of clothing in Lady Dai's tomb, many of them silk, decorated with beautiful raised-thread designs and with their colours still vibrant. There were silk accessories (shoes, socks and gloves) and transparent silk gauze robes, 'thin as dragonfly wings, light as fog'. The one wrapped around her body was 160 centimetres long, yet weighed only 48 grams, and another, with long sleeves, weighed 49 grams. In her son's tomb were silk books of classical texts (medicinal, astronomical, and philosophical), and three silk maps. However, it was the wonderful painted silk funerary banners (*ming-ching*), of a type never before seen, that are the true masterpieces. These banners were supposedly used during funeral ceremonies and then laid over the coffin.

The two-metre-long T-shaped banner from Lady Dai's tomb, called a *feiyi* or 'flying garment', has a red background with three distinct sections painted in heavy colours. The painting techniques and colours are of the highest quality. The iconography on the banner seems to illustrate a passage from an ancient text, where the souls are described as journeying to the 'four quarters of the universe as well as above and below' (D. Hawkes, *Ch-u Tzu: The Songs of the South*).

According to K. Linduff, in *The Tomb of Lady Dai*, the scenes represent 'the separation of the souls in the underworld' (lower section with two giant sea serpents) 'through the rites provided in the earthly realm' (middle section with Lady Dai's family offering sacrifices), 'to the return to the first ancestor of the race and to immortality' (upper section with Chinese deities and Daoist symbols). In the top left and right-hand corners are the crow, symbol of the sun, and the toad, symbol of the moon, thus pairing the cosmic forces of *yang* and *yin*.

The silk masterpieces from the tombs at Ma-wang-dui reveal the technological skill reached in silk manufacture by the time of the Han Dynasty. This precious commodity was in great demand from as far away as the Roman Empire to the west, and was used for 'buying' peace on China's northern borders. It is believed that in 110 BCE, the government had five million rolls of silk in storage, and caravans, like moving cities, carried skeins of silk thread and woven silk cloth along the Silk Road into Central Asia and beyond.

The silk masterpieces from the tombs at Ma-wang-dui reveal the technological skill reached in silk manufacture by the time of the Han Dynasty.

The extraordinary craftsmanship necessary to create lacquer ware made it treasured by nobility as a symbol of fortune and status. Red and black-coloured lacquer was used to coat objects of wood, bamboo, leather and hemp and then decorated (phoenixes, dragons, flowers, fruit whorls) and sometimes inlaid with gold and silver. The five hundred pieces of lacquer found in Lady Dai's tomb still retained a pearl-like sheen and were as freshly coloured as when they were first made. These items included bowls, trays, wine cups with two handles, folding screens, cosmetic boxes, as well as Lady Dai's four nesting coffins, the second of which was the most beautiful, with its black background painted with scenes of heaven: swirling clouds with strange sprits and peculiar animals floating around.

The Han Dynasty was a formative time in Chinese history and its sovereignty over regions as far afield as Korea, Central Asia and Vietnam, led to the spread of its material culture into these areas at the hands of soldiers and traders.

THE FEMALE NUDE

Venus de Milo, Colonna Knidia and other ancient Aphrodites

Kronos cast these (the severed genitals of Uranus) from the land into the surging sea ... and around them arose a white foam from the immortal flesh, and in it grew a maiden. —Hesiod, *Theogony*

Throughout the Greek and Roman world there were numerous images of Aphrodite (Roman Venus), the goddess of love, beauty and fertility, but none more renowned or influential than Praxiteles' masterpiece, the nude, life-sized Aphrodite of Knidos. This statue, now lost, set the canon for some of the loveliest of the surviving nude and semi-nude Aphrodites, such as the Venus de Milo in the Louvre and the Colonna Knidia in the Vatican's Pio-Clementine Museum.

Other renowned and beautiful Aphrodites include the Aphrodite of Arles, the Crouching Venus (Louvre) and the Venus de Medeci (Uffizi in Florence). It is only through these magnificent marble statues that we can gain some insight into the compelling appearance and workmanship of Praxiteles' famous nude, although none of them, according to ancient texts, equal the polished beauty of the original.

According to myth, Aphrodite arose from the sea, whether from the semen of Uranus, God of Heaven, or as the offspring of Zeus and the sea-nymph, Dione. It was said that she was carried by the waves to Cyprus where she was met by the gods Eros (Love) and Himeros (Desire) who

escorted her to the assembly of the gods. Her name may have originated from *aphros* the word for foam.

This goddess of seduction and sexual love wielded irresistible power over all living creatures and the gods. Sappho, the renowned Lesbian poet, wrote the *Hymn to Aphrodite* in which she addressed her as 'enchantress', imploring the goddess not to leave her in distress. 'Come thee now, dear goddess, and release me from my anguish. All my heart's desiring grant thou now. Now too again as aforetime, be thou my ally' (William Hyde Appleton, *Greek Poets in English Verse*).

Aphrodite was often worshipped in connection with marriage and as protectress of seafarers. Also, she was associated with the sacred prostitutes of wealthy Corinth, where, according to the Greek lyricist, Pindar (fifth century BCE), her sanctuary was renowned for its 'welcoming young ladies, servants of Persuasion' who were dedicated to Aphrodite's work. During Roman times, Strabo the geographer reported that her temple had 1000 prostitutes, and in Athenaeus' *Deipnosophiss* heavenly Aphrodite is described as bestowing on the sacred young prostitutes, 'the right to cull the soft beauty' of their desired embraces.

The first naked female in classical sculpture

Between 360–350 BCE, at the height of his career, the master Athenian sculptor Praxiteles was commissioned to execute a marble statue of Aphrodite by the people of Kos. After centuries of decorously draped female figures, he broke with tradition and created the first completely naked female statue in classical sculpture. It is not known whether he intended her nudity as an explicit embodiment of her sexual allure, or to signify her divine birth from the sea.

Rejected by the shocked people of Kos, the statue was bought by the citizens of Knidos in Asia Minor (south-west Turkey) and installed in their beautiful sanctuary to the goddess. Initially it created controversy as Praxiteles supposedly used his mistress, Phryne, as his model, but it

OPPOSITE: The famous marble statue of Aphrodite found on the Aegean island of Melos and now known as The Venus de Milo.

became the most admired figure of its day and for the next eight centuries. Pliny, the first century CE Roman natural historian, declared that it was superior to anything that Praxiteles and any other sculptor had ever done. Such was its lifelike essence and sensuous texture, that tradition has it that a young man hid in the temple to spend the night with it.

In his work *Imagines* 6, Lucian contemplates the ideal woman with the head of the Knidian Aphrodite whose gaze he described as being 'so liquid, and at the same time so clear and winsome'. In another text, *Amores*, the author describes a visit to Knidos to see the statue. 'We entered the temple. In the midst thereof sits the goddess—she's a most beautiful statue of Parian marble—arrogantly smiling a little as a grin parts her lips. Draped by no garment, all her beauty is uncovered and revealed, except is so far as she unobtrusively uses one hand to hide her private parts. So great was the power of the craftsman's art that the hard unyielding marble did justice to every limb …' (Pseudo-Lucian, *Amores*).

Praxiteles' Aphrodite of Knidos was a significant innovation in classical sculpture and all those who saw it were overwhelmed by its great visual power.

The original Knidian Aphrodite no longer exists; it was carried off to Constantinople where it perished in a fire in 476 CE. Fortunately, it was one of the most frequently copied statues by Hellenistic and Roman artists, many of whom followed Praxiteles' example of placing one hand over the pubic area, the first time such a gesture had appeared in Greek art. 'Venus herself, as she lays aside her robes, half stooping, covers with her left hand her modesty' (Ovid, *Art of Love*).

Most scholars see this as both hiding and revealing the sexual essence of the goddess, because the viewers' gaze is drawn to the pubic area. However, Christine Mitchell Havelock in her book *The Aphrodite of Knidos and her Successors: A Historical Review of the Female Nude in Greek Art*, maintains that the gesture is indicative of her fertility. Some of these statues are totally nude, some appearing to be in the process of robing or disrobing, with their garments lying tumbled over the water jar that stands nearby which may have been meant for bathing, or symbolic of the goddesses' eternal youth through ritual cleansing and renewal.

Like the original, the copies were meant to be seen from all angles. The author of *Amores* describes how the sanctuary of Aphrodite on Knidos 'had a door on both sides for the benefit of those who also wish to have a good view of the goddess from behind, so that no part of her be left unadmired'. Even the crouching Aphrodites, such as the Aphrodite of Rhodes, which were probably votive offerings rather than cult statues and capture the goddess in a twisting pose, were meant to be seen from all angles.

The most famous of the surviving Aphrodites is the Venus de Milo, found in 1820 by a peasant on the Aegean island of Melos. The 205 centimetre figure, sculpted ca. 130 BCE by Alexandros of Antioch, is often regarded as the personification of beauty with its ideal proportions, twist of the left leg and seductive Praxitelean 'S' curve of the torso. Although today it is minus its arms, the head is remarkably well-preserved. However, the Colonna Knidia in the Vatican is probably the closest to the original, while the Kauffman Head in the Louvre is believed to be a very faithful Roman reproduction.

Praxiteles' Aphrodite of Knidos was a significant innovation in classical sculpture and all those who saw it were overwhelmed by its great visual power. Hellenistic and Roman copies are all that the modern world now has to appreciate its magnificence.

RIGHT: A copy of the original nude Aphrodite by Praxiteles known as the Aphrodite of Knidos.

MILLIONS OF LITTLE PIECES

The Alexander Mosaic from the House of the Faun in Pompeii

... although he was so heavily outnumbered, [Alexander] not only gave the enemy no opportunity to encircle him ... but fighting in the foremost ranks put the barbarians to flight. —Plutarch, *Alexander*, 20

The Battle of Issus (333 BCE), which assured Alexander the Great's conquest of the Persian Empire, is often believed to be the subject of the most celebrated mosaic to have survived from antiquity. It is 'one of the great masterpieces of ancient art, a work whose beauty conjures up something of the astonishing achievement of artists otherwise known to us as mere names . . .' (Ada Cohen, *The Alexander Mosaic: Stories of Victory and Defeat*).

The mosaic was discovered in 1831 in the exedra (an open room overlooking the peristyle garden) in the House of the Faun, the most luxurious dwelling in Pompeii, having survived the destructive force of Vesuvius which buried the town in AD 79. This monumental mosaic, measuring 5.82 by 3.13 metres and composed of over a million and a half tesserae (pieces) no more than four millimetres in size, is displayed today in the National Archaeological Museum of Naples with other stunning mosaics from the same villa.

From 334 BCE, a sequence of events occurred which had a profound effect on Asia and the Mediterranean, including the Roman world. The Macedonian king, Alexander, crossed from

Europe into Asia where he confronted and defeated the Persian king, Darius III in the Battles of Granicus and Issus. He next laid siege to Tyre and Gaza and entered Egypt in 332 where he was installed as pharaoh and founded one of the greatest cities in the ancient world: Alexandria.

He returned to Syria and advanced on Mesopotamia to continue his pursuit of Darius whom he defeated at Gaugamela, in modern day northern Iraq, in 331. Darius fled and was killed by one of his own satraps (a provincial leader) and Alexander was proclaimed 'King of Kings'. Between 330-326 he conquered the north-west provinces of the Persian Empire and reached India before returning to Babylon where he died in 323.

After his death, his generals quarrelled over the division of his empire which eventually split into three great Hellenistic kingdoms ruled by the successors of his generals, Seleucis (Asia), Ptolemy (Egypt) and Antigonus (Macedonia). These kingdoms eventually fell to the legions of Rome between 149–30 BCE, but the Hellenistic cultures of Greece and the East captivated the Romans of this period, influencing both architecture and art in Rome and the provincial city of Pompeii.

The size and sumptuousness of the House of the Faun and the number of its exceptional mosaics, particularly the unique Alexander Mosaic, evoked the magnificence of oriental Hellenistic palaces.

BELOW: The heads of Alexander the Great and the Persian king, Darius from the Alexander Mosaic found in the House of the Faun in Pompeii.

The mosaic was probably produced towards the end of the second century BCE, copied from a fourth century Greek painting. Pliny, the Roman natural historian who recorded the Roman practice of copying from Greek masterpieces says, 'Philoxenus of Eretria painted a picture for king Kassander which must be considered inferior to none; it contained the Battle of Alexander against Darius' (Pliny the Elder, *Natural History*).

An actual battle or a symbolic moment?

One of the questions scholars have pondered over the years is whether the mosaic, and the painting from which it was copied, depicted a specific battle. Was it, perhaps, in the long tradition of battle imagery seen in Sumer, Egypt and Assyria, as well as in Greek heroic combat where 'close-ups of the chosen heroes, were set in interminable locations in confrontation with the enemy?' (*The Alexander Mosaic: Stories of Victory and Defeat*).

The inclusion of specific historical details copied into the mosaic was a departure from the totally heroic tradition of painting, and was the legacy of a new interest in Alexander's conquests. But the question remains: Was it a representation of the Battle of Issus or perhaps the Battle of Granicus (when Alexander is reported to have lost his helmet)? Some scholars believe that it did not depict a specific historical moment, although it was historical in that it gave an account of a Macedonian victory over the Persians and an accurate impression of dress, arms and weapons. Perhaps the helmetless Alexander was a device to glorify the young conqueror.

Why the aristocratic Satirii family, owners of the House of the Faun, spent so much money having an original Greek painting copied in mosaic on the floor of one of their rooms is unknown, but it is likely to have been associated with the Roman desire to possess Greek art and the status and prestige that accompanied it.

ABOVE: The monumental 18 square-metre Alexander Mosaic thought to represent the Battle of Issus fought between Alexander's Macedonian and Greek troops and those of the Persian king Darius.

It was in Hellenistic Greece and Macedonia that mosaic floors first became fashionable. They were composed initially of pebbles in contrasting colours, followed by the use of highly brilliant pieces of glass paste, shell, enamels, marble and terracotta (tesserae). Tesserae were sometimes cut into small squares, or shaped to suit the design as in the Alexander Mosaic. The mosaic's incredible detail and subtle gradations of the basic colours of white, red, yellow and black were made possible by the shape and minute size of the tesserae. Most floor mosaics in Pompeii featured a detailed central picture (emblema) surrounded with geometric designs. The Alexander Mosaic is unique 'in that it copied a very elaborate, historical, and extensive composition and occupied so much of the exedra floor' (*The Alexander Mosaic: Stories of Victory and Defeat*). There was no other like it in Pompeii.

Also rare were the number and quality of other mosaics in the House of the Faun. For over two centuries, the villa must have glowed with its luxurious mosaic panels which reflected not only the colourful world of Greece (the god Dionysus as a child riding a tiger, and Greek theatrical masks with long curling wigs) but also the exotic world of Egypt. Themes from the Nile delta (Nile fowl with lotus flowers in their beaks, snakes, crocodiles and a hippopotamus) decorated the threshold of the room that featured the Alexander Mosaic. Although mosaics originated as a practical form of

decoration on floors, they were later used as wall friezes, to decorate fountains, pools, columns and even the vaulted roofs of public baths.

It is difficult to 'read' the Alexander Mosaic, and there have been any number of interpretations over the years. However, the general effect on the viewer is 'one of turmoil, confusion and panic on the part of the Persians, contrasted with the forceful forward charge on the part of the Greeks, the whole being very intense, compact and charged with emotion' (*The Alexander Mosaic*).

Despite some damage to the mosaic, the Macedonian and Persian kings can be idcnitified. Alexander, presumably on his famous horse Bucephalus, is risking his own safety by leading the cavalry into battle himself. He is depicted without a helmet and wearing a breastplate featuring the

> This monumental mosaic, measuring 5.82 by 3.13 metres and composed of over a million and a half tesserae (pieces) no more than four millimetres in size, is displayed today in the National Archaeological Museum of Naples.

Gorgon's (a female monster) head. Surrounded by his helmeted Macedonians, he pierces an enemy with his lance. It has been suggested that this dying Persian is Oxyathres, Darius' brother, who was supposed to have sacrificed himself for the king.

Darius in his chariot, drawn by four black horses, seems to be in a state of anguish as he desperately extends one of his arms, appearing to command his frightened charioteer to turn to meet Alexander. Fallen horses, trampled soldiers, and an assortment of weapons are in the foreground while a dead tree with twisted branches is in the background. It has been suggested that the tree may have been meant to symbolise the death of the Persian defenders and the end of the Persian Empire. However, it is just as possible that it was meant to represent a landscape devasted by war.

In 2005, a copy of the Alexander Mosaic was installed in the original location in the House of the Faun. It took a team of nine from the International Centre for the Study and Teaching of Mosaics in Ravenna, Italy, 22 months to make.

OPPOSITE: A mosaic of an Egyptian scene from the same house as the Alexander Mosaic.

A DIONYSIAC INITIATION

Life-sized paintings from the Pompeian Villa of the Mysteries

...The pleasures of drinking and feasting were added to the religious rites, to attract a larger number of followers. When wine had inflamed their feelings ... all sorts of corruption began to be practised ...

—Livy, *Rome and the Mediterranean*, Bk. 39.8

Just outside Pompeii is the Villa of the Mysteries, once owned by the urbane Istacidii family. In a private room measuring 6.7 x 4.5 metres is 'an ancient spiritual document' and the finest specimen of a genre of painting known as megalography: twenty-nine life-sized figures painted against an entire architectural background. All four walls of the room are covered with scenes believed to depict the process of initiation into the mysteries of the god Dionysus (Bacchus).

The number and continuity of the scenes, as well as the state of their preservation, make this controversial fresco the most important surviving representation of the mysteries which Livy described so disparagingly in his official version of the cult. Since the discovery of the murals in 1909, there has been a great deal of conjecture concerning their interpretation.

The worship of Dionysus, a god of wine, fertility, seasonal death, rebirth and joyous life, is believed to have been introduced into southern Italy about 200 BCE after Rome's conquests of

Greece and the East. Originally a primitive initiatory wine cult in which drunkenness was a sign of possession by the god, the cult was gradually absorbed into Greek culture, evolving into a more complex mystery religion. The intoxicating effect of wine and trance-inducing techniques, such as ecstatic dancing to pipes, drums and clashing cymbals, were believed to liberate the initiate to return to a more natural state of being. Because the cult was a celebration of everything that was outside societal restraints, it was not surprising that many of its original devotees were women and others on the margins of society: slaves, foreigners, even outlaws, for all were regarded as equal within the cult.

According to the classical sources, on certain feast days, ritual processions were held high in the Greek countryside. 'Following the torches as they dipped and swayed in the darkness, they climbed the mountain paths with head thrown back and eyes glazed, dancing to the beat of the drum which stirred their blood . . . in this state of *ekstasis* they abandoned themselves, dancing wildly and shouting 'Euoi!' (the god's name), and at that moment of intense rapture became identified with the god himself. They became filled with his spirit and acquired divine powers' (Hoyle, *Delphi*).

As the cult spread around the Mediterranean it took on many different forms, often absorbing local divinities. In Italy, Dionysus/Bacchus merged with the local god Liber (Liberty). At first, only women attended and only on three days of the year, but it was supposedly transformed by Paculla Annia, a priestess from Campania (the area around Vesuvius) by admitting men and extending the celebration of the rites to five times a month.

As in other places, it initially appealed only to the lower classes, but eventually became more widespread throughout society. Because official Roman religion was impersonal, those seeking a

ABOVE AND FOLLOWING PAGE: Part of the life-sized wall painting thought to have represented various phases of a female initiation into the mysteries of the god Dionysus.

more emotional involvement with a god were attracted to mystery cults. They 'offered an escape from worldly reality into mystic communion with the gods and the promise of a blessed life after death' (M. Grant, *Cities of Vesuvius*).

According to Livy, the cult of Bacchus spread through Italy like a 'contagious disease' and during the Bacchanalia (a Latin name for the rites of Bacchus), 'men, apparently out of their wits, would utter prophecies with frenzied bodily convulsions: matrons attired as Bacchantes, with their hair dishevelled and carrying blazing torches, would run down to the Tiber, plunge their torches in and bring them out still alight—because they contained a mixture of live sulphur and calcium' (*Rome and the Mediterranean*).

Livy's official fiction presents a picture of sexual abuse, and criminal activities ranging from murder to forgery. In 186, the Roman Senate, convinced that the secret and excessive nature of the Bacchanalia was a threat to public order and a possible source of political conspiracy, issued a senatorial decree suppressing all Bacchic societies. However, the practice of the cult by individuals was not forbidden and it continued to flourish, particularly in the cities of Campania. The paintings in the Villa of the Mysteries at Pompeii were painted in the first century BCE, over a century after the cult was officially banned.

There is no doubt that some people in Pompeii were light-hearted in their attitude to the cult, but many worshippers, perhaps like the owners of the Villa of the Mysteries, appear to have had a deep and serious attachment to Dionysus/Bacchus, and sought initiation into the Dionysian *thiasos*, or community, in this world and the next. Because the paintings seem to express the emotions of a religious experience and because the main participants are women, they probably depict an actual initiation endured by the matron of the house for whom the god would have been both a source of sensual and spiritual hope.

Like the mysterious initiatory rites they depict, the exact meaning of the frescoes has remained a mystery. Only those who were initiated ever knew their secrets and any interpretations of these scenes are only guesswork. It appears that a young girl is about to be initiated into the mysteries of Dionysus in preparation for marriage and her transition to the next stage of her life. The human marriage is linked with the sacred marriage of Dionysus and Ariadne who by her marriage to the god was endowed with eternal life.

Various features of Dionysiac initiation are appropriate to a wedding: 'the flagellation imparting fertility, and the revelation of the phallus' (R. A. S. Seaford, 'The Mysteries of Dionysus at Pompeii', from *Pegasus: Classical Essays from the University of Exeter*). Both initiation into the mysteries and marriage were important rites of passage. Once the initiation was completed, not only would the girl become a woman but she would become a mythical follower of Dionysus—a maenad (or satyr if a male)—and ensured of a blessed afterlife.

Initiation rites

Most initiations, during which the initiate is radically changed, followed a similar pattern: separation; purification; instruction; revelation; ordeal; the eating of a special meal and the assumption of a special garment. Many of these elements appear in the fresco cycle.

There seems to be three parts to these frescoes: the preliminaries, the initiation into the world of the divine, and the adorning of the bride and the marriage bed. In the preliminaries, the girl crosses the threshold and the preparations begin. A young nude boy, wearing actor's boots, reads from a scroll (possibly prayers or the liturgy of the ritual). The girl, in a change of garment, carries an offering tray of sacramental cake (ceremonial meal) and a priestess removes the covering from a basket while another attendant pours water into a basin in which the priestess is about to dip a laurel sprig (purification).

The bride/initiate then passes an old Silenos (companion to Dionysus) playing a ten-stringed lyre, and moves into the mythical nature realm of the god where a young male satyr (half-human and half-goat) is playing a pan flute, while a maenad (nymph) suckles a goat. The girl is about to enter a new psychological state of mind necessary for a rebirth. All the elements of the initiation are there. There is the revelation of the sacred contents (*sacra*) in the basket (*liknon*); the divine couple (Dionysus sprawled across the lap of Ariadne); the divination of the future as the young satyr stares into a bowl perhaps seeing the death of youth; the mask (perhaps used to terrify the initiate, but also as a symbol of throwing off the old mask in preparation for the new), and the winged flagellator.

The climax of the rite is shown in the agony on the face of the initiate and the lash across her back; a dancing maenad with celebratory cymbals, and the offer of the thyrsus, the symbolic rod of Dionysus topped with a pine cone, as a symbol of the completion of the ordeal. The third part of the cycle shows the girl preparing for her 'divine' marriage with the god who will ensure her fertility as an actual wife, and the final stage in the transition from girlhood to matronhood in the form of the older woman on the marriage bed looking back in serenity.

Unlike the members of the Istacidii family who perished during the eruption of Vesuvius in 79 CE, the stunning, vividly coloured and enigmatic paintings that decorated their walls survived almost intact.

BANQUETING IN STYLE

Silverware from the vicinity of Mount Vesuvius

Silverware, my very own silverware, is my great passion.

—Petronius, *Satyricon*

In 1895, during the excavation of the Villa of the Pisanella at Boscoreale not far from Pompeii, 109 pieces of beautiful silverware were found in a chest hidden in a well in the *torcularium* (a room containing the olive and wine presses). Thirty-five years later, while renowned archaeologist Amedeo Maiuri was excavating in one of the largest houses in Pompeii (the House of the Menander), he located a treasure trove of Roman silverware, unique in its variety and superlative workmanship. The 118 silver objects (cups, bowls, plates, vases, spoons), were wrapped carefully in wool and cotton, hidden in the bottom of a wooden box in the cellar. Almost three quarters of a century later in 2000, 20 pieces of silver tableware were discovered in a wicker basket in the *triclinium* (dining room) of a complex at Morigene, not far from Pompeii.

Much of the silverware found in the Menander and Boscoreale hoards was embossed in elaborate yet delicate mythological, landscape and vegetal motifs, and seems to reflect the influence of the great Hellenistic centres of Pergamon and Alexandria. This was confirmed by the names of craftsmen incised on some pieces. In the House of the Menander collection, the drinking vases were in pairs and the plates and bowls in sets of four.

Three particularly stunning vessels from the first century BCE reveal great technical ability and elegant taste. One features a bucolic landscape, much like that described in idyllic literature; another by the same artist, Apelles, depicts Hercules performing his labours. The third, a *kantharos* (drinking vessel), is decorated with olive twigs and fruit. The total collection is housed in the National Archaeological Museum in Naples.

Amongst the vessels in the Boscoreale treasure in the Louvre is a superb goblet with skeletons grouped in four scenes under garlands of roses. The skeletons represent the Greek poets and philosophers Sophocles, Menander, Zeno and Epicurus and each is accompanied by an inscription such as 'enjoy life while ye may' and 'life is a theatre'. Two of the Moregine cups are decorated with what appears to be Egyptian motifs, but the significant features are the portraits of Antony and Octavian. It has been suggested that they were produced to commemorate the signing of the Treaty of Brundisium in 40 BCE which helped to avert a chaotic civil war throughout the Roman Empire.

Wealth and prestige, wining and dining

What do we know about who owned these silver table settings? Because silverware was rare in the Roman world until the first century BCE, ownership of any fine objects made from the precious metal was regarded as one of the signs of social and economic status. Pliny asserted that refined Romans collected the finest antique silver decorated with themes from classical mythology and poetry.

Amedeo Maiuri concluded that the owner of the House of the Menander was from the highest level of society. He suggested the house belonged to a member of the Poppaea *gens* (clan) which included Poppaea Sabina, the second wife of the Emperor Nero. There was no doubt that from the time of her marriage to Nero, Poppaea Sabina was one of Pompeii's favourite daughters, and that members of her family owned another house (House of the Golden Cupids) and a villa in the countryside at Oplontis. Since the silver

> Much of the silverware found in the Menander and Boscoreale hoards was embossed in elaborate yet delicate mythological, landscape and vegetal motifs, and seems to reflect the influence of the great Hellenistic centres of Pergamon and Alexandria.

ABOVE: Part of the embossed silverware found in the House of the Menander in Pompeii.

represented a considerable investment, all that can be said of the owner of the House of the Menander is that he was a wealthy Pompeian.

The owner was probably socially and politically active, as the grand house had five public reception areas. Recent archaeological work done on the house in the late twentieth century by Richard Ling, revealed that the owners had at some stage expanded to incorporate an adjacent property, and around 60 CE, they demolished an earlier part of the house to create more luxurious reception rooms, service quarters and stables. Even after the disastrous earthquake of 62 CE, seventeen years before the eruption of Vesuvius, they had initiated a large redecoration program.

An integral part of the social and political life of well-to-do citizens in Pompeii was the dinner party; it was part of the ritual which bound a patron to his large network of clients and friends. Several still life paintings of silver table settings in Pompeian houses and tombs indicate that feasts and banquets were occasions for the city's elite to advertise their wealth and social status by flaunting or displaying their silver and glassware, their cooks' latest sweet and savoury dishes, and best wines which young handsome male wine waiters, one to each guest, kept flowing during the meal according to etiquette. After-dinner drinking was often heavy and dinner parties could last well into the night. Whether the collection found in the House of Menander was ever used at such banquets is not really known, but K. S. Painter, in his 2001 *The Insula of Menander at Pompeii; The Silver Treasure*, suggests that the silver was used for no more then eight people and possibly for open-air dining.

The owner of the Boscoreale treasure—or at least the house where it was found—is believed to be the famous Pompeian banker and moneylender, M. Caecilius Jucundus. However, it is possible that the silver was not his. There is documentary and archaeological evidence suggesting silver plate could be used or held as security by others. Jucundus also had a house in Pompeii where 150 wax tablets were found with details of his business: tax farming, lending money to merchants, as well as renting and selling land, properties, and slaves. Many entries were receipts for loans. It is possible that some part of the silver in his villa may have been security for a loan.

The owner of the abandoned Morigene hoard are unknown although they were fugitives fleeing the eruption of Vesuvius.

Why had the silver hoards in the House of the Menander and the Villa of the Pisanella been hidden: one in a cellar and the other in a well? One suggestion is that it may have had something to do with the massive earthquake of 62CE and the frequent quakes prior to the eruption of Vesuvius.

These three silver hoards bear witness to the refinement of the Pompeian elite and their luxurious lifestyle at the beginning of the imperial period, as well as to the artistic skill of the Campanian metal ateliers.

ACTION, DRAMA AND EMOTION
Monumental Hellenistic sculptures

At the same time as, with his hands, he strives to tear away the knots, his fillet soaked with slaver and dreadful poison, he also raises a horrifying shriek to the stars ... —Virgil, *Aeneid*

The anguish and desperation of Laocoon, the Trojan priest fighting the sea serpents in Virgil's *Aeneid* described above, is also depicted in one of the great masterpieces of Hellenistic art from the first century BCE. The sculptural group of Laocoon and His Two Sons in the writhing grip of the snakes, with its violent muscular movement, high drama and extreme emotion, contains many of the elements common to Hellenistic sculpture. The Winged Victory (Nike) of Samothrace, one of the greatest treasures in the Louvre, also displays some of the typical Hellenistic features: energetic movement and theatricality, while the stunning masterpiece of the Dying Gaul, revealing the agony and anguish of the defeated warrior, is an example of a new type of hero in art.

The term 'Hellenistic' generally refers to the period from the death of Alexander the Great (323 BCE) to the victory of Augustus over Antony and Cleopatra at Actium (31 BCE), and the prevailing art and culture at the time, although there was no clear-cut starting and ending point. Hellenistic art was often compared unfavourably with the work of the Classical Greek artists. However, when the Laocoon was discovered buried in a vineyard in Rome in 1506,

Michelangelo declared that the statue had a profound effect on him and gave him the inspiration for the muscular movements of his own work.

The luxurious courts of Hellenistic monarchs (Ptolemies, Antigonids and Seleucids) and the cosmopolitan outlook of the Mediterranean world, with its better

understanding of foreign, non-Greek-speaking peoples, provided the background for much of the innovative and diverse art of the period. Unlike the Classical period when most great artists were likely to come from Athens, the work of Hellenistic artists came from places like Alexandria, Rhodes and Pergamon. The themes also varied.

Whereas the Classical focused on the idealised human figure, the Hellenistic sculpture was more realistic: ageing old fishermen with prominent veins and sinews, a drunken old woman, a dwarf, a hunchback, a boy picking a thorn from his foot. Foreign gods (Serapis from Egypt and Helios, patron god of Rhodes) entered the artistic repertoire, as did different ethnic groups (the superb bronze head of an African Berber and the Dying Gaul).

The Winged Nike, a personification of victory, came from the Rhodian school of sculpture and was found on the north-western Aegean island of Samothrace in 1863. Rhodes was the most powerful naval state in the Aegean around 200 BCE and it is believed that this statue was dedicated by the Rhodians to the sanctuary of the Great Gods on Samothrace, for a victory by their fleet. Even today, without head and arms, this impressive 2.5 metre *Victory*, braced against the wind, with her garments billowing around her as she tries to land on the prow of a ship, creates a stunning visual effect. 'With her huge and meticulously feathered wings outspread, she strides energetically forward, her torso twisted in one direction, her hips in the other, producing a boldly contorted effect . . . the full curves of her body are visible through her finely pleated chiton as it presses and moulds her body and thighs . . .' (Lucilla Burn, *Hellenistic Art: From Alexander the Great to Augustus*). Despite its power, the Nike appears almost weightless.

OPPOSITE: The monumental Hellenistic sculpture known as Laocoon and his Sons reveals the high drama and emotion of much of sculpture of the time.

The sculptors Agesander, Polydorus and Athenodorus, also from Rhodes, using all their technical skill, produced a piece of sensational realism in Laocoon and His Two Sons. This sculpture was based around the story of the Wooden Horse of Troy. Laocoon, priest of Apollo (or Poseidon), warned the Trojans not to trust the Greeks by bringing the wooden horse into their city: 'Trojans, trust not the horse. Whatever it be, I fear the Greeks, even when bringing gifts' (Virgil, *Aeneid*), but the Trojans ignored him and, in his anger, he threw a spear at the horse. By attempting to interfere with the fated course of events, he infuriated the gods who sent sea serpents to destroy him and his sons. This powerful sculpture is in the Vatican Museum.

Realism and pain

The Dying Gaul was part of the victory monument set up by the Attalids of Pergamon after their defeat of the Celtic-speaking Galatians of Asia Minor in the 220s. There is something noble in the image of this strong, nude 'barbarian' with his neck torc (a necklace made of twisted metal) and long moustache, head drooping onto his chest as his life ebbs away. Such was the pathos that this figure evoked in the viewer that it became one of the most copied of Hellenistic pieces. It also reflects a change in attitude as people gained a wider perspective of the world around them.

Although traditional themes such as athletes continued to be used, the Hellenistic artists attempted to show an individual's experience with greater realism, such as in the bronze of the seated boxer. Here is not an idealistic depiction of an Olympic hero, but one of an ageing boxer whose experience is etched on his battered face with its clearly defined scars inlaid with copper.

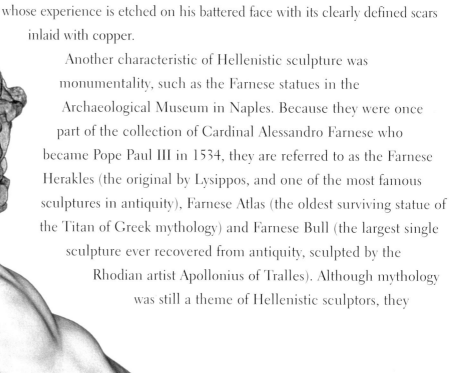

Another characteristic of Hellenistic sculpture was monumentality, such as the Farnese statues in the Archaeological Museum in Naples. Because they were once part of the collection of Cardinal Alessandro Farnese who became Pope Paul III in 1534, they are referred to as the Farnese Herakles (the original by Lysippos, and one of the most famous sculptures in antiquity), Farnese Atlas (the oldest surviving statue of the Titan of Greek mythology) and Farnese Bull (the largest single sculpture ever recovered from antiquity, sculpted by the Rhodian artist Apollonius of Tralles). Although mythology was still a theme of Hellenistic sculptors, they tended to depict legendary heroes, like Herakles, in a different light, and to focus on more obscure myths.

The Farnese Herakles was found in the Baths of Caracalla in Rome, along with the Farnese Bull. The awesome scale, powerful proportions and musculature of the Herakles seem appropriate for the huge bath complex which covered 13 hectares and could accommodate 1600 bathers at a time. Despite having successfully completed the 'Twelve Labours' imposed on him by Eurystheus, including stealing the golden apples that would eventually ensure his immortality, Herakles is not depicted in triumph. He is shown resting on his lion-skin-covered club, not so much in thoughtful relaxation, but in a state of physical and mental exhaustion after the struggles of his 'Labours'.

The Farnese Bull depicts Dirce, second wife of the king of Thebes, being tied to a wild bull by Zeto and Amphion as revenge for her mistreatment of their mother. The 2.1 metre-high Atlas is shown with the weight of the world on his shoulders in the form of a unique celestial globe. It has been suggested that the artists who created these statues may have been reflecting the lifetime struggle experienced by all humans.

Rather than being inferior to Classical sculptors, Hellenistic artists were innovative, and their works were varied, bold and full of emotion, drama and movement. 'Anguish and fear replace classical repose. The emotional tensions and suffering which had previously been idealised were now conveyed directly through agitated gestures, facial expressions and muscular strain' (John Boardman in *The Birth of Western Civilization*).

ABOVE: The Winged Nike, found on the island of Samothrace in the north-western Aegean, is a magnificent example of Hellenistic sculpture.

45
DEFINING MOMENTS

The coinage of the first two Caesars

'This is violence!' Caesar cried, and at that moment, as he turned away,
one of the Casca brothers with a sweep of his dagger stabbed him just below
the throat ... Twenty-three dagger thrusts went home as he stood there.

—Suetonius, *The Twelve Caesars, Julius Caesar*, 82

A ncient Roman coins are not rare, and hoards are often found in areas that were once
under Roman control. Some finds, of course, are more spectacular than others, especially
if they contain an overwhelming number of *aurei*, gold coins that were never in daily
circulation. However, despite their value as a gold treasure, these coins, as well as silver *denarii*
and bronze *sesterti*, are more valuable as a source of socio-political information.

Coins show how various powerful individuals, like emperors, chose to present themselves:
as a great military leader, a statesman or even as a god. Roman coins became an important
medium of propaganda, especially those minted from the time of Julius Caesar in the late
Republic, to the early years of the Empire under Augustus and the Julio-Claudian emperors
(Tiberius, Gaius, Claudius and Nero). Those covering the years 44–27 BCE are particularly
valuable as they reveal a number of defining moments in Rome's history.

OPPOSITE: A gold aureus of 28 BCE depicting Octavian as imperator, one year before he adopted the name
of Augustus. On the reverse he claims 'he restored to the people of Rome their laws and their rights'.

The silver denarius, first minted in 217 BCE, became the standard coin of the Roman Republic and the Empire. Republican coins generally featured gods, legendary heroes or famous ancestors of the 'moneyers' who minted them. Gold issues were rare in the late Republic. By the first century BCE, coins began to depict contemporary events, and generals often minted their own silver dinarii in order to pay their troops. This change in coin type corresponded with the career of Julius Caesar who, between 58–50 BCE, campaigned in Gaul (modern France) during which time he is believed to have been engaged in thirty pitched battles, captured over 800 towns and exacted an annual tribute of 400, 000 gold pieces.

Two coins issued in 50 and 48 BCE commemorated his subjection of Gaul which offered Rome vast resources and added an area twice the size of Italy to Rome's territories. One of these coins features an elephant (symbol of Caesar) trampling a dragon or a Gallic trumpet (symbol of the Gauls). The second coin depicts a Gallic warrior, possibly Vercingetorix, against who Caesar fought the hardest battle of his career.

While Caesar was in Gaul, a small group of Senators and long-time enemies manipulated the political situation, forcing him to take action which initiated a Civil War. After his eventual victory, a subservient Senate offered him unprecedented titles and honours, including that of Dictator for Life in 44 BCE. In the same year he introduced a revolutionary change in coinage with portraits of himself occupying the place on the obverse of coins normally reserved for gods, heroes and renowned ancestors. This series featured his titles at the time such as CAESAR DICT. PERPETVO (Dictator for Life).

Never before had the image of a living individual been placed on a coin. Caesar believed that the days of the Republic were over, that it was 'a mere name without form or substance' (Suetonius, *Julius Caesar*). However, he was ahead of his time in believing that one-man-rule was needed to maintain peace throughout the empire. His enemies, who put an adverse interpretation on everything he said and did, believed he wanted to make himself king. Sixty of them, including a former friend, Marcus Junius Brutus, conspired to assassinate him, to save the Republic.

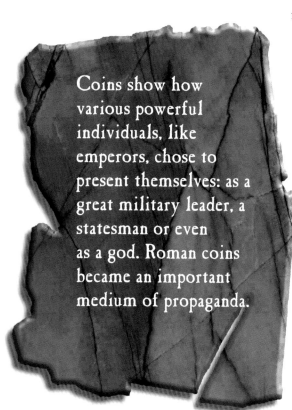

Coins show how various powerful individuals, like emperors, chose to present themselves: as a great military leader, a statesman or even as a god. Roman coins became an important medium of propaganda.

On 15 March 44 BCE, a date that the Roman calendar called the Ides of March, he died from 23 stab wounds. During the following two years, Brutus struck a series of coins, including at least two of gold, commemorating Caesar's death. On the reverse of these rare coins was the cap of liberty (an ancient symbol of freedom) flanked by two daggers and the abbreviation EID (ibus) MAR (tiis), the Ides of March, a clear statement of the date, purpose and method of the assassination. Interestingly, the portrait of Brutus is on the obverse. What was regarded as an objectionable innovation by Caesar became the norm.

The assassination of Caesar, which did not restore the Republic, resulted in chaos and upheaval. Caesar's heir and adopted son, his grand-nephew Gaius Octavius, changed his name to Gaius Julius Caesar Octavianus, and with the help of Mark Antony, avenged his father's murder; the assassins were defeated at Philippi in 42 BCE. In the same year the Senate made Caesar a god. Suetonius stated that a comet, seen over Rome just after Caesar's death, was believed to be his soul ascending into heaven. Octavian came to be known as *divi filius*, son of a god, which was a useful piece of propaganda during the hostilities that erupted between Mark Antony and himself over control of the Roman Empire. In 37 BCE, he issued the first of a series of coins depicting himself as DIVOS IVLIVS.

The empire was divided between the two men with Antony given the east, including Egypt, where he met the charismatic Cleopatra, married her and fathered a number of children. After a victory in Armenia he returned to Egypt and bestowed extravagant honours on her. An extraordinary denarius minted in 34 BCE shows a portrait of Cleopatra on the reverse with the title 'Queen of Kings and of her sons who are kings'. Antony's political miscalculations led to civil war with Octavian, whose victory at Actium in 31 BCE was celebrated with the issue of a coin with the title IMPERATOR.

Following the suicides of both Antony and Cleopatra, Octavian marched into Egypt, making it a province of Rome. This momentous event was commemorated on a denarius in 28 BCE

ABOVE: Reverse of a silver denarius of Brutus that was minted to celebrate the murder of Julius Caesar on the Ides of March.

which shows Octavian Caesar on one side and a crocodile, symbol of Egypt, on the other with the inscription AEGYPTO CAPTA. Octavian returned to Rome and, in 27 BCE, accepted the name of Augustus and began a new era in Roman history: one-man rule of the Roman world.

Propaganda

The demise of the Republic, which Julius Caesar had foreseen, was finally brought to an end by his adopted son. Coins were now issued in gold, silver, bronze, copper and orichalcum (brass) with the minting being shared between the Emperor (gold and silver coins) and the Senate (the lesser valued coins).

In 18 BCE, to emphasise his divine ancestry and the deification of Julius Caesar, Augustus had a coin struck depicting a comet with eight rays and a flaring tail with DIVVS IVLIVS inscribed across it. On the obverse is the head of Augustus wearing an oak wreath, the *crona civica*, which symbolised that it was Caesar Augustus who had saved the citizens of Rome from the destructions of the civil wars of the Republic, and who brought peace and prosperity to the Roman Empire.

Under Augustus (27 BCE–14 CE), coinage was used with great effect as propaganda, especially in the pretence that he and the Senate shared the rule of the Empire. A coin representing him as he wished to be known, as *pater patriae*, 'father of his country', was issued in 2 BCE. Augustus ushered in a cultural Golden Age, and except for a few military campaigns to secure the borders of the empire, it was a time of peace, stability and prosperity.

A series of victory coins were struck for campaigns conducted by his stepsons Tiberius and Drusus (the sons of Livia). Others reflected the problems he had organising the succession of a member of his own family (the Julians). He issued a series of aurei when he adopted his grandsons Gaius and Lucius Caesar, and made them his heirs. Unfortunately both died as young men and he was forced to name his ageing stepson, Tiberius (a Claudian), as his successor.

Tiberius' accession marked the beginning of what is referred to as the Julio-Claudian period (14–68 CE). Although peace and prosperity continued in the Empire, at the courts of Tiberius, Gaius, Claudius and Nero, there was intrigue, ambition, murder, attempted murders, terror, promiscuity and even incest. The coinage of the period featured some of the royal women (Livia, Agrippina the Elder, Agrippina the Younger and Poppaea) who instigated or played a part in many of these incidents. The death by suicide of Nero at only 31 brought to an end the supremacy of the Julio-Claudians.

46

AN EXPERIMENTAL TECHNIQUE

Rare Roman cameo glass

The eye is particularly caught by a sepulchral urn ... most beautifully executed by the hand of the artist, and so transparent that you would think it a native amethyst ... encompassed with white figures.

—Girolamo Tetzi, *Aedes Barberinae*, 1642

The extract above refers to the finest and most famous of Roman cameo glass vases, the so-called Portland or Barberini Vase, now in the British Museum. When Tetzi made his comment in the seventeeth century, the vase was owned by Cardinal Francesco Barberini, nephew of Pope Urban VIII and was displayed in his palace on the Quirnal hill in Rome, visited by 'all travellers of taste and judgement'.

After 150 years in their family's collection, Donna Cornelia Barberini was forced to sell it to pay for her considerable losses at cards. It was taken to England, and after several owners, was bought by the Duchess of Portland, hence its name. At the same time another magnificent cameo vase, the *Blue Vase*, was lying undisturbed under layers of solidified ash and pumice in Pompeii where it had been since that fateful day in 79 CE when Mount Vesuvius erupted. It is now displayed in the National Archaeological Museum in Naples, the most valuable piece among three thousand objects of Roman glass in the collection.

The experimental Roman technique of cameo glass grew out of the Hellenistic craft of gem

engraving. Some of the finest craftsmen came from Alexandria in Egypt and specialised in making cameos from banded sardonyx by cutting the stone's separate layers to different depths, so that a light-coloured portrait head could stand out against a darker background. One of the largest and finest cameos of the period is the so-called Tazza Farnese or Farnese Bowl which is another of the treasures in the Naples Museum. It was fashioned from a single piece of sardonyx agate, and the inside bottom of the bowl features a magnificent cameo decoration of seven figures which some experts believe is an allegory of the Nile and creation; others believe it celebrates the Golden Age founded by Octavian/Augustus after his defeat of the last of the Ptolemies (Cleopatra) (*American Journal of Archaeology*).

These views depend on the date and origin of manufacture which, like the subject matter, is controversial. It is uncertain if it was made at the court of the Ptolemies in Alexandria between 100–31 BCE, or if an Alexandrian craftsman was working for the Emperor Augustus between 31-10 BCE. Another stunning onyx cameo is the renowned Gemma Augustea which features Augustus as Jupiter and was carved to celebrate the victories won by his heir, Tiberius, in Pannonia.

The discovery of glass-blowing in the first century BCE speeded up and simplified glass manufacture so that even the poorest inhabitants of the Roman Empire were able to afford glassware for daily use. However, surviving examples of Roman cameo glass, like the Portland Vase and Blue Vases are extremely rare, due to the restricted period in which this innovative technique was practised (from ca. 27 BCE–ca. 68 CE); the technical challenges imposed in creating a multi-layered matrix; the skill involved in carving the finished glass, and the time taken to complete one piece. Only the wealthy Roman senatorial class and imperial family could have afforded these exquisite vessels. An attempt in the nineteenth century to reproduce the Portland Vase in glass took master craftsmen three years to achieve.

It is still uncertain how the ancient cameo glass workers created these amphorae-like vases. Modern experimentation suggests two possible methods. One involves placing a globular bubble of the background colour into a hollow outer blank of the overlay colour, allowing the two to fuse and then blowing them together to form the final shape of the vessel. The second method requires that the background blank be shaped to the desired size and form and then dipped into a vat of molten glass of the overlay colour. Whichever method was used, the

OPPOSITE: The Portland Vase, an example of rare Roman cameo glass. Its decorative theme has given rise to numerous interpretations over the centuries.

ancient craftsman had to have a precise knowledge of the proportions of the two pastes to make them fuse without breaking. The preferred colours were a dark translucent blue background with an opaque white layer on which the engraver (*diatretarius*) would carve the decorative motif.

There is no doubt about the theme of the 32-centimetre-high Blue Vase found in 1834 in a cemetery just outside the walls of Pompeii. It features a Dionysiac scene of cupids harvesting grapes and making music under a trellis, with grapevines sprouting from a mask of Dionysus (god of wine and fertility). In Pompeii during the first centuries BCE and CE, the cult of Dionysus (Bacchus) offered an 'escape from worldly reality and into mystical communion with the god and the promise of a blessed life after death' (M. Grant, *Cities of Vesuvius*). The vase was obviously associated with the rites of death.

Unlike the Blue Vase, the decorative theme of the Portland/Barberini Vase, thought to have been originally 35 centimetres high (it lost its tapered base in antiquity), has given rise to numerous interpretations over the last four hundred years. A naked young man entwines his arm around a woman who holds a snake-like creature, while a bearded man looks on and a cupid flies overhead. On the other side, a seated woman holds a sceptre and a young man looks at a reclining woman holding a torch.

Possibly the most favoured interpretation is that the scene depicts the marriage of the sea goddess Thetis (mother of Achilles) and Peleus. If this is the case, the vase may have been presented

ABOVE: The renowned Gemma Augustea carved from onyx and depicting Augustus with the goddess Roma.

as a wedding present. On the other hand, there are those who associate the scenes with the Golden Age of Augustus and Virgil's *Aeneid*, in which the birth of Augustus occurred, according to the propaganda of the day, when Apollo visited his mother Atia in the form of a snake.

Reproduction, vandalism and reconstruction

Before the Barberini Vase was sold to the Duchess of Portland, it was owned by Sir William Hamilton, the British Ambassador to the Court of Naples. He wrote to his good friend, the noted ceramicist, Josiah Wedgwood, 'I saw the vase every day for above a year, and protest I admired it more and more'. When he took it to England, he urged Wedgwood to visit London and see the vase which was 'the very apex of perfection', with perhaps the possibility of copying it in his revolutionary jasper ceramic ware.

For four years, Wedgwood, his son and several renowned artists experimented and struggled to copy the famous cameo vase in ceramic. Eventually, in 1789, he announced, 'I have now the pleasure to find my imitation of this vase, after strict comparison with the original, has given perfect satisfaction to the most distinguished artists in Britain'.

In 1810, the original Portland Vase was loaned to the British Museum, but in 1845, a drunken vandal threw a statue at the display case and smashed it to pieces. Although it was repaired satisfactorily, it has undergone two more reconstructions (in 1948 and 1987).

Most Roman cameo glass production occurred over a period of no more than two generations from the late first century BCE to the early first century CE and, although there was a brief revival in the fourth century CE, it was not produced again until the eighteenth century. The Portland Vase is considered to be one of the crowning achievements of the entire Roman glass industry, and the famous First Edition copies made in jasper by Josiah Wedgwood in the eighteenth and nineteenth centuries are not only in museum collections around the world, but fetch a fortune at auction.

Surviving examples of Roman cameo glass, like the Portland Vase and Blue Vase are extremely rare, due to the restricted period in which this innovative technique was practised (from ca. 27 BCE–ca. 68 CE).

Part V

1st Millennium CE

A cultural turning point, synthesis and synergism

47

FACES IN THE SAND

The Faiyum mummy portraits

... the awareness of eternal life was to impart a new accent to the individual face, as the proximity of the corpse was to do in the Faiyum.
—Andre Malraux, *Voices of Silence*, 1953.

In the late nineteenth century, a dubious art dealer called Theodor Graf obtained a large number of painted mummy portraits from the local inhabitants of el-Rubayat in the oasis of el-Fayoum (Faiyum), about 100 kilometres south-west of Cairo. Around the same time, the eminent British Egyptologist Sir Flinders Petrie was excavating in Hawara in the south east of the Faiyum when he came upon a Roman cemetery. In 1888, he recorded that he was about to give up digging in the area when one of his workers found a mummy with a painted portrait on a wooden panel placed over its face. He was fascinated by the beautifully drawn head of a girl, in soft grey tints. In its style and mode it was entirely classical without any Egyptian influence.

Petrie excavated sixty of these portraits, some as fresh as the day they were painted. More were discovered in Antinoopolis, Thebes and Memphis, but because most came from el-Rubayat and Hawara they are referred to as the Faiyum mummy portraits.

Conserved in Egypt's arid climate, they comprise the most outstanding body of ancient portable art to have survived. They are exceptional in that they are 'Egyptian in their symbolism,

OPPOSITE: A mummy portrait of a woman from el-Rubayat in the Egyptian Faiyum area. This is one of the most beautiful of the Faiyum portraits.

Greek in their pictorial technique and Roman in their social context' (Berenice Geoffroy-Schneiter, *Fayum*).

The men, women and children who gaze directly out of these portraits with large, dark eyes are not idealised, but surprisingly human and individual. There is 'the severe matron displaying her jewels; the young girl with a mischievous smile and bright eyes quivering with life; the young man with sensual lips and the beginning of a moustache . . . here a woman who looks bored . . . steeped in a gentle melancholy; here one who frowns, anxious and bitter; here a man with the brutal look of a soldier, a scowl on his rough face'.

Who were these people with Greek names like Hermione, Demos, Tenos and Eutychus, dressed in the latest Roman fashions and buried according to Egyptian funerary customs in an Egyptian oasis?

For millennia before their burials, the Faiyum supported a relatively dense population. Although referred to as an oasis, it was watered by a branch of the Nile which fed into a lake (Lake Moeris in antiquity) in a depression 45 metres below sea level. The area supported abundant vegetation, teemed with wildlife such as crocodiles, and was a playground for the Egyptian pharaohs and nobles. Periodically land was reclaimed from the lake; the first major project occurred in the nineteenth century BCE when the Egyptian kings moved their capital to the area and were buried in the same vicinity.

Over a thousand years later, the first Greeks settled in Egypt. In the middle of the seventh century BCE, Greeks from Asia Minor, in the service of the Egyptian king Amasis, were given land for a Greek town (Naukratis) in the Delta as a commercial centre for those who wanted to settle in Egypt. In 332 BCE, Alexander the Great took possession of Egypt and founded the city of Alexandria. After his death, Egypt came under the control of one of his generals, Ptolemy, and a dynasty of Greco/Egyptians ruled Egypt as pharaohs for 250 years.

People from all around the Mediterranean with Greek, Jewish, Syrian, Libyan and African backgrounds flocked to the cities of

Conserved in Egypt's arid climate, they comprise the most outstanding body of ancient portable art to have survived. They are exceptional in that they are 'Egyptian in their symbolism, Greek in their pictorial technique and Roman in their social context'.

Alexandria, Naukratis and Ptolemais. To increase productivity, the Ptolemies introduced further reclamation schemes in the Faiyum and settled Greek and foreign soldiers and their families on land there in return for military service.

Three cultures intersecting

By the first century BCE, the Greek-speaking urban elite saw themselves as both Greek and Egyptian. However, the Romans were looming on the horizon and in 30 BCE, the Ptolemaic dynasty of Queen Cleopatra came to an end. Egypt became a province of Rome, and the people of the Faiyum part of the diversity of that empire. After generations of Roman administration, Egypt consisted of a complex mixture of indigenous Egyptians, descendants of the Greeks and Macedonians, and Roman citizens. In the first two centuries CE, it is possible that the wealthy elite, who were able to afford mummification and expensive portraits, saw themselves as Egyptian, Greek and Roman.

The Roman practice of fitting a naturalistic representation of the deceased above the elaborately bandaged body was common in Egypt during the first few centuries CE. The painting technique used in the portraits, however, originated in Greece centuries earlier. Mummy images were usually painted on a primed wooden panel, or more rarely, directly onto the stretched linen shroud. The technique most frequently used was referred to as 'encaustic', from the Greek *enkaio* 'to burn'. It involved dissolving the pigments in hot wax. Because the pigments dried quickly, the artist had to work at great speed using a hard tool such as a spatula rather than a brush.

The advantage of this method is that in the hands of a talented artist, the portrait glowed with colour and the paint seemed to retain its fluidity. Tempura painting, that is, where the colours are mixed with water, was employed less frequently. The colours used were the four Greek primaries: white, yellow ochre, red earth and black, although these were often supplemented by rose madder, a pink dye from a herbaceous plant, and with shades of purple and green, used especially for clothes. In one masterpiece, the purple clothes of a woman seem to be accented in porphyry, an extremely expensive purplish-red pigment.

Gold leaf was used occasionally for backgrounds and details such as wreaths and diadems (headbands). Since gold in ancient Egypt was regarded as the flesh of the gods, the use of this material suggests the sacred nature of the portrait. For example, the seven petals on the golden diadem encircling the head of one man, suggests he was a priest of Serapis (a Greek version of the Egyptian god Osiris). The anonymous painters also used the Greek technique of a single light source casting shadows and highlights on the subjects' faces.

While the clothing, jewellery and hairstyles are those of imperial Rome, the complexions and facial structure of the subjects reflect the melting pot that was Egypt in the first two centuries CE. An unusually large and unique portrait in 'tondo' (circular format) depicts two men of obviously mixed race. Their facial resemblance suggests that they were brothers, one perhaps no more than a teenager. The other has a darker complexion and his expression appears somewhat bitter. The portrait of a young woman has been dubbed 'the European' because of her pale skin, another referred to as the 'Jewish Woman', and one of a gaunt-faced dark man suggests that he may have been an Ethiopian.

Even though the artists are anonymous, some portraits reveal the hand of a great master while others are the cruder work of simple craftsmen. One of the most controversial issues regarding these mummy portraits is whether they were painted while the person was alive or after they had died. Flinders Petrie believed that the subjects posed for the paintings. Perhaps they originally hung in their houses and were later cut to size to fit the mummy assemblage. Since most were separated from the mummy when discovered, there is probably no definitive answer, although the portraits of young children suggest that they, at least, may have been painted after death.

For a long time after their discovery these realistic portraits, painted in the Greek style on Egyptian mummies found in a Roman province, were treated as unclassifiable curiosities by museum curators who were unsure whether to display them in Egyptian, Greek, Roman or Coptic departments.

'Created nearly two thousand years ago and, until recently, all but overlooked by scholars and by the public alike, these ancient faces still engage the modern viewer by the directness of their gaze and their evocation of a long-gone society. The athletes, the learned men and women, soldiers and priests, children, adolescents, and old people are rendered in rich colours with the freshness of yesterday' (Philippe de Montebello, Director of the Metropolitan Museum of Art, 2000).

A UNIQUE SYNTHESIS

Greco-Indian art from ancient Gandhara

It seems highly probable ... that the unknown artist who created the initial model (for the Buddha) was ... both artist and philosopher, who belonged both to Greece and India. —Mario Bussagli, *L'art du Gandhara*, 1996. p.378

The unique and rare Greco-Buddhist art from the area known in ancient times as Gandhara was lost until the nineteenth century. This ancient kingdom was located in the north-western part of the Indian subcontinent on the northern side of the Kabul River. It covered parts of eastern Afghanistan, but its main centres were Peshawar and Taxila in present-day Pakistan. It was not until British soldiers and administrators began taking an interest in the ancient history of the Indian subcontinent that the existence of Gandhara and its importance in Buddhist iconography was realised.

From 1848, large numbers of Buddhist carvings and statues in terracotta, stucco and blue-grey schist flecked with mica were found throughout the Peshawar Valley. Gandhara was the source of the first Buddha figures, and its magnificent works of art incorporated Hellenistic styles within a Buddhist context. No other art combines western and eastern sculptural traditions in such a beautiful and refined way. It was Alfred Foucher, the French archaeologist, who first coined the term 'Greco-Buddhist art' in the early twentieth century and he considered the freestanding Buddhas of Gandhara as 'the most beautiful and probably the most ancient of the Buddhas' (Sir John Marshall, *The Buddhist Art of Gandhara*).

The main Greek features in this synergistic Greco-Indian Buddhist art included Corinthian columns; decorative scrolls and fruit garlands; Hellenistic deities such as Dionysus, Atlas, and the Greek wind god Boreas; mythological figures such as Herakles; winged Cupids holding wreaths; fantastic animals of Greek origin (tritons, centaurs and sea monsters), and groups of devotees in Greek dress, drinking from amphorae and playing instruments. These features were fused with Buddhist elements to depict the life of the Buddha in visual form from the first century BCE.

> Gandhara was the source of the first Buddha figures, and its magnificent works of art incorporated Hellenistic styles within a Buddhist context.

Buddhas were depicted in typical Hellenistic pose with a Greek hairstyle (*krobylos*) in which the hair was knotted on top, and garments (*himation*) with voluminous drapery rather then the Indian *dhoti* or loincloth. They were shown sitting on a throne under a leafy canopy to represent the Bhodi tree with legs folded under, or standing in niches of Greek style surrounded by realistic bare-chested Bodhisattvas looking like jewelled Indian princes, and Greek and Indian deities. Atlas was substituted for the Indian *Yaksa* (benevolent nature spirit); Vajrapani, the protector of Buddha, was depicted as Herakles, and winged angels called *asparas* became the winged cupids holding wreaths over Buddha.

Possibly the earliest depiction of Buddha in human form is found in Greco-Buddhist style on the magnificent gold and ruby Bimaran casket, displayed in the British Museum. It has been dated to the late first century BCE or early first century CE. Charles Masson found this masterpiece of Gandharan art in the nineteenth century in a stupa (a Buddhist mound-like structure) in eastern Afghanistan. It is only seven centimetres high and was found in a steatite box with inscriptions stating that inside were relics of the Buddha. Its high relief features Greek realism, Greek poses, garments and hairstyles, as well as Greco-Roman arched niches while Hindu deities Brahma and Indra/Sakra and several devotees surround the Buddha.

Due to its strategic location on the crossroads between ancient Iran and Central Asia, Gandhara was a centre of multicultural influences. From the sixth–fourth centuries BCE, it was part of the Persian Empire until Alexander the Great marched into Gandhara in 326. He left

OPPOSITE: A Gandharan Buddhist bodhisattva depicted in typical Hellenistic pose with Greek hairstyle and garment.

Greek and Macedonian troops and governors to rule his most eastern territories, and after his death in 323, the area became part of the Hellenistic empire of his successor in Asia, Seleucis. In 317, an Indian king, Chandragupta Maurya (founder of the great Maurya Empire), conquered the Macedonian-occupied areas west of the Indus River and later defeated Seleucis when he tried to regain his territory.

Chandragupta signed a peace treaty with the Hellenistic monarch in 305, which included a marriage alliance and, in return for 500 elephants, Seleucis gave up his Indian territories, including Gandhara. The Greek population remained in the area under the rule of Chandragupta's grandson, Ashoka the Great (273–232 BCE) who embraced the teachings of the Gautama Buddha. Ashoka is said to have sent many Buddhist missions to western Asia and South-East Asia. His *Edicts*, some written in perfect Classical Greek, indicate that many Greeks within his empire became Buddhist monks and helped the spread of Buddhism.

With the demise of the Maurya Empire, Gandhara was conquered by the Hellenistic Bactrians (from the area of modern-day Afghanistan) who, in 180 BCE, founded the Indo-Greek Kingdom in the northern subcontinent. Its most famous king was Menander who ruled from Taxila in Gandhara and became a Buddhist. It is believed that elements of Greek mythology and iconography were introduced into the Indian subcontinent via the coins produced by these kings and a fusion of Hellenistic and Buddhist elements started to appear in art.

The spread of a religion and its art

Between the first–third centuries CE, Gandhara reached the height of its power under the Kushans, a horde from Central Asia. During the rule of King Kanishka (128–151 CE), a distinct form of Buddhism (Mahayana Buddhism), which accommodated the ordinary people, emerged and flourished. Stupas became centres of devotional worship and places where the stories of the historical Buddha and his previous lives as a Bodhisattva (Buddha-in-waiting) could be expressed in visual form to the illiterate masses. Gandhara became the holy land of Buddhism and Greco-Buddhist art communicated the deeply human approach of this Buddhist faith. Standing Buddhas and Bodhisattvas were erected in monasteries and carved into hillsides.

Buddhism and its Greco-Buddhist art spread into Afghanistan where two monumental Buddhas, 55 and 37 metres high, were carved into the sandstone cliffs of the Bamyan Valley 2500 metres above sea level. The details of these statues were modelled from mud mixed with straw, coated with stucco and originally painted in brilliant colours, the larger wore a red robe, the smaller a blue one. Faces and hands were golden. Traces of the painting were still visible in the 1970s. These were the largest examples of standing Buddha carvings in the world and were listed as a UNESCO World Heritage Site.

In 2001, the Taliban, the ruling fundamentalist Islamic regime of Afghanistan, ruthlessly destroyed these treaures. Koichiro Matsuura, head of UNESCO, said in the media at the time, 'it is abominable to witness the cold and calculated destruction of cultural properties which were the heritage of the Afghan people and indeed of the whole of humanity'. The irony of this destruction is that the builders of the Buddhas may have been the ancestors of the modern Pashtuns, the ethnic group which formed the core of the Taliban. Many Pashtuns from Peshawar and Kandahar claim descent from Alexander the Great and his Macedonians.

It was not the first time that these massive statues had been attacked. Aurangzeb, the last of the Mughal emperors of India, who introduced strict Sharia law, attempted to destroy them by artillery fire in the early 1700s, and Nadir Shah, an Iranian military leader who conquered Afghanistan in 1738, also directed cannon fire at at them. For centuries they were left virtually untouched, until a 2001 decree declared them an affront to Islam and ordered them to be totally destroyed. 'All we are breaking are stones,' said a Taliban militia leader.

What the Taliban destroyed were not simply stones, but part of a long legacy of Greco-Buddhist art, a fusion of two great ancient cultures.

ABOVE: The gold Bimaran casket inlaid with garnets, is a Gandharan relic container and the best example of goldsmithing to survive from early India.

49
LORDS OF SIPAN

Ceramic and metal masterpieces from the Moche culture of northern Peru

The Moche buried fine gold and pottery so alluring that in decades of excavation archaeologists have rarely found a major tomb unplundered.

—Dr. Walter Alva, archaeologist and Director of Brunning Archaeological Museum, Peru

The term 'Moche' refers to a culture that flourished in the river valleys along the arid coastal plains of northern Peru between the first–seventh centuries CE. It is believed that the centre of this theocratic state was the great complex referred to as *Huacas del Sol y de la Luna* in the lower valley of the Moche River, five kilometres south of the present city of Trujillo.

The sacred 'pyramid' shrine, *Huaca del Sol* (monument to the sun), built of over one million adobe bricks, was the largest pre-Columbian structure in Peru but was destroyed in the sixteenth century during looting by Spanish conquistadors looking for gold. The nearby *Huaca de la Luna* (monument to the moon) remained largely intact. Although the Moche people had no form of writing, they left a vivid artistic record of their way of life and religious practices in their unique ceramic vessels and stunning objects in gold, silver and copper.

The Moche *huacas* scattered along the river valleys became a prime target for bands of *huaqueros* or grave diggers, and for decades looting had been a regular pastime for many of the

OPPOSITE: A copper and gold Moche death mask.

poor sugarcane farmers of the Lambayeque Valley. On a February night in 1987, a group, armed with shovels and torches, stumbled upon what turned out to be the richest site of pre-Columbian treasures ever found in the New World.

These raiders penetrated a tomb in the Huaca Rajada, near the village of Sipan. An unemployed mechanic, named Ernil Bernal, pushed an iron rod through the floor of a burial chamber and was almost buried in a shower of

gold, silver and bones. The men carted out eleven rice sacks of treasure that night but, as is often the way with thieves, they began to quarrel. The rest of the story involves a mafia-backed Italian financier with suitcases and cardboard boxes stuffed with money; furtive meetings; smugglers; overseas art connoisseurs; an informant; a predawn police raid on the home of Ernil Bernal and his death by shooting; angry Sipan villagers and a Peruvian archaeologist, Dr Walter Alva.

When shown the confiscated loot from Bernil's home, Dr Alva knew the villagers had found an elite Moche burial ground. Despite the recovery of the eighty-three priceless pieces, the police had arrived too late to save the rest of the treasures and they began appearing on the international antiquities market leading to a worldwide undercover investigation which led to prosecutions and the return of at least one of the treasures (a gold backflap) in 1998.

Dr Alva surrounded the Sipan site with barbed wire, and toting a gun against further armed thieves, began an excavation that would unearth the burials of many Moche dignitaries, three of them still intact and filled with wondrous treasures of gold, silver, copper and semiprecious stones. The first of the tombs contained the body of a warrior/lord (the Lord of Sipan) about 40 years old who is estimated to have died around 290 CE. Two young women were at his side and a young warrior with a golden shield lay at his feet.

He was covered in, and surrounded by, magnificent items revealing the incredible skill and sophistication of Moche metallurgists in the processes of alloys, casting, welding and repousse: a

ABOVE: A Moche culture excavation site. OPPOSITE: A gold Moche crab deity.

crescent-shaped headdress of hammered gold, a gold death mask, a sceptre and gold backflap that covered the back of the lower torso; a necklace composed of ten gold beads each depicting a spider in the centre of a web with its body in the form of a human head, and necklaces of gold and silver peanut beads. Here was actual evidence of the imposing and ornate costumes and ornaments worn by the great Moche warrior/priest lords previously seen in art participating in ritual sacrifice.

Dr Alva excavated the tomb of another Lord of Sipan and a High Priest, and between 1997 and 1999, three more extraordinary tombs of Moche elite were found at the site of San Jose de Moro in the lower Jequetepeque Valley. Some of these included the bodies of high-ranking women dressed in priestess costumes similar to those shown on ceramics and temple walls, where the women were depicted catching the blood of sacrificed victims in cups and handing them to the warrior/priest to drink.

Although the metal artefacts are magnificent, it is the two-coloured (cream and red/brown) stirrup-spouted pottery for which the Moche culture is best known, particularly the unique 'portrait ceramics' modelled on individual male faces of different ages and personalities. These ceramic masterpieces gave archaeologists their first insight into Moche life. The moulded figures and fine-line paintings not only depict houses, clothing, jewellery, animals, everyday events, and burials, but 'warrior priests bedecked in imposing ornate garb orchestrating ritual warfare; slitting captives throats, drinking their blood and hanging their de-fleshed bones from ropes, and participating in acts of sodomy and fellatio. All in the context of structured ceremony' (Colleen P. Popson, 'Grim Rites of the Moche', *Archaeology*).

Amongst the vast number of sexual acts represented in the art, vaginal intercourse was only ever depicted being performed under an elaborate roof, possibly a shrine, by a male in ceremonial garb and a female wearing her hair in two plaits ending in snake heads surrounded by other figures in poses of supplication.

Gruesome sacrifices

Who were these people who made such stunningly beautiful artefacts and yet engaged in the most grisly of sacrificial practices?

Moche society was based predominantly on farming. The rivers flowing from the Andes sliced through the coastal desert creating oasis-like valleys. Sophisticated irrigation schemes with mud-brick aqueducts and a network of canals extended the productive farmlands and made the support of a dense population possible. Their gruesome ceremonial practices of ritual sacrifice appear to have revolved around rain in the Andes, the fertility of the valleys, and the continuity of the social organisation as a whole. These ceremonies were carried out by a warrior/priest leader and a class of priests and priestesses on the *huacas* which were constructed on platforms, some reaching over 30 metres in height.

When archaeologists first found stone reliefs and pottery painted with scenes of throat-slitting, decapitation, bloodletting and consumption, they regarded them as too gruesome to be taken literally. However, archaeological discoveries soon revealed that these ritual activities were actually carried out by members of the ruling elite, like the Lords of Sipan.

Dr Steve Bourget of the University of Texas uncovered a ceremonial plaza with the remains of seventy systematically dismembered bodies of young men, embedded in mud, with marks on their neck vertebrae that indicated that their throats had been cut. It appeared that the young Moche warriors engaged in ritual combat, confirming the pottery scenes of warriors in the same attire fighting each other. Those who lost were bound, led up to the top of the *huaca* and sacrificed. Discoveries of other bodies with what appear to be deliberate mutilations indicate that, at certain times, enemy warriors were used to appease the fearsome-looking deity referred to as the Decapitator, who took the form of a human, spider, crab, octopus or scorpion, and carried a crescent-shaped knife in one hand and a severed head in the other.

After six centuries, the Moche culture declined, possibly due to environmental factors and the human reaction to them. Climatologists taking ice cores from glaciers in the Andes found

ABOVE: Moche culture treasures revealed.

that over the last hundred years whenever there was drought in the mountains, the coastal areas suffered heavy rains (El Nino). During the period from 500–650 CE, there had been a thirty-year drought in the mountains followed by thirty years of heavy rains and snows.

Assuming the reverse situation applied to the coast, the Moche would have been faced with a mega El Nino starting around 560. The unusual rainy period might explain the ritually slain bodies embedded in mud found by Dr Steve Bourget and the heavily eroded *huacas*. The number of Moche settlements engulfed in sand dunes could be evidence of an extended drought. As the ruling elite lost their power, the people may have turned on them, and each other, for control of the limited resources.

In 2006, almost twenty years after the looting at Sipan, a magnificent Moche gold mask depicting a sea goddess with spirals radiating for her face, turned up in a lawyer's office in London and was returned to Peru.

50

FROM PAGAN TO CHRISTIAN

The Mildenhall Treasure of Roman silver

Bacchic imagery had a long history in Greek and Roman art, and this example, on a magnificent silver vessel, is one of the finest to survive from the late-Roman period. — British Museum

S ometime in the mid-fourth century CE, a collection of some of the finest Roman silverware was buried in the Fens of East Anglia. The area had been occupied since the Romans first conquered Britain in 47 CE. It was a prosperous and well-populated area due to its production of grain and wool, as well as its river access. Almost 1500 years later, in 1942, and at the height of the Second World War, a Suffolk ploughman by the name of Gordon Butcher is supposed to have found a large metal dish in land near Mildenhall.

He showed it to his boss, Sydney Ford, a collector of antiquities and together they dug another thirty-three items (dishes, bowls, goblets and spoons) from the snow-covered field. According to the story, Ford stuffed them into a sack, took them home, cleaned them, and believing they were pewter, placed them on his mantlepiece. They were not recognised as silver until 1946 when they were classified as 'treasure' and appropriated by the authorities.

OPPOSITE: The Great Dish (Oceanus Dish) is the most outstanding piece of silverware from the Mildenhall Treasure. At its centre is the face of the sea god.

268

Later, the silver was acquired by the British Museum. For fifty years, scholars have questioned the provenance of the stunning tableware, the largest hoard of Roman silver ever found in Britain.

The most magnificent piece in the collection is the highly decorated *Oceanus Dish*, so-called for the face of the sea god, with a beard of seaweed and dolphins emerging from his hair, staring out from the centre. This large circular platter has a diameter of 60.5 centimetres and weighs 8.256 kilograms. There are two decorative bands around Oceanus which feature Bacchic scenes and mythological marine creatures. The inner frieze is decorated with scallop shells and sea nymphs riding a seahorse, a triton (half-man, half-fish), a sea stag and a ketos (a dragon-like sea monster).

The wide outer band features what looks like a drinking competition between Bacchus, the god of wine, and the hero, Heracles. The god, resting a foot on his panther, holds a bunch of grapes in one hand and his thyrsus (staff) in the other, while a drunken Heracles is supported by two satyrs (mythical male devotees of Bacchus). Silenus passes more wine to the god while the goat-legged Pan and maenads (nymph devotees of Bacchus) are engaged in frenzied dancing.

The Bacchic motif is continued in two smaller platters (satyrs and maenads dancing, Pan holding a shepherd's crook, Pan playing a syrinx (a pan flute) and a maenad playing a double flute). These and the Great Dish probably came from the same Mediterranean workshop. Another large dish, with a 55-centimetre diameter and engraved geometric designs and inlays of black niello (silver sulphide), may have been produced at a different workshop.

A fluted bowl, 40.8 cm in diameter, with alternating plain and foliate panels, has swinging handles, the ends of which are shaped like the heads of swans. Its central motif features a six-pointed star formed by two interlocking triangles (the hexagram). This bowl may have been for washing hands at the table. Several interesting pieces, referred to as goblets, could just as easily have served as stemmed platters when turned upside down. Amongst the collection are five ladles which originally featured handles in the shape of dolphins. Of the eight spoons, five are inscribed.

In contrast to the pagan scenes shown on most of the pieces, the spoons appear to have been associated with Christianity and were possibly associated with christenings. Three identical ones feature the engraved Chi-Rho symbol, consisting of the superimposed first two letters of Christ's name in Greek, Chi (X) and Rho (P), between Alpha and Omega ('I am the beginning and the end'). Emperor Constantine, the first Christian Roman Emperor, is believed to have adopted this symbol in the early fourth century CE as his monogram. The inscriptions on the other two spoons refer to specific individuals. One reads 'Papittedo Vivas' ('long life to Papittedus'), the other, 'Pascentia Vivas' ('long life to Pascentia').

Did all of these pagan and Christian artefacts belong to the one person? And if so, who was the owner? Probably the answer to this will never be known, but there are a few pieces of information that can be used for making a reasonable guess.

Mystery and conjecture

Because the hoard is of such high quality, the owner must have been wealthy and of high rank in Britain, perhaps a Roman provincial administrator. There was considerable unrest in Britain at that time with Picts and Scots marauding the province from the north and Saxon pirates menacing the south-east. Had the owner, who appears to have been a Christian, buried his wealth for safekeeping?

Christianity had spread through the Roman Empire long before it became the official religion under Constantine. It was probably introduced to Britain by merchants from the eastern Mediterranean or by troops garrisoned there. Although three British Bishops attended the first Christian council of the western Roman Empire in 314 CE at Arles in southern Gaul, the Church in Britain was still 'a small body of believers concentrated in urban communities and governed as elsewhere by a hierarchy led by a bishop. It was of little consequence in the general life of the province' (W. H. C. Friend, 'Pagans, Christians, and the 'Barbarian Conspiracy' of AD. 376 in Roman Britain', *Britannia*).

One of the silver plates bears the inscription 'Of Eutherius', and it has been suggested that this may have referred to a high official known to have served the Emperor Julian (360–363 CE) whom Christians vilified, calling him Julian the Apostate or the Pagan Emperor. He was the last of the emperors in the line of Constantine the Great, and it is ironic that he was also the last non-Christian emperor. His father was the half-brother of Constantine and Julian was born in the capital of Constantinople. When Constantine died in 337 CE, his heir, Constantius II, killed many members of the families of Constantine's half-brothers. Julian was spared because of his youth but this purge of his family left its scars. He was put under the care of a Scythian eunuch and brought up in the Greek philosophical tradition. Later he studied in Athens under the Neo-Platonist scholar Priscus. He recorded that he had given up Christianity when he was 20 and become an adherent of the traditional Greco-Roman deities in 351.

The emperor Constantius realised that the empire was too big for one man to rule and there was a need for an imperial presence in the western part of the empire, including Gaul and Britain. He pressed the scholarly Julian to become 'Caesar', a subordinate emperor in the west, to restore order along the Rhine frontier and to deal with the growing problem of the Picts and Scots in Britain. Once in Gaul, Julian sent the leader of his military, a Christian by the name of Lupicinus, to Britain in 360 CE to deal with the barbarian attacks. Perhaps Lupicinus was the owner of the silver? Had Julian or Eutherius given him the Oceanus Dish?

> **Because the hoard is of such a high quality, the owner must have been wealthy and of high rank in Britain, perhaps a Roman provincial administrator.**

Julian's military successes and popularity in Gaul aroused the suspicion of Constantius and he tried to weaken him by demanding that he send some of his best military units to the East, but Julian's troops reacted by proclaiming him Emperor. Not sure whether he could trust his British commander, Lupicinus, Julian had him recalled to Gaul. Was that when Lupicinus buried his silver, hoping to retrieve it at a later date? If so, the opportunity would never present itself, as Julian had Lupicinus arrested. He then marched east for a showdown with Constantius, who died before this could occur. Julian became the sole ruler of East and West. It was then he attempted to revive the pagan traditions of Rome, and abolish the privileges that had been granted by his predecessors to the Christian churches, hence the name 'Julian the Apostate'.

Whether Lupicinus was the Christian owner of the silverware who could not return to retrieve it, and whether he was presented with some of the platters, decorated with pagan themes, by Julian, will probably never be known. Despite a lack of context for the silverware, the curator of the British Museum chose it in 2002 as one of the top ten British treasures in the museum.

A SEMINAL ART

The hidden murals of the Caves of Ajanta

Whoever studies the art of China and Japan, at whatever time he begins, starts on a long road that will lead him ultimately to Ajanta.

—Laurence Binyon, Director of the British Museum, 1930

I n 1819, officers in the British imperial army were on a tiger hunt in the forests of the western Deccan in the Indian state of Maharashtra. They sited their prey silhouetted against what looked like the carved entrance to a cave high on a cliff above the gorge of the Waghora River. When they investigated, they discovered not one, but a series of carved caves. Today these are referred to as the Ajanta Caves after the small town 480 kilometres inland from Mumbai.

The thirty-one caves are not the result of natural processes, but were painstakingly hewn by hand from the cliff over many centuries by dedicated Buddhist monks and artisans to serve as prayer halls and monasteries. They are filled with masterpieces of sculpted and painted religious art. The stunning murals which cover walls, ceilings and pillars 'reach rare heights of aesthetic expression' producing 'a sense of sublime harmony' (Benoy K. Behl, 'Ajanta, the Fountainhead', from *Frontline*).

They have been described as a seminal art, the 'fountainhead' of the world's Buddhist paintings. Not only are they among the greatest works of Indian art, but they are also the best source of information on court life in India during the fifth century CE.

The earliest of the caves are believed to have been carved and painted somewhere between

271

1ST MILLENNIUM CE

the second and first centuries BCE. However, the later paintings done at the height of the Gupta period when the Mahayan form of Buddhism had evolved are the most magnificent. The Gupta Empire of Northern India, which reached its peak in the fifth and sixth centuries CE, is regarded as the Classical Age of Indian history. Peace, law and order, and great cultural achievements in religion, education, mathematics, Hindu and Buddhist art, and Sanskrit literature, marked the Gupta period. It was during this time that Indian Buddhist art became influential in East and South-East Asia.

One of the mysteries of the jewel-like paintings with their minute and precise details is the question of how they were painted in the semi-darkness of the caves. Even with lamps and mirrors to magnify the diffused light, the ancient artisans would have been working in extremely poor light, and yet the beauty of the work is overwhelming. The rough walls, ceilings and pillars were first covered with a mixture of mud, cow dung, vegetable matter and rock grit about three centimetres thick and then smoothed over with lime plaster.

The colours: yellow and red (ochre), black (lamp soot), white (lime) and blue (lapis lazuli) were blended into numerous vivid and subtle hues. The artisans who executed these murals came from a long creative tradition documented in a treatise called the *Chitrasutra* which provided guidance for the artist in things such as perspective, volume and shading. Yet each artist was expected to look inward and impart his own vision into his work. He knew 'that the material world was a veil of illusion' and he was expected to 'lift that veil and look beyond' ('Ajanta, the Fountainhead', from *Frontline*).

LEFT: One of the jewel-like paintings from the Ajanta Caves featuring King Mahajanaka about to leave his royal life to become an ascetic.

A 'sublime and compassionate view of life'

Indian art can never be understood outside the context of the spiritual philosophy of the people. The *Upanishad* philosophical texts from the ninth–eighth centuries BCE had a long-term and profound effect on later religious thought. The texts stressed the unity of all creation and the ecstasy that could occur when experiencing something truly beautiful, whether in nature or art. At the moment of bliss, the veils of illusion would be lifted and the individual would become aware of his or her unity with the divine and the whole of creation. This was the purpose of the artists who painted the Ajanta Caves.

Today the caves are numbered, but not in chronological order. For instance, Cave 1 with its 20 pillars supporting the ceiling was painted during the fifth century CE. The ceilings of the caves are generally covered with flowers, fruit, animals and mythical creatures, but the spectacular roof of Cave 2 gives the impression of a cloth canopy with a mandala (a geometric pattern) of the cosmos. The paintings on the walls are predominantly parables of a virtuous life taken from the *Jatarka* tales (stories of the Buddha in his previous incarnations, when he was on the road to enlightenment).

They reveal what it was like in the royal courts of ancient India. Some of the most magnificent of the paintings are The Bodhisattva Padmapani, The Dying Princess, Yashodhara and Rahul, The Dark Princess, and The Queen Persuading King Mahajanaka. These paintings reveal peace, tenderness, humility, grief and poignancy combined with elegance, grandeur and drama. It is particularly through the eyes of the figures that the ancient artists expressed emotions. The forms of the eyes represented in the Ajanta paintings follow those mentioned in the *Chitrasutra* as meditative; peaceful; lovelorn; frightened; weeping; angered, and pained.

Possibly the greatest of all the Ajanta masterpieces is The Bodhisattva Padmapani or 'Lotus Bearer'. According to Mahayan Buddhism, a bodhisattva was an enlightened being who had decided to stay on earth to help others. The Padmapani reveals a sublime peace even though surrounded by the queen, ladies

RIGHT: A carved Buddha from the Caves of Ajanta.

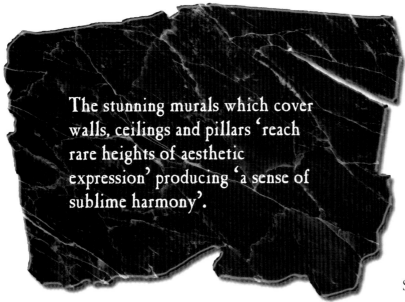

The stunning murals which cover walls, ceilings and pillars 'reach rare heights of aesthetic expression' producing 'a sense of sublime harmony'.

of the court, playful monkeys and musicians. Another Bodhisattva, The Vajrapani or 'Bearer of the Thunderbolt', with his glorious headdress, is believed to represent the majesty of spirit.

In the same cave is the poignant scene of the Queen Persuading King Mahajanaka not to give up his royal status to take up the life of an ascetic. She employs a beautifully attired dancer to try to distract her husband and prevent him from leaving. Other scenes show sad palace attendants; King Mahajanaka taking a ritual bath; riding out of the palace with a meditative look already in his eyes, and standing before a hermit in great humility.

The Dark Princess, also found in Cave 1, is believed to be one of the most beautiful images of a woman ever painted. In Cave 16 is the story of the conversion of Buddha's half-brother, Nanda. His wife is grief-stricken (*The Dying Princess*) on being told that her husband is going away. 'For pathos and sentiment . . . this picture cannot be surpassed in the history of art' (John Griffiths, official painter for the British Government in India in the nineteenth century).

For 'grandeur and tenderness', according to Laurence Binyon, 'there is nothing more impressive' than the painting of Yashodhara and Rahul in Cave 17 which depicts Yashodhara, the wife of the Buddha, covered in jewels, with her son Rahul, asking for the child's princely inheritance, but the Buddha has nothing to offer except his begging bowl ('Ajanta, the Fountainhead', from *Frontline*). Cave 17 is remarkable for the number of paintings to have survived and in the depictions of apsaras or celestial nymphs, particularly the dark-skinned one wearing a jewelled turban.

Hidden from the sixth -nineteenth century, these paintings have nonetheless faded and are damaged in places. The famous Indian art historian and photographer, Benoy K. Behl, photographed the Ajanta paintings, and with the help of technical experts in a number of fields, dedicated eight years to digitally reproducing fifty of the masterpieces in their original glory. In his words, 'the paintings of Ajanta are one of the most valuable treasures of the art world as they enshrine a sublime and compassionate view of life'.

52

THE SPIRIT OF BYZANTIUM

The Ravenna mosaics of Justinian and Theodora

No other work of art ... conveys the spirit of Byzantium with so much eloquence as do these two mosaics.

—Otto G. von Simson, *Sacred Fortress: Byzantine Art and Statecraft in Ravenna*, 1948. p.27

The Italian city of Ravenna on the north-east Adriatic coast possesses the world's richest collection of fifth and sixth century mosaics. These mosaics, which glow from the walls and ceilings of numerous religious buildings, most notably the Basilica of San Vitale, are judged by many to be far superior in artistic quality and iconographical significance than those from any other city of the ancient world.

Of all the mosaics, with their vivid and sharply contrasting colours, the most famous are the two panels on either side of the apse of San Vitale which feature the Emperor Justinian (527–565 CE) and his renowned Empress Theodora. These are two of the few surviving examples of Byzantine secular art. 'In the Justinian and Theodora mosaics we are confronted with a new style, the Byzantine, in which the artistic traditions of East and West have found expression in a coherent and independent whole' (Michael Gough, 'The Ancient to the Medieval World: Bridge of Faith', from *The Birth of Western Civilization*).

Since the late fourth century CE, the whole geographical and political landscape of the Roman Empire had changed. In 395, the Roman Empire was permanently divided into the Western and Eastern empires. The Eastern Roman Empire was ruled from Constantinople, the former Byzantium, while the capital of the Western Roman Empire was moved from Rome, first to Milan and then, from 404 CE, to the Adriatic city of Ravenna.

While the Eastern Empire flourished, the Western Empire was progressively weakened and dismembered by barbarian hordes (Vandals, Goths, Angles, Huns and Franks) until only the Italian peninsula was left. History records that the end of the Western Roman Empire occurred in 476 CE with the sacking of Rome by the mercenary, Odoacer, who became the first barbarian king of Italy, but he was defeated by Theodoric, the king of the Ostrogoths, who ruled an Ostrogothic Kingdom in Italy from Ravenna, supposedly as a vassal of the Emperor in Constantinople.

When Justinian came to the throne of the Eastern Roman Empire (the Byzantine Empire) in 537 CE he was already married to Theodora, who is regarded as possibly the most powerful woman in Byzantine history despite her lowly and dubious background. Her father was a bear trainer in the Hippodrome in Constantinople where she performed as a mime. Later she became a full-time actress, a term synonymous at the time with 'prostitute'. According to the writer, Prokopius, who lived at the time, Theodora was a common courtesan and a performer in 'low comedies' who, when on stage, delighted in 'letting herself be cuffed and slapped on the cheeks … raising her skirts to reveal to spectators … feminine secrets'.

He also claimed she was promiscuous, 'picnicking with ten young men or more . . . and dallying with them all the whole night through' (Prokopius, *Anekdota*). At age 16 she went to Africa as the companion of an official and remained there for four years. On her way home to Constantinople she spent some time in Alexandria. There she was converted to Monophysitism, a Christian sect that believed in the wholly divine nature of Jesus Christ. Orthodox Christians believed in 'the full humanity and full divinity of Jesus' as set out in the *Chalcedon Creed* of 451 CE.

At 20 years of age Theodora changed her former life, settled in Constantinople near the palace and became a humble spinner of wool. Justinian, the nephew of the emperor, captivated by her charm, intelligence and wit, made her his mistress. Due to the recent passage of a law allowing intermarriage between people of different social classes, Justinian married Theodora in

OPPOSITE: Part of the magnificent Theodora Mosaic showing the Roman Empress Theodora. The mosaic is located with that of the Emperor Justinian in the choir of the church of San Vitale in Ravenna.

525. As spectacular as her rise so far had been, her subsequent achievements, as unofficial joint ruler with Justinian, are far more notable.

She took an active role in the affairs of Constantinople and Justinian appears to have treated her as his intellectual equal. Justinian reformed and codified the Roman law. Theodora either influenced or initiated reforms of her own with regard to the rights of women. Laws were passed that prohibited forced prostitution, granted women rights in divorce cases (guardianship of children), and allowed women to own and inherit property. She also established convents and hospices such as the Convent of Repentance, to shelter former prostitutes. Together she and Justinian sponsored the building of churches in Constantinople, including the rebuilding of Hagia Sophia.

Justinian believed in an empire united politically and religiously, ruled from Constantinople under a Christian Emperor pursuing an orthodox policy. For him this involved establishing religious uniformity by punishing any 'disturbers of orthodoxy' within the empire, such as pagans (Hellenic and Egyptian forms of worship), Jews, and the heretical Christian sects (Arrians who regarded Jesus as wholly human, and Monophysites). His persecution of the Monophysites caused great discontent throughout the empire, but Theodora, herself a Monophysite, worked to mitigate the laws against the sect and provided safe shelter for Monophysite leaders who faced opposition from the majority Orthodox Christians. Although never able to convince Justinian to alter his official religious policy, she was successful in ending their persecution.

Church and state

The Emperor's policy also included reclaiming the western provinces that had once been part of the Roman Empire and were now under barbarian rule. In 540, his commander, Belisarius, conquered the Ostrogothic Kingdom in Italy and Ravenna became the western capital of the Byzantine Empire. The stunning domed, octagonal Basilica of San Vitale had already been started. Justinian's appointee, the Archbishop Maximian, completed it and is believed to have been the inspiration for the mosaics.

The stylistic perfection of the San Vitale mosaics present a political-religious message based on the view that the emperor combined the functions and authority of the imperial Roman Caesars with those of the Pope of the Roman Church, a concept known as Caesaropapism. They were a form of propaganda which was intended to reveal Justinian's defence of orthodoxy against heretical forms of Christianity, and also to present Theodora as benefactress.

The mosaic of Justinian is in the most holy part of the church, on the right hand side of the altar. The Emperor is richly dressed in a cloak of royal purple with a gold halo encircling his glittering crown depicting the divine splendour of the representative of Christ on earth. The halo gives him the same aspect as that of Christ in the dome of the apse as he receives the saints into Paradise. The Emperor, surrounded by a retinue of court officials, holds a gold paten or shallow dish used for the bread of the Eucharist.

Apart from Justinian and Maximian, whose portrait is strictly historical, two others are thought to depict Belisarius, the great military commander, and an individual called Julianus Argentarius, the banker who is believed to have contributed to the building of San Vitale. The twelve people in Justinian's retinue are symbolic of the twelve apostles. The chevron (a bent bar in an inverted V-shape) on his shoulder, indicates his supreme military power over the Christian Roman Empire, and the shield of the military officer bears the Chi-Rho, the symbol of Christ that became the monogram of Constantine, the first Christian emperor. Maximian carries a jewelled cross, a priest swings a censor and another carries the ornate-covered gospel.

In the opposite panel, on the left side of the altar, is the luminous image of Theodora who appears almost goddess-like in a purple gown with golden halo and jewels, surrounded by the ladies of her court. The emphasis is on the chalice used in the Eucharist, a symbol of her beneficence. Another symbolic reference to her imperial donations is the Three Magi (Wise Men who brought gifts to Jesus) on the hem of her gown.

> In the Justinian and Theodora mosaics we are confronted with a new style, the Byzantine, in which the artistic traditions of East and West have found expression in a coherent and independent whole.

The medium of the mosaic was especially appropriate for the decoration of churches 'in whose interiors the straight surfaces of the walls alternated with the curves of arches and semi-dome. Better than a painting, the mosaic, with its myriads of tesserae so arranged to catch the light in all its moods would have induced a religious atmosphere, and at night, against the flickering glow of lamps and candles, must have glittered and sparkled like rich jewelled brocade'. ('The Ancient to the Medieval World: Bridge of Faith', from *The Birth of Western Civilization*).

53

CULTURAL SYNERGISM ALONG THE SILK ROAD

The paintings and carvings in the Mogao Grottoes of Dunhuang

Thousands of miles connecting the site with the Western States;
the famous Yang Gate has been here a thousand years.

—*Twenty Hymns to Dunhuang*, sixth Hymn, eighth century CE

Close by the ancient Yang Gate, where the northern and southern routes of the Silk Road converge before entering China proper, is Dunhuang, once a remote Han Dynasty fortress. There, according to tradition, in 366 CE an ancient Buddhist monk, named Yuezin, had a vision which led him to carve out and decorate the first of 492 meditation grottoes out of a ridge, referred to as 'Singing Sands Mountain'. Thirty-two kilometres outside Dunhuang, this series of remarkable caves are referred to as the Mogao Grottoes or the 'Thousand Buddha Caves'.

Over more than five centuries, a community of dedicated and skilful monks carved and decorated these beautiful images. With their priceless 45,000 square metres of wall paintings and 2415 painted sculptures, they comprise the world's greatest repository of Buddhist art. The variety

OPPOSITE: A mural from the Mogao Grottoes near Dunhuang in western China. This early painting reflects traditional Indian style: red background and figures with oval faces, pendant earlobes and jewelled crowns.

of the images, the richness of the colours, the skill of the ancient artists, and the excellent state of preservation make the Mogao Grottoes a treasure house on a colossal scale.

The site also possesses great significance for both China and India; it is an area of cultural synergism. Buddhist cave art started in India, moved to Central Asia, where it assimilated local elements, and then into China where it was eventually transformed in the fifth and sixth centuries into a unique Chinese style. The decoration of the Tang period (618–907) reveals 'realism in portraiture and the beginnings of perspective in landscape painting' (Edward L. Shaughnessy, *Ancient China: Life, Myth and Art*).

Dunhuang, an oasis town, was established by the Han emperor, Wu, in 111 CE to control trade routes west and to protect China from their Hun enemies of Central Asia. It became a bustling centre due to the 7000 kilometre lines of caravan trails that led from Dunhuang across Asia to the Roman Empire. It was not just exotic merchandise that passed along the Silk Road, but Chinese and foreign envoys and monks from the Buddhist kingdoms of Gandhara (part of present-day Afghanistan and Pakistan) as well as Khotan and Kucha in Central Asia.

The Middle of the Han dynasty was a time of religious ferment in China. When the earliest missionaries arrived six centuries after the life of the historical 'Buddha' (Siddartha Gautama), Buddhism was considered a religion of foreigners. In order to impart its concepts, the foreign monks used the idiom of Daoism and for a time there seemed little difference between the two. Eventually learned Buddhist monks were employed as palace advisors and, with royal and aristocratic patronage, the new religion took hold.

Many Chinese found its teachings appealing. It addressed questions concerning suffering, the causes of which were people's desires and attachments which inevitably lead to disappointments and anxieties. It also offered a fully developed version of the afterlife and the prospect of salvation, a code of conduct to live by, and helped transcend class differences in hierarchical Chinese society. It appealed also to women. Many Chinese became monks and nuns, although the vow of celibacy meant that they had to break away from the cult of the ancestor. By 477 CE there were 6478 Buddhist temples in China and 77,258 monks and nuns. For centuries large numbers of monks were employed in translating the Buddhist sutras, or texts, into Chinese.

Every part of the caves' surfaces are covered with painted and sculpted images of meditating buddhas and *bodhisattvas* (enlightened beings) sitting in niches, surrounded by disciples, deities and a myriad of flying figures from nude Indian winged angels, Kucha figures with their Persian scarfs, and Chinese *yuren* or flying fairies floating across the sky trailing their coloured banners. The layout, themes and artistic styles of the caves reflect varied political situations and chronicle changes that occurred in Chinese Buddhist thought.

Themes and styles

Despite revealing the specific imprint of their own times, the murals can be divided into a number of themes. There are illustrated stories of the Buddha's life and the workings of dharma and karma, concepts of Hindu cosmology which were taken for granted by the historical Gautama; mythological and Buddhist tales, and illustrations of the Buddhist texts (sutras). Two fascinating murals even give a detailed bird's eye view of a famous monastic complex hundreds of kilometres from Dunhuang in the mountains of Shaanxi province, and an elite Chinese brothel in Dunhuang with its courtyards and elaborately dressed women attending to male patrons.

The earliest murals reflected the traditional Indian style: with red-ochre backgrounds and figures with long curling hair, oval faces, large eyes, pendant earlobes, wearing garlands and jewelled crowns. Bodhisattvas and royal individuals were dressed in the garments of India and of Central Asia. Later, the figures became more slender and oval faces were replaced with thinner and leaner ones similar to those in the tombs of the surrounding areas. Landscapes were added to the stories to provide a time frame for particular historical events.

> The variety of the images, the richness of the colours, the skill of the ancient artists, and the excellent state of preservation make the Mogao Grottoes a treasure house on a colossal scale.

When the Wei Dynasty emperor, Xiaowen, introduced the ideology and art of southern China into the north, the Bodhisattva figures began to resemble the Chinese aristocracy. The background colour changed from red/ochre to white and the oranges, violets, blues and greens used in the art of the south added vibrancy. For a brief period (557–581) when the Northern Zhou emperor married a Turkik princess (modern day Turkistan), the former 'western style' of Kucha and Kizil returned to the Dunhuang caves. During the Siu Dynasty (581–618), two styles predominated. One was a sparse style with 'simple strokes, a light mood and an elegant finish' and the other, 'a detailed, exquisite and extremely beautiful dense style' (Zhang Yanyuan, Tang art historian). Over time, the buddhas, bodhisattvas and supernatural deities underwent a transformation. They became sexless, heavenly beings, losing all signs of gender. The original depictions of the bodhisattvas as strong men became more feminine, with graceful postures and soft and beautiful eyes.

By the Tang Dynasty, Buddhism had become an integral part of Chinese life: monasteries ran schools, became gathering places for the Chinese literati, and were a significant economic force in the community. As well as paintings and sculptures, the Magao Grottoes are known for their manuscripts, written in several different languages on a wide variety of topics. In 1900, a Daoist priest involved in the renovation of the caves discovered a sealed chamber containing more than 10,000 manuscripts written between the fifth-tenth centuries, including the oldest surviving printed book containing a copy of the *Diamond Sutra*, dated to 868. Not all were Buddhist texts. One of them was a star map of the seventh century, made with astounding accuracy without the aid of telescopes. Some texts were educational, ranging from mathematics to etiquette and aspects of moral behaviour.

Just as the remote desert oasis town of Dunhuang had been a melting pot, the paintings in the Mogao Caves were a mingling of Chinese, Indian and Central Asian styles.

In 755, a military rebellion, led by a governor of non-Chinese background (An Lushan) was fought over eight years. Many believe that this rebellion was the end of China's ancient history, for the Tang court's brilliance never really recovered. As the state's international status weakened and it found itself in economic difficulties, there was a backlash against Buddhism. In 841, the government ordered the demolition of 4600 monasteries and the suppression of Buddhism as a 'foreign' religion.

Just as the remote desert oasis town of Dunhuang had been a melting pot of military men, merchants, travellers and Buddhist monks from the Han to the Tang Dynasties, the paintings in the Mogao Caves were a mingling of Chinese, Indian and Central Asian styles. After the brilliance of the Tang period, when trade along the Silk Road was severely curtailed, Dunhuang was left in isolation, the murals of the Magao Grottoes beautifully preserved by its remoteness and desert climate.

54

A MOUNTAIN MAUSOLEUM

Tang pottery and the six steeds of Zhaoling

A line of tombs winds skyward up the slope
Where mountain beasts keep to their leafy lair ...

— Du Fu, Tang poet, *Re-passing Zhaoling Mausoleum*

After an initial period of military expansion by the first Tang Emperors of China, a sophisticated and cosmopolitan culture developed, marked by peace, stability and flourishing international trade. The early Tang period (618–755 CE) is regarded as a Golden Age in Chinese culture. Unlike the emperors of earlier dynasties, Tang rulers looked outward. Foreign merchants in large numbers, some travelling by sea, others along the Silk Road, came to the populous capital of Chang'an (modern Xi'an) to sell their exotic wares, passing on different belief systems and cultural styles in the process.

The Tang adapted many of these foreign influences and combined them with local styles. The dynamism and tolerance of this dynasty is reflected in the exquisite pottery they produced, much of which was prepared as *mingqi*, 'articles of the spirit' or 'objects of the afterlife' to be placed in the tomb to provide continuing sustenance, protection, companionship and entertainment for the deceased.

One of the greatest burial sites in China was that of Zhaoling, where the second and possibly the greatest of Tang Emperors, Tai Zong (Li Shimin), was buried high on the peak of

Jiuzong Mountain. One hundred and sixty-seven tombs of nobles, generals, royal attendants and chieftains of minority nationalities were built lower down on the mountain. The whole cemetery complex had a circumference of 60 kilometres and covered 20,000 hectares.

All walks of life represented

The tombs contained large numbers of round-bodied glazed vessels as well as human figures, each with unique postures, subtly-detailed facial expressions, elegant gestures and clothing. There are court ladies, some dressed in Persian-style fitted bodices and pleated skirts, with painted faces and chignon hairstyles, as well as people from all walks of Chinese life: military officials, servants, grooms, falconers, musicians, dancers and wine bearers.

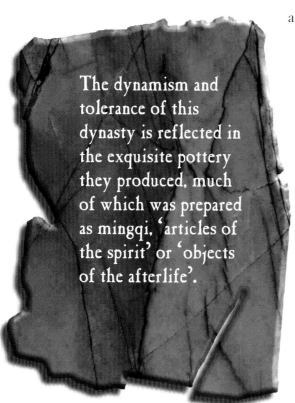

The dynamism and tolerance of this dynasty is reflected in the exquisite pottery they produced, much of which was prepared as mingqi, 'articles of the spirit' or 'objects of the afterlife'.

There were figures of foreigners, often depicted with exaggerated features such as large hooked noses, and foreign animals like the Bactrian camels that were so important in the caravans that plied the Silk Routes. Some of these camel figurines were shown carrying foreign products or bearded Central Asian musicians, indicating the Chinese interest in the exotic, and the importance of the silk trade to the economy. The much-loved horse with its small head, long neck and powerful body, was depicted in endless poses: standing still; walking; bearing loads; neighing; carrying women in active pursuits, and others shown with their grooms.

The hallmark of Tang pottery is what is termed *sancai* (three-coloured) glazed earthenware in straw, amber, browns (iron oxide) and rich green (copper oxide). Sometimes a rare dark blue was included (cobalt oxide). These brilliant lead glazes were applied either in a controlled or random way, to different parts of a pot or figurine and allowed to run together during firing at about 900°C, creating unique patterns and colour mixes. Both vessels and figures were often left with an unglazed section at the base. The highpoint in the production of Tang pottery was in the early

ABOVE: Two sancai ceramic horses, 79 centimetres tall, found in a Tang burial.

part of the dynasty where the craftsmen surpassed any of their predecessors, producing more finely modelled and individualised figures. The glazes were also more colourful and shinier than previously.

'These sculptures provide a fascinating glimpse into the cosmopolitan, multicultural society of Tang-dynasty China, apparently so beloved that the Chinese hoped to recreate it in the afterlife' (*Chinese Dynasty Art Special Exhibit*, Frank H. McClung Museum).

The importance of the horse to the Tang in their military conquests, and as a measure of wealth and power, is reflected in the number of horses in China by the middle of the seventh century (recorded as over 700,000). Huge quantities of silk were exchanged for the prized horses used by the

nomadic horsemen of Central Asia. Six chargers ridden by Emperor Tai Zong (Li Shimin) in his decisive battles were immortalised on stone screens 2.5 metres high and 3 metres wide on both sides of the entranceway of his mountain mausoleum (Zhaoling). He commissioned six paintings of the horses by a leading artist to be used as models by the sculptors.

The bold lines and unique postures of the horses reveal their power, individuality and liveliness. At least four of them were hit with arrows in battle. Along with their names and description, the Emperor included words of praise for each horse. Te Quinpiao (fatty prince) was yellow with a white mouth; Qing Zhui, a black and grey, was hit by five arrows in the chest; Shi Fachi, a red horse, was hit by four arrows in the chest and one on the back; Sa Luzi, a purple-looking horse, hit by one arrow on the front, was the only horse whose image was accompanied by a human figure, a bodyguard who pulled the arrow from him; Quan Maogua, a curly-haired yellow horse, was hit by nine arrows, and Bai Tiwu was a black horse with four white hoofs. Not only are they excellent examples of sculpting, but are also rich historical sources.

Two of the bas-reliefs (Sa Luzi and Quan Maogua) were stolen by treasure hunters and shipped to the USA in 1914 and are now in the Museum of the University of Pennsylvania. Four years later, the other four images were broken into pieces when robbers again attempted to send the treasures to the United States. They were recovered and restored, and are now in the Shaanxi Provincial Museum in Xian.

ABOVE: A sancai ceramic Bactrian camel with bearded foreign musicians.

SACRED, SENSUAL AND EXUBERANT

Hindu treasures of the Deccan

To the western eye, these gods and goddesses are, given their sacred function, almost shockingly beautiful. Divinity, and sensuous, sexual beauty seem to be inextricably mixed.

—Joanna Pitman, *Chola: Sacred Bronzes of Southern India*, The Royal Academy

All the elements that comprised Hinduism crystallised during the great Gupta Empire (fourth–sixth centuries CE) although its roots went back over thousands of years. The sources of Hindu teachings are the Vedic Poems, believed to be the word of God delivered at the dawn of creation and passed down orally before being written in Sanskrit ca. 1500 BCE. Due to its tolerance of diversity, and its lack of a founder or hierarchy, Hinduism, known to its followers as Sanatana Dharma (the eternal way of life), readily absorbed, reinterpreted and assimilated the beliefs and practices of many groups of people, which created variations across India. The Great God of Hinduism is Shiva, timeless, formless, spaceless, omnipresent, residing in everyone and everything as pure consciousness. For the benefit of devotees, and to help them focus on God, Shiva has been given many attributes and forms. The myriad of male and female deities in the Hindu pantheon are regarded as aspects of the Divine, and their worship is a personal activity.

The Hindu art that emerged during the Gupta period has been described by art historian Dr Ananda K. Coomaraswamy as 'at once abstract and sensuous, reserved and passionate'. Some of the

most beautiful images of Shiva were executed during this period, particularly the form of Shiva as half-male, half-female (Ardhanarishvara).

To the Hindus, everything in life was an expression of the Divine, including the human body. Even human sexuality was regarded as a metaphor for the union of the human soul and the Divine. Hindu artists saw the erotic and sensual as an integral part of life and were adept at portraying the human form, including those of the deities, as soft and sensual or curved and voluptuous. They excelled particularly at representing the female body, the epitome of which was the Goddess Uma. Uma/Parvati was the Great Goddess, consort of Shiva, often shown alongside him in sculptures, and whose presence was of great importance in temples if Shiva's beneficence was to be directed to the devotee. This beautiful and benign goddess was the daughter of Himavan, Lord of the Mountains (Himalayas) and was often depicted as a divinity in her own right. In her active form as destroyer of demons she is referred to as the warrior goddess, Durga.

For five hundred years after the demise of the Gupta Empire, it was the kingdoms of the Deccan, the vast plateau of central and southern India that continued the Hindu artistic tradition. Between the fourth–ninth centuries, the Pallava kings who ruled in the Eastern Deccan began the building of magnificent stone temples for which Southern India became known. Outside of Chenai, at Mahabalipuram, on the coast of the Bay of Bengal, is the world's largest open-air sculptural bas-relief called Gangacatarna or 'The Descent of the Ganga'. This is part of a series of carved rock shrines.

The Descent of the Ganga 'is a masterpiece of classic art in the breadth of its composition, the sincerity of the impulse which draws all creatures together round the beneficent waters, and its deep, fresh love of nature' (Rene Grousset, *Civilizations of the East*). This relief was carved from a granite cliff divided by a deep cleft. When it rained, water cascaded down the cleft in a simulation of the great River Ganges (Ganga). The Pallava sculptors used the cleft as a focus for their composition, which was based on a Hindu myth.

A sage named Bhagirath appealed to Ganga, a river appearing as the Milky Way in the heavens, to fall to earth to purify the ashes of 6000 of his ancestors who had been murdered. Ganga was unwilling, fearing that her descent would be too much for the earth to bear, but Shiva agreed to break the sacred river's violent power as it fell by catching it in his tangled hair. This magnificent relief is 13 metres high and 29 metres long and extends out on both sides of the cleft. Serpent deities (*nagas*), which symbolise water are carved into the symbolic Ganges, while on either side,

1ST MILLENNIUM CE

OPPOSITE: Bronze statues of the Hindu god Vishnu and his two consorts Bhu, earth goddess, and Shri, goddess of prosperity, from the Chola culture of southern India.

emerging from the rock face, are adoring deities, people and animals (deer, lions, monkeys, elephants, even a cat and mice) approaching Ganga to pay homage. The sky is filled with flying gods all celebrating the descent of the celestial river. The ascetic, Bhagirath, is seen standing on one leg, all skin and bones, performing a purificatory spiritual discipline (*tapas*). Beside him is the god Shiva with his attendants (*ganas*), and below is a Vishnu shrine.

Between the eighth–tenth CE, the kings of the Rashtrakutu Dynasty in the Central Deccan produced one of the greatest masterpieces of Indian sculpture: Mehesamurti (Trimurti), a six-metre-high, three-headed sculpture of Shiva in the man-made Caves of Elephanta near Mumbai. The Mehesamurti depicts three Shiva forms and attributes: Aghora, the destructive form of Shiva; Ardhanarishvara, the half-male, half-female form; and Mahoyogi, the serene, meditative ascetic. The latter is the most serene and peaceful of the three.

Nowhere is the synthesis of the sensual and sacred seen better than in the stone and bronze statues of the deities made during the Chola period. The Chola was a Tamil Dynasty that originated in Tanjore and ruled, not only the South-Eastern Deccan (Tamil Nadu) from the ninth century CE, but also which at its height, spread to Sri Lanka, the Maldives, parts of the Malay Archipelago and Indonesia. Possibly the most splendid of the Chola bronzes are the depictions of Shiva as Nataraj or Lord of Dancers, 'a manifestation of primal rhythmic energy . . . the clearest activity of God which any art or religion can boast of.'

The Shiva Nataraja depicts the endless cosmic dance of creation, preservation and destruction whose purpose is to release humans from the illusion of 'self' and of the physical world. Although Shiva Nataraja statues may vary slightly, they all contain the same symbolism. The god stands on a lotus pedestal and is surrounded by a ring of fire representing the eternal cycle of existence. In his upper left hand he holds a flame to spark the destructive, yet purifying circle of fire, and in his upper right hand he holds the drum, the beating of which sets creation in motion. His lower left hand points down to his raised foot which signals release from ignorance while his raised right hand assumes the symbolic gesture 'without fear'. Shiva's other foot is implanted on the demon dwarf, Muyalaka, to stamp out ignorance without which enlightenment cannot occur. Within the folds of the god's braided and jewelled hair is a writhing cobra, a skull and a small personified image of the Ganges River.

According to the mystic, philosopher and poet, Sri Aurobindo, the finest Hindu sculpture contained a spirituality which was never found in the art of Greece. It was exuberant and 'belonged to an entirely different world of imagination, one that did not correspond to the classical ideals' (*The Foundations of Indian Culture*).

A WINDOW INTO CLASSIC MAYAN SOCIETY

The Bonampak murals and Jaina figurines

These people used certain letters with which they wrote in their books about ancient subjects ... We found many books written with these letters, and since they held nothing that was not falsehood and the work of the evil one, we burned them all. —Bishop Diego de Landa, *Report of Things in Yucatan*

In 1946, the local Lacandon Maya in the southern Mexican state of Chitapak, not far from the Guatemalan border, led an American photographer named Giles Healey to a previously unknown site in the tropical rainforest. They called the site 'Bonampak' or 'Painted Walls' after the brilliantly coloured murals painted on the walls of three rooms in a small temple on top of a stepped pyramid base. The Bonampak Murals, dated to ca. 776–795 CE, are the most complete set of paintings of the ancient Americas and the most significant. They have survived almost intact despite more then 1200 years in the tropical rainforest.

The site was abandoned soon after the completion of the paintings, and water leaking through the roof deposited a transparent layer of calcium carbonates over the murals, bonding them more tightly to the walls. Professor Mary Miller of Yale University calls them 'an elaborate visual pageantry'. They are invaluable as sources of information for life at the court

of Bonampak's final and greatest ruler, Lord Chan Muan who reigned during the last quarter of the eighth century. They depict royal ceremonies, dancing, musical performances, battles, presentation of tribute from foreign nobles, human sacrifice and the practice of bloodletting, as well as providing evidence of musical instruments, weapons of war, the elaborate costumes worn by the elite and the social hierarchy.

On the island of Jaina on the other side Mexico, off the coast of the Yucatan Peninsula, a Mayan burial ground was unearthed, yielding up a series of unique cult figurines, only a few centimetres tall. These were usually clutched in the hands of the dead. Their beauty, detail and realism are astonishing, even portraying facial traits and expressions. They provide glimpses into upper class Mayan society and it is possible to determine the rank of many individuals by their elaborate costumes, jewellery and headgear.

Some of the tiny statues are hollow and filled with clay pellets to form a rattle; others have holes to serve as whistles, perhaps to help the soul to its final resting place in the underworld. The island was originally named 'House Over the Sea' and since the underworld was associated with water, Jaina Island may have been regarded as the entrance to Xibalba or the Maya Underworld. The figures still retain some of their original bright colours, particularly the striking turquoise, referred to as Maya Blue, which was also used in the murals. It was produced by mixing a natural clay called palygorskite and a derivative of indigo, and was remarkable for its resistance to chemical solvents and biodegradation.

There were three main areas of Maya settlement: the mountains of Guatemala and the southern Mexican highlands of Chiapas; the central Mesoamerican lowlands south of Tabasco, stretching as far as eastern Belize and western Honduras; and the northern Cameche to the tip of the Yucatan Peninsula. Although the Maya can be traced back to the first millennium BCE, the Maya Classic Period covered the years from ca. 250–900 CE and, during these centuries, towering artificial mountains or pyramids (*witz*) were erected, along with other ceremonial monuments such as vast plazas, ball courts, stairways and temples in the numerous and populous Maya cities such as Copan, Tikal, Uaxactun, Palenque, Uxmal, Mayapan, and Chichen Itza.

OPPOSITE: A brilliantly coloured section of the Bonampak Murals depicting members of the court of Lord Chan Muan, Bonampak's final and greatest ruler.

Warring, bloodletting and ceremonies

It seems that warfare was a natural condition among the independent Maya city-states which were never part of a centralised administration under a supreme ruler. The chief purpose of warfare was as a source of captives, whose sacrifice and lifeblood was offered to the gods (returning energy to the Cosmos). Warfare and sacrifice also enhanced the rulers' status, particularly if a captive was a rival king.

In the Bonampak Murals there is evidence of a battle that took place on 6 August, 792 at the same time as an important astronomical phenomena appeared in the skies: the appearance of the constellations which marked the place where the Maize God would supposedly be reborn. Amongst the Jaina figures is an individual referred to *Halach Uinic* or 'The True Man', who was a hereditary governor or war chief. He is shown seated on a bench or a circular throne perhaps made of wood and leather in a dignified pose. His face is tattooed and he wears a detachable helmet comprised of a serpent's head with exotic feathers and a shirt over his loincloth. His breastplate is decorated with jade beads and his sumptuous outfit is completed with earrings, bracelets and sandals. A fan rests on his knee.

The murals also show the presentation of captives to a richly attired Lord Chan Muan. The captives look down at their hands. Their nails have been ritually pulled out and their fingers are bleeding. Other forms of sacrifice and bloodletting included slicing the victim's chest and extracting the dripping heart to offer to the gods.

Bloodletting wasn't restricted to captives. It was carried out by the elite, both men and women, and regarded as a privilege. A ceremony of ritual bloodletting by royal and noble women, depicted at Bonampak, shows them seated on thrones piercing their tongues, passing a chord through the puncture and offering up their blood. Men also used sharp knives or the spines of stingrays to cut and draw blood from their penises, as the genitals had an especially potent life-giving energy. A priestly Jaina figure is shown seated above a bowl and, judging by the position of his legs, he is drawing blood from his genitals. Such bloodletting may have been used to go into an ecstatic state and enter the supernatural realm.

All Mayan ceremonies were magnificent spectacles, with sacred music, masked dancers and priestly and noble participants dressed in extravagant costumes. The decoration in the first room at Bonampak depicts the child heir to the throne being presented in a ceremony with costumed dancers and musicians playing a variety of instruments including wooden trumpets (*Hom-Tahs*)

OPPOSITE: A stone bust of the Mayan Maize God.

and drums. The priests and nobles are shown getting dressed for the ceremony and Chan Muan is donning a vivid costume of jaguar pelts, feathers and a boa constrictor.

Both noble men and women were tattooed, a process carried out by means of a scarring technique, and wore large headdresses and jade jewellery. The kings dressed according to the specific occasion — as war leader or civil ruler — and carried an appropriate symbol of authority. On top of their long jewelled hair, they wore massive headdresses, some rising to a metre in height, covered with elaborately designed textiles and decorated with jade, shell and feathers, particularly the highly prized long bright plumes of the quetzal bird. The enlarged lobes of their ears were filled with ornaments and their teeth were probably filed and inlaid with jade. For certain occasions, a huge bird beak was moulded over their noses.

The Jaina figures show that kings and lords often donned the ceremonial padded outfits of the ball players, a ritual game played in the temple ball courts. The murals and Jaina figures reveal that on ceremonial occasions women wore an ankle-length, tunic-like blouse known as a *huipil*, like those still worn in Guatemala. The *huipil* was covered in geometric designs of diamonds and dots. These were symbols of the cosmos. A diamond motif symbolised the four cardinal directions of the universe while a tripod of dots represented the hearthstones that featured in the Maya creation myth.

By 800 CE, the Maya who produced the Bonampak Murals abandoned their settlements, perhaps due to deforestation, depleted soils and overpopulation. Some of the settlements were burned to the ground which may indicate that the environmental damage led to extreme food shortages and violent conflicts between city-states. By 900 CE, the forest began to reclaim the main areas of Maya settlement although some centres in the Yucatan survived until the arrival of the Spaniards.

In 1995, art historian Mary Miller, concerned about the continuing deterioration of the Bonampak Murals, initiated the Bonampak Documentation Project. The aim was to record every detail of the paintings using infrared film which would reveal previously invisible details. Sponsored by the Getty Foundation and National Geographic, her team painstakingly recorded the walls of the three rooms. Between 1996–99 the data was assembled, and over the next two years a team of artists and pigment experts meticulously hand-painted a nine-metre-long reconstruction of the murals, 50 per cent of the original size. This was produced and displayed in the Peabody Museum of Natural History at Yale University.

BIBLIOGRAPHY

Balter, M., *The Goddess and the Bull*, Free Press, New York, 2005

Burn, L., *Hellenistic Art: From Alexander the Great to Augustus*, The British Museum Press, London, 2004

Carter, H., *The Tomb of Tutankhamun*, Sphere Books Limited, London, 1973

Castledon, R., *Minoans: Life in Bronze Age Crete*, Routledge, London, 1990

Cernenko, E. V., *The Scythians 700-300 BC*, Osprey Publishing Limited, Oxford, 1983

Cohen, A., *The Alexander Mosaic: Stories of Victory and Defeat*, Cambridge University Press, Cambridge, 1997

Cottrell, L., *The Bull of Minos*, Sutton Publishing Limited, Gloucestershre, 2003

Cunliffe, B., *The Ancient Celts*, Penguin Books, London, 1999

Curtis, J., & Tallis, N., (ed.) *Forgotten Empire:The World of Ancient Persia*, British Museum Press, London, 2005

Curtis, J., *Ancient Persia*, British Museum Press, London, 2000

Diehl, R., *The Olmecs: America's First Civilization*, Thames and Hudson, 2004

Doumas, C., *Cycladic Art*, The British Museum Press, London, 1983

Durando, F., *Greece: Splendours of an Ancient Civilization*, Thames and Hudson, London, 2005

Ebrey, P. B., *Cambridge Illustrated History: China*, Cambridge University Press, Cambridge, 1996

Gere, K., *The Tomb of Agamemnon*, Profile Books, London, 2006

Geoffroy-Schneiter, B., *Fayum Portraits*, Assouline Publishing, New York, 2004

Hawass, Z., *Hidden Treasures of Ancient Egypt*, National Geographic Society, Washington DC, 2004

Hawass, Z., (ed.) *The Treasures of the Pyramids*, White Star Publishers, Vercelli, Italy, 2003

Higgins, R., *Minoan and Mycenaean Art*, Thames and Hudson, London, 1997

Hobbs, R., *Treasure: Finding our Past*, British Museum Press, London, 2003

Hodder, I., *The Leopard's Tale: Revealing the Mysteries of Catalhoyuk*, Thames and Hudson, London, 2006

Hoving, T., *Tutankhamun; The Untold Story*, Penquin Books, 1980

Kenoyer, J. M., *Ancient cities of the Indus Valley Civilization*, Oxford University Press, Oxford, 1998

Neils, J., *The Parthenon Frieze*, Cambridge University Press, Cambridge, 2001

Phillips, C., *The Lost History of Aztec and Maya*, Anness Publishing Limited, London,2004

Quilter, J., *The Treasures of the Andes*, Duncan Baird publishers, London, 2005

Robins, G., *The Art of Ancient Egypt*, British Museum Press, London, 1997

Schulz, R., & Seidel M., (ed), *Egypt: The World of the Pharaohs*, Konemann, Cologne, 1998

Shaughnessy, E., *Ancient China: Life, Myth and Art*, Duncan Baird Publishers, London, 2005

Zettler, R., & Horne, L., *Treasures form the Royal Tombs of Ur*, Marquand Books, Seattle, 1998.

INDEX

304